JUSTICE INC

The Intellectual Bodyguards, Book 1

JB Phillips

Quail Valley Publishing

CONTENTS

NOW ISN'T THE TIME
April 2019

Rev. Jamaal Wilkes leaned back in the chair and placed his feet on the mayor's desk as he looked around the room. The office was decorated with the requisite photos of the mayor with other politicians, celebrities, and athletes, as well as signed jerseys and other sports memorabilia. "Really, Chuck, you need to update your office. Your furniture looks like it has been here since the Depression. And those drapes make this place look like a Tijuana whorehouse. But I digress. So, what's it going to be, Chuck?"

Mayor Charles Benton took a deep breath, put his head in his hands, and closed his eyes. Jamaal was the only person on Earth that he wouldn't punch in the nose for calling him Chuck. And Jamaal knew it. "Jamaal," he said softly, "we go back a long way. You know I'd do anything for you, but I can't do this."

Jamaal shook his head. "Don't say that you'd do anything for me and then refuse to do something for me. What is that called? Oh yeah, hypocrisy. After all I have done for you over, what has it been, twenty years? You have forgotten that I was the one who got you into this office. Regardless, you're goddamn straight that you'll do anything for me. Maybe you need to reconsider your position." Jamaal didn't say it, but his tone conveyed "or else."

Charles opened his eyes and glared at the man he had essentially raised as one of his own. One mistake over twenty years ago, and Jamaal had never let him forget about it. In recent years, the younger man had used their secret like a leash to control his surrogate father. Charles knew he would never have had a successful political career without Jamaal, but every man has limits as to what he can tolerate. Jamaal was pushing him to the edge. What Jamaal wanted him to do would be political suicide, and Charles had his eyes set on a higher office. The mayor shook his head.

"You know I support what you want to accomplish, but now simply isn't the time," Charles said slowly. "It wouldn't be politically acceptable. Half the council fights damn near every proposal I make simply because I made it. And this campaign would make the fight over zoning back in the 1990s look like a stroll through the park. Houston has come a long way from the good-old boy network that ran the city for decades, but the city isn't ready for what you propose. Hell, other than Seattle, San Francisco, and maybe Austin, it would be dead on arrival almost anywhere else in the country. These kinds of policies take time to implement. You must plant the seeds, nurture them to maturity, and then you can reap what you have sown." The mayor thought for a moment. "You are trying to hit a home run when a series of singles will net the same result and be easier to achieve. You need to curb your enthusiasm and be patient."

Jamaal laughed. "Sometimes your grammar is simply atrocious. That is a lame excuse, Chuck, even for you. You need to grow a pair. Need I remind you that you have a re-election campaign coming up in seven months? Just because you are the incumbent doesn't guarantee re-election. Look at the first Bush. You have a couple of serious challengers, and you are going to need every penny that I can direct your way. That old lady who's running might be more appreciative of my efforts. And she might even be open to my proposal. After all, she keeps shouting that you aren't progressive enough, and she is right. What's her name? Martha Wilkerson? Yes, that's it. Maybe I'll call her and offer my services."

Charles struggled to control his anger. He desperately wanted to beat Jamaal to a pulp, but he knew that attempting to do so would be a mistake. First, it wouldn't look very good for the mayor to get into a fistfight with a visitor to his office. And second, he had every reason to believe that he'd come out on the worse end of a brawl. Though he was in decent shape for a fifty-five-year-old, Jamaal was a black belt in Brazilian Ju Jitsu. Charles had been a Golden Gloves champion in Houston many years prior, but he was now a middle-aged man. And he had a stomach bulge and graying hair to prove it. No, trying to beat the daylights out of Jamaal would be dumber than supporting his proposal.

"I'm not saying that I would never support your plan. I just don't think this is the right time. It will be very controversial and contentious, and it isn't a brilliant strategy to make radical proposals leading up to an election." The mayor thought for a moment. "But once I get re-elected—"

"If you get re-elected," Jamaal interjected. "Don't count your chickens...."

Charles ignored the attempt to anger him further. "When I am re-elected, I can do a lot more. I won't be able to run for mayor again because of term limits. Then, I can support you and not worry about the political fallout. I won't be running again until the gubernatorial race in 2026, and if your plan blows up in our face, voters will have forgotten about it by then. The average voter has the memory of a rock."

Jamaal frowned and narrowed his eyes. "Sometimes I think that you have no goddamn sense at all. If you made this your main campaign promise, you'd get the vote of every renter and poor person in the city. That's nearly half of the people in Houston. And you'd probably get most of the votes from those guilt-ridden white progressives. Yes, it's audacious. But greatness only comes to those who will take bold steps. And if you proposed this now, that Wilkerson bitch wouldn't have anything to complain about. Hell, she might even drop out of the race and endorse you."

Charles shook his head and looked out his window towards Tranquillity Park. He chuckled to himself at the irony. The mood in his office was anything but tranquil. That was usually the case when Jamaal visited. Charles could see a small encampment of homeless people in the park, even though it was illegal to camp in public parks. I'm going to have to get on the police chief's ass, he thought. Those people should be rounded up and moved somewhere where I can't see them. "There is no justification for taking such actions. How would I sell it to voters? If I had made this a part of my campaign from the beginning, it might be easier. But there is no way to make a strong case at this time. I'd need something to justify such a drastic action at this point in the game. If I supported your proposal without adequate justification, I'd look crazier than Sheila Jackson Lee."

"That's chickenshit," Jamaal shouted. "The justification is that rents are soaring and have been for years. Homelessness is at an all-time high. Hell, people are camping out in the park in front of City Hall. And nobody likes their landlord. If you put the reins on those greedy sons-a-bitches, you'd be a hero. This is such an easy sell that my dog could do it."

Charles took another deep breath and stared at Jamaal. How did it come to this? he asked himself silently. He had known long ago that Jamaal was intelligent and resourceful, but he never thought that the precocious young boy would turn into such a manipulative adult. To the public, Jamaal was a passionate and sincere advocate for the poor. Few people saw his seedier side, and Charles was one of those people. Did I sell my soul to the devil? he wondered. A devil who poses as a man of God?

"I can see—" Jamaal stopped as a thought occurred to him. Charles might be a cowardly idiot, but he was a useful cowardly idiot sometimes. Admittedly, Charles had come through many times in the past and supported legislation that was beneficial to Jamaal and his agenda. For now, Jamaal thought, I'll keep my wagon hitched to Charles. "Perhaps you are right. Now isn't the time, but if we lay our foundation, a year from now will be perfect. I can start working clandestinely to build support among some of the other ministers and the housing activists. We will slowly build our coalition and create a growing demand for bold measures. Then, you can announce your support. You'll just be following the will of the people."

Charles smiled and sighed in relief. "That's a great idea. So, we're okay, Jamaal?"

"We're just fucking wonderful, Chuck." Jamaal tipped his fedora at the mayor and strode from the office.

THIS IS GOING TO BE FUN

October 2019

"So, Justin, have you given any more thought to my idea?" Pratik Shah asked his roommate and best friend.

Justin Walker nodded. "Yeah. I still have mixed feelings. I don't know anybody in Houston, and I'm not sure how I would like the summer heat. But I must admit that I am growing weary of these cold winters. However, the weather isn't the primary source of my hesitation. I am not convinced that we can operate a successful business as intellectual bodyguards."

"I understand," Pratik said. "Starting a business can be scary, particularly when it is something new. Many times, my dad has talked to me about his decision to leave India and start a business in Houston. It was an enormous risk, but he wanted a better life than he could have in India. There are a lot more opportunities there today, but thirty years ago it was a pretty poor nation. He didn't want his family to grow up without opportunities. I don't know if this idea of mine has any merit. But I know I don't want to wake up one day thirty years from now wondering, what if? What if I had tried? I might fail, but I won't need to live with regrets for having refused to try. A good friend of mine once admonished me to not live with regrets, and

I am going to take his advice."

Justin laughed. He was that friend. It was typical of Pratik to use Justin's words against him to make a point. It made it very difficult to disagree. Justin liked Pratik because he listened carefully and took ideas seriously.

Pratik continued. "We would have never met if you hadn't taken a risk. What you did was audacious, but truly great things can only happen when you are willing to be bold. This is my chance to be bold, and I intend to take it. And it would be a lot better if you were on that journey with me. To be honest, I think that my chances of success are much better with you as a partner. But don't do it for me. If you think it's the right thing to do, then do it for yourself. If you don't think that it is the right thing to do, then say no. Be selfish."

Justin closed his eyes and leaned back on the sofa. In 2018, he had walked into Ohio State's first football practice of the season. He marched up to the head coach and introduced himself. "And who the hell is Justin Walker?" the coach demanded. Justin explained he was the team's next placekicker. The coach scowled and remarked that he didn't recall recruiting a Justin Walker to be the team's placekicker. Justin smiled and said, "I am here to correct that oversight."

Justin was given a tryout and became the youngest football player in Ohio State's long, storied history. In the last game of the regular season, he kicked a fifty-five-yard field goal to beat Michigan as the clock ran out. Just after the ball left his foot, a Michigan player slammed into his planted left leg and tore the ligaments in Justin's knee. The surgery to repair the knee was successful, but Justin did not want to risk another injury and the possibility of being a cripple for life. Justin quit the team. He had fulfilled his dream of being the kicker for the Buckeyes, and that was enough for him. Besides, he had a full-ride academic scholarship and could stay in school.

In the few months that he had been on the team, Justin had gained twenty pounds of muscle and developed a daily exercise regimen. He continued that after leaving the team. He was a strapping young man standing just over six feet tall and weighed just over one-hundred-eighty pounds. His flaming red hair, which he wore shoulder length, was as striking as his arctic blue eyes. He often joked that he was the ultimate patriot—he was red, white, and blue.

Pratik, on the other hand, was the size of a garden shed. He was 6'8" tall and weighed two-hundred-seventy pounds, none of which was fat. He was an imposing figure, and as agile as a cheetah. During high school, he won nearly every honor that could be given to a football player in Texas. He had received offers of an athletic scholarship from a dozen major schools, but he decided to play football for Ohio State. Both he and Justin were freshmen in 2018 and quickly became friends.

In his first and only season with the Buckeyes, Pratik won many awards, including being named to several All-America teams. He seemed destined for greatness in the National Football League. But after he witnessed Justin's injury, he came to the same conclusion as his friend. He didn't want to risk an injury that would leave him hobbled for life. Pratik quit the team, thereby forfeiting his athletic scholarship. He applied for and received several academic scholarships, and his parents made up the difference. They had long thought that football was too dangerous and were relieved when Pratik gave up the sport.

Both Justin and Pratik would graduate in December with double majors. Justin majored in philosophy and psychology. Pratik majored in philosophy and business. Graduate school wasn't appealing to either, but neither young man was certain what industry would be best for applying their knowledge. A month before, Pratik had suggested that they become intellectual bodyguards and set up shop in Houston, his hometown. As a native Ohioan, Justin thought moving to Texas might be a bit of a culture shock. Weren't Texans still riding horses and wearing a six-shooter on their hip? Justin had jokingly asked. "No," Pratik had deadpanned. "At least in my neighborhood, there were no cowboys. But there were a lot of Indians."

Justin pushed his thoughts aside and finally spoke. "Looking back, what I did was pretty crazy, but it worked out well. I had a plan, and if we go ahead with this, we'll need a plan. We are going to be two recent college graduates offering a service nobody has ever heard of. This will not be easy, but if I have to wrestle alligators, there is nobody else in this world that I'd rather do it with than you."

Pratik smiled. "Thanks Justin. I agree we need a plan—a business plan. We'll need to figure out who might be a potential client and how to reach them. That's just business 101."

"I know that I've brought this up before, but I see a lot of obstacles," Justin said. "Almost nobody will know that they need us. If someone threatens them with a gun or a knife, they can easily see the danger. But when they are threatened by bad ideas, they can't see the danger."

Pratik nodded. "Yes, when someone is threatened with a gun or knife, the danger is in the moment. But an intellectual threat takes much longer to play out. Sometimes it takes years or even decades. Most people don't see that. We are certainly going to face some challenges in convincing them of the danger they face."

"We are not only going to have to convince them they need an intellectual bodyguard," Justin replied, "but we're also going to have to educate them about what that is." Justin paused a moment. "I'm not even sure what that kind of service looks like. Even if we figure all of this out, we don't have any experience doing this. We look more like physical bodyguards than intellectual bodyguards.

"I think that we have a lot more experience than might be obvious. Over the past two years, how many philosophical papers have we written? How many debates did we have in classrooms? And we also had that little tiff with Antifa. We've been honing our skills as intellectuals. I know it's not exactly the same, but we are both pretty good at expressing our ideas.

"We both know that the world is filled with bad ideas," Pratik continued. "We have to look for those who are most being victimized by those ideas. Since they likely accept the same premises as those attacking them, they are going to be defenseless. We see it all the time in the news. Someone complains that a policy goes too far, but he doesn't challenge the morality behind it. If we publicly give them a moral sanction, we can get their attention. The pen is mightier than the sword."

Justin frowned. "Yes, but we need to focus our efforts. A friend once told me that a business can't be all things for all people. A business must pick a market to target."

Pratik laughed. He was that friend. It was typical of Justin to use Pratik's words against him to make a point. It made it very difficult to disagree. Pratik liked Justin because he listened carefully and took ideas seriously.

"I agree. We should pick two or three issues to focus on. Two obvious topics are business regulations and property rights violations, but that's probably too broad. Focusing on either could send us in a dozen different directions."

"I have an idea," Justin exclaimed. "Why don't we study what's going on in Houston? We can offer our services to people across the nation, but it might be easier to start locally. We can see what is going on politically and culturally in Houston. Maybe that will help us identify what issues are hot, and we can focus on them."

"That's a great idea. We can start doing that today. Let's identify some websites to follow. The websites for newspapers, radio stations, and television stations are obvious. And there are probably lots of bloggers and independent journalists covering the city. I will start compiling a list of the media sites. Why don't you make a list of alternative news sources? Then we can decide which are worth following."

"Sounds like a plan to me," Justin replied. They gave one another a fist bump as they said in unison, "This is going to be fun."

YOU ARE MISSING A GOLDEN OPPORTUNITY

March 2020

amaal stood in the doorway to Mayor Benton's office. As always, he wore a custom-made suit and a fedora. He smiled as he surveyed the room. "Charles, it looks like you took my advice and redecorated. I notice a new souvenir or two since my last visit. But you still have this hideous furniture and the whorehouse drapes," he said as he walked toward the bookshelf. Jamaal picked up a football and looked at the signature on the ball. "Should I be impressed that you got the Texans' quarterback to autograph a ball for you?" He turned suddenly and flipped the ball to Charles. The ball bounced off the desk and landed on the floor. "Sorry," Jamaal said while laughing, "I thought you were going to break to the outside."

"What do you want, Jamaal? I have a busy afternoon," the mayor said with an obvious tone of irritation. He found he was getting annoyed by Jamaal more easily with each passing week.

"Yes, yes. I know. You must shut down the Livestock Show and Rodeo. That's going to piss off a few people." Jamaal settled his tall, lean body into a chair while placing his fedora and feet on Charles' desk. The reverend wondered if the mayor would ever object to the disrespect he showed while in the office.

"How do you know that?" the mayor demanded. Jamaal has placed a spy in my office, the mayor thought. Fewer than twenty people knew about the shutdown. But that is a problem for another day, he decided.

"I have my sources." Jamaal waved his hand dismissively. "If the cowboys and cowgirls didn't like you before, this will seal the deal. They spend eleven months preparing to spend a month playing in cow shit, and you are going to spoil their fun." Jamaal shook his head. "I pity the fool."

Charles frowned. "Shutting down the livestock show and rodeo is necessary. In case your source failed to inform you, we have a public health emergency. It was confirmed today that an individual who tested positive for COVID was at the livestock show yesterday. Who knows how many others are infected and walking around exposing others? There are seventy thousand people in the petri dish we call NRG each night to watch the rodeo and listen to that God-awful country music that they love. We can't risk exposing so many people to this virtuous virus."

Jamaal held up his hands. "I think you mean virulent. But save that bullshit for the public. I am not criticizing you, Charles. I am just pointing out an obvious fact. This will not help your popularity with the red-neck crowd. Not that they really matter in Houston politics, but statewide is a different matter. And you are thinking statewide, aren't you, Chuck?"

"Whatever," Charles shouted. "Why are you here?"

"I was nearby and thought I'd drop in to say hello to my old friend. We are still friends, aren't we?"

"You tell me, Jamaal. You are the one who makes demands and threats."

"I am shocked that you see it that way, Chuck. What you consider demands are simply requests that you use your power to further our shared goals. And I have never threatened you. I have simply reminded you of your obligation to me."

Charles waved his hand at Jamaal. "Don't bullshit me, boy—"

Before Charles knew what was happening, Jamaal was on

his feet and reaching across the desk to grab the mayor by the front of his shirt. Jamaal pulled Charles across the desk until their noses were six inches apart. "You fat shit," Jamaal snarled. "I am not your boy. I am your guardian, and you better not forget that." Jamaal pushed Charles backwards into his chair and returned to his own seat. "Since you are going to be busy issuing orders, why don't you implement the plan we discussed last year? A year ago, you said that if you were re-elected that you would endorse my proposal. I helped you keep your seat, but you have done nothing to repay your debt to me."

"Now isn't the time. I still can't justify measures that radical. And, in case you didn't get the memo, I am dealing with a pandemic. That is much more urgent than renter protections. Besides, I am already doing something unprecedented in shutting down the freaking rodeo. As you said, that alone is going to piss off a lot of people. If I propose renters' protections in the mist of a pandemic, well, that would just be throwing gasoline on the fire."

Jamaal shook his head. "You really need to take some grammar lessons. I'm sure the city budget would allow a little money for the mayor to learn how to speak properly. Anyhow, this is the same old story. Now is never the time for you. Oh well, don't say that I didn't warn you."

"What the hell does that mean?" Charles shouted.

"Think about it, old man. You are missing a golden opportunity to be a hero to the working class."

Charles leaned back in his chair and closed his eyes. I don't need this today, he thought. I had to make a tough decision, and this little punk is just wasting my time. No matter what I decide, I'll be criticized. If I allowed the rodeo to continue, hundreds, perhaps thousands, would get COVID and die. And I'd be blamed. But shutting down the rodeo is going to ruin a lot of lives. How do we do this calculus to figure out the best policy? Breathing deeply, Charles felt himself relax and opened his eyes. Jamaal had left the room.

* * *

Justin and Pratik had arrived in Houston in late February. To familiarize Justin with his new home, Pratik had been taking him around the city to see sites and attend events. Since it was rodeo time—three weeks of celebrating all things agricultural and cowboy—they were at the NRG complex to enjoy the day at the livestock show and carnival. That night, they would attend Justin's first rodeo and a concert by the country music icon Willie Nelson. Justin hated country music, but he had developed his opinion of that genre from hearing his grandmother play country music every morning when he visited her in his youth. He concluded that the basic message of country music was: my wife ran off with my best friend, my dog died, and I can't drink enough whiskey to kill the pain. That wasn't something that Justin wanted to listen to, but Pratik convinced him that country music had progressed beyond that cynical period. "Country music today isn't your grandmother's country music," Pratik explained.

As Justin and Pratik walked through NRG Center, Justin felt himself being overwhelmed by the sights and sounds of his first livestock show. Having grown up near several farms, he was familiar with cows, horses, chickens, and several other animals. But this was something else entirely. There were hundreds of animals of nearly every variety he could think of. All of them seemed to be tended to by individuals just a few years younger than him. He had never experienced such a thing, and he found it amazingly inspiring.

"The livestock show," Pratik explained, "gives kids an opportunity to raise and exhibit animals and do other things related to agriculture. They compete for scholarships. Talking to them can be very interesting. A few years ago, I talked to several girls who had refurbished an old tractor and were displaying it."

"I didn't realize that there were so many farms in Houston," Justin said.

"There probably aren't any farms in Houston," Pratik

responded. "These kids come from all over the state. I think that some are even from neighboring states. But many of the counties adjacent to Harris County are heavily agricultural." Patrik pointed to a steer with horns that were nearly eight feet from tip to tip. "That there is a Texas longhorn."

"That's crazy," Justin squealed. "Those horns are huge."

When they got to the front of the exhibition center, they noticed vendors frantically placing signs that announced huge discounts on merchandise. "What is going on?" Justin asked one vendor.

"The mayor is shutting us down as of seven this evening because of this COVID thing," the man said. "We need to get rid of this merchandise any way we can. Would you boys like to buy a pair of boots?"

Justin thought for a moment. "I think I will. But I'll pay full price. It sucks that you are being forced to close, and I don't want to benefit from your misfortune."

"This is going to hurt many people," Pratik said. "This must be a big event for you vendors, and you are going to lose a lot of income. That doesn't seem fair that you must suffer through no fault of your own."

"I hear you," the man said. "I get a third of my annual income from this one event. But I can't do anything about it. I need to cut my losses and do what I can to make it through this bullshit."

Justin and Pratik looked at each other and nodded. They both realized that their first clients might be emerging before their eyes.

WE MUST EACH DO OUR PART

March 2020

Judge Marta Escobar's assistant, Tilde Garcia, motioned for Jamaal to enter the judge's office. Escobar extended her hand and offered a firm handshake. The judge did not preside over a courtroom. A peculiarity of Texas law gave the top county official the title of Judge. Escobar presided over the county commissioners court, which was the county equivalent of a city council. "To what do I owe this pleasure, Rev. Wilkes?"

"I understand that you have a meeting with the mayor tomorrow, and I—"

Escobar interrupted him. "How do you know that?" Christ, she thought, this man of God has a spy in my office.

Jamaal smiled as he looked around the room. The walls were deep purple, and the drapes were gold. The furniture was modern and looked new. No pictures or documents adorned the walls, and the bookshelves were bare. Perhaps she hasn't had time to hang anything, Jamaal thought. After all, she's only been in office a few months. But this room looks regal and is a far cry from Charles Benton's pathetic office, he thought. "I have my sources. But that's not important at the moment. Nearly a year ago, I presented Charles Benton with a proposal to ease the suffering of Houston's most vulnerable citizens. While he has feigned support for my proposal, he has yet to take any action. To be frank, I don't think that he ever will. You seem like a woman who likes to take bold action, and so I have come to make my proposal to you. Charles doesn't know that I am here, and I would prefer to keep it that way."

Escobar and Jamaal stared at one another. That's one desirable woman, Jamaal thought as he looked at Escobar. She had light brown skin, black hair that fell just below her shoulders, and a very attractive figure. Jamaal couldn't detect any makeup. Pictures don't do her justice, he concluded. I bet she's a firecracker in bed. From my experience, Latinas usually are. I have to get me some of that, but today's not the day. Maybe when this is over. He smiled at the thought. As their silence lingered, Jammal noticed the judge was also smiling.

As Escobar studied Jamaal, she estimated his height at 6'3". Even in his finely tailored suit, it was obvious that he was in excellent shape. His hair was closely cropped, and his face was cleanly shaved. His eyes sparkled, but she couldn't decide if it was because of amusement or because of deviousness. Escobar liked devious men, but only if they were on her side. I wonder what he looks like naked. I'll have to find out, but today's not the day, she thought. Maybe when this is over. "Okay," she nodded, "I'll give you thirty minutes. Then I have to finish preparing for a press briefing."

"To announce a stay-at-home order," Jamaal remarked, as if he were reporting baseball scores. Escobar raised her eyebrows. "Like I said, I have my sources. But let's not waste any more time with things that aren't important."

For the next twenty minutes, Jamaal explained his proposal. Escobar listened attentively, only speaking to ask a few questions for clarification. He concluded by saying, "As I mentioned, Charles has expressed support for this plan, but he refuses to take action. He says that the time isn't right, he can't justify it, or some other excuse. I assume he doesn't really support this plan. I think you are better than that. Further, if my understanding is correct, you have the authority to act unilaterally."

This guy really knows how to lay on the bullshit, Escobar thought. I like his proposal, and it fits perfectly with my own ambitions. Charles is right. Now isn't the time, it can't be justified. But if I play my cards right, in another month it would be welcomed. And because of the public health emergency, I can do it by executive order rather than needing to convince those stupid commissioners. This is brilliant, but I will need to be careful with this guy. I can't allow him to steal my limelight. If he will go behind the mayor's back, he'd do the same to me.

Escobar hid her excitement behind a straight face. "That is an interesting plan, Rev. Wilkes. There is a lot to digest, and I'm not sure that I have the authority to implement any of the measures you propose. I will need to have my legal team look into it. Thank you for sharing this with me. I will give it serious consideration." She glanced at her watch. "I'm sorry to cut this short, but I need to finish my preparation for the press briefing." Escobar stood and escorted Jamaal from her office.

Returning to her desk, Escobar sat with a heavy sigh of relief. Looking upward, she crossed herself and muttered, "Thank you, Jesus. This is a miracle."

* * *

An hour later, Escobar stood at the podium, looking at the assembled media. She had changed into her lucky dark purple pants suit. Good things always happened when she wore it. As she looked around the room, it appeared that every news outlet in the county was present. Good, she thought, everyone in Harris County will soon know who is boss. The media seemed to sense that something big was about to happen.

"As you know, we are facing the greatest public health threat this nation has seen in a century. The severity of this threat requires a dramatic and decisive response. Therefore, I am ordering all non-essential businesses, including restaurants, bars, gyms, churches, and hairdressers, to close as of 6 p.m. today and to remain closed for at least two weeks. By the end of the day, we will supply a complete list of which businesses may continue to operate and which must close. We are still trying to determine which businesses are essential and which are not." An audible gasp came from the media.

"In addition, all individuals are required to wear a face mask when in public. Masks have been proven to slow the spread of the virus. While surgical masks are preferred, such masks are currently in short supply. Therefore, any type of facial covering will suffice for the purposes of this order. The important thing at this time is for us to contain any airborne particles that may contain the novel coronavirus and any form of face covering, no matter how crude and unscientific it may be, is essential to this goal.

"Further, gatherings of more than six people are prohibited, even in private homes. Large groups present a vulnerable situation and must be minimized. We've seen what is happening in Italy, Japan, and lots of other places. It would be foolhardy to think that what is happening in Third World countries can't happen here. And when in the presence of others, you must maintain a distance of at least six feet. This social distancing will reduce the chance of spreading the virus. Combined with the wearing of masks, these precautions will stop the spread of the virus. We must each do our part.

"I know that this will be painful for all of us. However, I am following the advice of the county's top public health professionals. The science shows that the coronavirus is easily spread to others who are in close proximity. These measures should reduce close contact with others and provide protection for those times when we must be in public.

"If we all do our part, we can stop the spread of the virus. Scientists have told me that these measures will prevent our hospitals and health care professionals from being overwhelmed. In other communities, the number of confirmed COVID cases has skyrocketed, and their hospitals have been filled to capacity. We want to flatten the curve—to keep the increase in new cases to a level that hospitals and health care professionals can comfortably manage. I don't want to look back on this and regret not doing what I should of.

"If we all cooperate, we should be able to return to normal in two weeks. Thank you. I will not be answering questions today." Escobar turned and walked away. She stopped suddenly and returned to the podium. "One last thing," she said, "the baseball season opens in a few weeks. Go Astros!" The media looked at one another in bewilderment as Escobar turned and walked out of the room.

WE NEED TO WORK TOGETHER

March 2020

Marta Escobar stood in the doorway to Mayor Benton's office. She smiled as she surveyed the room. It was smaller than her office and looked like it had last been updated during the Truman Administration. Yes, she thought, it's much better to be the county judge than the city mayor, especially during a public health emergency.

Mayor Benton stood as she approached his desk and extended his hand. "Judge Escobar, I'm pleased to finally meet you in person."

Escobar smiled. "The pleasure is all mine, though I suspect that what I am about to tell you won't be so pleasurable."

Charles nodded and motioned for her to take a seat. She sat with a posture that suggested a stern upbringing and studied Charles' face. Neither wore a face mask, despite the judge's order the previous day. Charles, she thought, is showing his age. His face is pudgy, she noted, and most of his hair is gray. His eyes look fatigued, which isn't surprising given the public health emergency both of us are dealing with.

This guy won't give me any problems, she thought. He looks like he is out of his league. "Mayor Benton, as you know, the governor has declared a public health emergency. Such a declaration grants each county judge extraordinary powers. I exercised some of those powers yesterday. At a time like this, my primary responsibility is public safety. This is an issue of life or death. We have seen what this virus has done in other locales. I will do whatever it takes to save lives, but I am already hearing complaints about the measures that I have implemented. I can take the criticism. It's a part of the job, as I'm sure you know."

"Yes, we can't please everyone," the mayor agreed. "We have to do what is best for the public. And that will obviously upset some people. Shutting down the rodeo wasn't popular, but it was the right thing to do. Just like your order yesterday."

"Exactly. I came here today to ask for your support. A firm statement to that effect would be beneficial to all and appreciated by me. I was just elected last November, and this is the first time that I have held a public office. I have yet to develop the reputation that you have, and your support would convince many people to be more compliant. The last thing we need right now is a bunch of right-wing lunatics causing problems. A united front from public officials will help silence the critics and building support from the public. We need to cease the day."

Charles grimaced. He had no problem supporting the judge, but he didn't want to become too closely associated with her. He would support her from a distance. There were rumors she held some very radical ideas. Some said that she was to the left of Castro, but most people with that opinion were conservatives. Regardless, he didn't want to be tied too closely with Escobar. Nor did he want to be her toady. "Certainly, I can issue a statement in support of your measures."

Escobar shook her head. "I'm sorry, but that won't suffice. I need you to appear at a press conference with me to announce that the city and county are working together on our pandemic response. As they say, a picture is worth a thousand words. A joint appearance would send a much stronger message than a written statement."

"But," Charles objected, "so far I haven't heard how we are working together. What role will the city be playing in this?"

Escobar smiled. "I haven't decided yet. I have a few ideas that I am exploring, but trust me, it will be an important role. For now, your role will be to support me. You can do that, can't you?" Her tone implied that she was issuing an order, not asking a question.

This is bullshit, Charles thought. This woman is a political newcomer, and she has more power than me. Christ, she's not even thirty years old, and she's acting like she is my superior. He gasped when he realized she was his superior at the moment. The county judge was given far more emergency powers than a mayor. The reason was simple and made sense. Many Texans did not live in a city, but all of them lived in a county. In an emergency, rural Texans would have nobody watching over them if emergency powers were only given to mayors. And if anybody needed to be watched over, it was those yellow dog Republicans. Charles chuckled as he thought of that term—it had long been used to describe Southern voters who would vote for a yellow dog before voting for a Republican. Now, it was rural Texans who were equally stubborn and refused to vote for a Democrat. He couldn't remember when Texas became a red state, but he seemed to think that it was during the Reagan era.

"Well?" Escobar finally asked impatiently. "I have a press conference scheduled for this afternoon. You will join me, won't you?"

Charles shook his head. "I have meetings all afternoon with department heads to decide how we are going to implement yesterday's orders. I really don't have time to attend a press conference."

Escobar stared icily. "I suggest you find the time. Your absence will be duly noted, and the press will probably wonder why you are hiding from the public during this public health emergency. We need to work together, Mayor." Escobar stood. "Have it your way," she said, "but don't say that I didn't warn you. We can work together, or…." She held her hands out with raised palms.

This is one bossy bitch, Charles thought. She sounds just like

Jamaal. But she holds all the cards at the moment. When this is over in a few weeks, her powers will return to normal. In the meantime, I should probably suck it up and be a team player. "Okay," he said meekly. "I'll be there."

SHE SEEMS LIKE A POWER LUSTER

March 2020

"What do you think, Justin?" Pratik asked. They had just watched Marta Escobar's latest press briefing. She had announced further closures, including schools and day care facilities, as well as more restrictions on individual activities.

"This is like something out of a dystopian novel," Justin said as he shook his head. "There is certainly a lot that we don't know about this virus, but closing businesses and forcing people to stay home isn't the proper response. Nothing good can come from that. She's treating us like children who can't make rational decisions."

"Yes," Pratik responded, "Escobar should just provide us with information, make suggestions on how to reduce our risk, and let us decide for ourselves what risks we will take. She said that if we don't wear a mask, people will die. She didn't bother to explain how this can happen if an individual isn't infected. It can't, but unfortunately, most people won't identify that fact. This looks like a power grab to me, and she is using the pandemic as an excuse.

"This is akin to arresting people because they might commit a crime. We arrest people when there is evidence that they actually committed a crime, not merely because they have the potential to do so. I can understand quarantining those who are infected—they pose an objective threat to others. But there must be evidence that the person is actually infected. Escobar essentially is quarantining everyone, whether or not they are guilty.

"This is going to be a disaster for many businesses. As one example, restaurants are going to have food spoiling. They have no income and will have to replace the food when they are allowed to reopen. Even worse, the workers are going to suffer horribly. Many live paycheck to paycheck, and two weeks without income is going to make it almost impossible to pay their bills."

Justin frowned. "Escobar didn't even address that. She expects people to live without a livelihood. Either she hasn't identified that fact, or she doesn't care. Neither of those is good. She didn't mention any alternatives to a lockdown, which suggests to me she didn't consider them. She claims that this will save lives, but she is going to wreck a lot of lives in the process. And she didn't utter a peep about what would happen if this lockdown doesn't work. How long will she continue disrupting our lives?" Justin thought a moment before continuing. "I know little about her, but she sure seems like a power luster."

Pratik nodded. "Escobar insisted that she's following the science. Scientists can tell us about the virus, how it spreads, and what we can do to reduce our risk, but they shouldn't be setting government policy. Government's purpose is to protect our rights, not protect us from disease. In their zeal to protect us, they are trampling on our liberties. Nothing good can come from that. Epistemology trumps epidemiology. Escobar implies she is stopping people from making bad choices. She's also stopping us from making good choices. If an individual makes a terrible choice, then he suffers the consequences. If Escobar makes a terrible choice, then all of us suffer the consequences."

Justin smiled sadly. "I like that point. There may be a silver lining to this dark cloud. We have a lot of potential clients. These business owners need a consistent, rational argument against these dictates. We need to figure out how to reach them."

"One problem I see," Pratik said, "is the diversity of businesses affected by this. It will affect them in different ways. Each will have their own particular concerns and issues. We couldn't possibly address all of them. I think we should either focus on one or two different industries or develop a message that applies to multiple industries."

"Property rights," Justin replied, "obviously apply to every business. They should be free to produce and trade as they think best. That includes the freedom to determine what precautions to take to keep employees and customers safe, and employees and customers should be free to decide if those measures are acceptable. Those who aren't infected should be free to live their lives."

"There is also freedom of association," Pratik added. "That's essentially an application of property rights, but it may not appeal to many people. Property rights aren't the sexiest of topics."

"Yeah," Justin said, "people don't care about property rights until it is their property that is threatened. Part of our challenge will be to explain the importance of the right to property. The lockdown is making it impossible to exercise three crucial aspects of that right—production, trade, and use. And that affects everyone. We can defend the broader principle and then use particular industries or businesses or individuals as concrete examples."

"I like that idea, Justin. But how are we going to reach our potential clients? Their businesses are closed, so we can't go to their facility. Developing a list of emails or addresses would take forever."

"We do have that list of media outlets and bloggers that we put together when we were in Ohio. That is one way to get our message out." Justin paused as he considered a thought. "We could also start our own blog. That would give us a forum to reach everyone in a single fell swoop. We could write articles for our blog and then send links or the articles to the media and bloggers. That isn't ideal, but it is a good start."

Pratik nodded and smiled. "Agreed. Let's spend the rest of the day thinking about the blog. We'll need a name, a web host, and some other details. A list of topics to address would also be good. We could get a blog set up in an hour, but we need to give some thought to it. A little time planning now could save us a lot of time and grief in the future."

Justin shook his head sadly. "Too bad Escobar didn't follow that advice. This couldn't have been thought out very well. There are going to be a lot of problems and grief in the coming weeks. She said nothing about that, other than to warn us that there will be hardships. Like we needed her to tell us that. You don't need an MBA to know that shutting down businesses is going to be harmful to owners and employees."

"Maybe we are getting ahead of ourselves," Pratik said. "We need a name for our business, and then we need to do the legal paperwork. That can be done online and doesn't take long, but it still needs to be done. We need a name that captures the essence of what we do and is easy to remember."

Both thought a moment. "What is it we do?" Justin asked.

Pratik grimaced. "That is a good question, and difficult to answer in a few words. I'd say that we want to stop injustice."

"Let's phrase it in terms of a positive," Justin said. "The positive is always more powerful than a negative."

"Okay, good point. We seek justice for those being subjected to unjust intellectual and political attacks."

"That's it," Justin said excitedly. "That's our name. Justice Inc."

IDEOLOGUES ARE ALWAYS DANGEROUS

March 2020

"Elections have consequences," Roger Mason ranted on air. "Harris County voters elected Comrade Escobar, and we are paying the price. I warned you last fall, and now my predictions are coming true." Roger Mason was Houston's most popular radio talk show host. An outspoken conservative with libertarian leanings, he outraged many and entertained all. He didn't hesitate to express his opinions on any issue, even if he knew little about it, and he didn't care who he offended. Many thought he was offensive simply to draw attention to himself, and it was a claim that had merit. However, like many who don't care about offending others, he was easily offended himself.

The forty-year-old had grown up in Victoria, about one-hundred thirty miles southwest of Houston. After graduating from the University of Houston, he worked for several different newspapers and radio stations. When he was thirty, he cajoled a friend who was the general manager of a local radio station to give him an hour of airtime on Sunday. The station was struggling, and the manager figured he had nothing to lose. Mason soon developed a following and within two years he was on the air three hours every weekday morning. A short time later, the station became profitable because of Mason.

Mason was just under six feet tall, and though not muscular, he was a solidly built man. He visited his barber weekly to keep his blond hair carefully trimmed in a flattop. Though born in 1980, he was devoted to the styles and culture of the 1950s. His bump music featured Buddy Holly, Jerry Lee Lewis, and Little Richard. Reflecting his bohemian inclinations, he also sported a soul patch.

"This lockdown is nothing more than a power grab. I told you last year that the Comrade wants to control your life. Now that you have elected her, she is doing just that. Who is she to decide what businesses are essential? To the workers who she has tossed out of work, their job is essential. To the business owners who have been forced to close, their business is essential. Comrade Escobar has no right to decide who is essential and who isn't. I say that Comrade Escobar isn't essential.

"And this mandate that we wear a rag on our face.... Well, that's just ridiculous. Masks don't work. Wearing one because the Comrade demands it is nothing more than a sign of obsequiousness. This is a test by Escobar to see how obedient you will be. You can bet the liberals will be quick to don their masks to signal their virtue. As for me, I am not a sheep. I will not be led to the slaughter. Nor will I wear a face diaper, and if Escobar doesn't like it, she can arrest me.

"I encourage all of you to do the same. She can't arrest all of us, and the more of us who resist, the greater the pressure on her to rescind these orders. I encourage businesses to remain open and defy the Comrade. We still need to work, eat, and play. The pandemic hasn't stopped our need to live.

"We have rights, and we need to protect them. We can't let some would-be dictator trample on our freedom.

"Comrade Escobar says that she is trying to save lives. She has a funny way of doing that since she is destroying lives. And trust me, this lockdown will destroy lives. We will soon see businesses close for good. Homeowners will soon be unable to pay their mortgage. We will soon see renters unable to pay their rent. People won't be able to put food on the table or go to the doctor. Everywhere we look, we will soon see suffering and destruction. That isn't saving lives, and to claim that it is, well, that's just intellectually dishonest. But what do you expect from a Marxist?

"This virus is no more threatening than the common cold, which I might remind you is also caused by a coronavirus. The Comrade and her ilk are manufacturing a crisis in order to control our lives. That tactic is right out of the Marxist playbook. Far too many of you will sacrifice your liberties for the perception of safety. But as Benjamin Franklin once remarked, 'They who can give up essential liberty to obtain a little temporary safety, deserve neither liberty nor safety.'

"Voters made a huge mistake in electing Marta Escobar. We can mitigate the damage of that mistake by resisting her and her mandates. Now is the time for civil disobedience. Escobar talks about the need to be united. I agree. We need to be united against her and her egregious attempt to take away our God-given rights. If we passively accept this lockdown, we will certainly see worse in the future.

"Despite her claims, the Comrade isn't being guided by science. She is being guided by Marx and Lenin and Saul Alinsky. She is being guided by Leftist ideology, and ideologues are always dangerous. They are unwilling to consider any ideas or opinions that differ from their own. They rigidly stick to their dogma, come hell or high water. Mark my words, if we allow her to get away with this, we will see more controls and restrictions. We will experience hell right here on Earth.

"Many of you probably think that I am being melodramatic, and my words are hyperbole. Trust me, I am not exaggerating. And the time to realize that is now, before it is too late.

"Escobar is rejecting God, just like her commie friends. She believes rights come from the State, not God. And what the State giveth, the State can taketh away. As an agent of the State, Escobar has just taken away our God-given rights.

"Escobar talks about flattening the curve, whatever the hell that means. I'd like to flatten her nose and teach her a lesson. But violence isn't the answer. We need to express better ideas consistently and coherently. We need to awaken the patriots and recruit new ones."

THE BOLD SEIZE
THE MOMENT

April 2020

Lia Patel and Roderick Jackson opened the church door and warily stared into the building. Other than a faint light in the sanctuary, the room was dark. They had received a call saying that Rev. Jamaal Wilkes wanted a meeting with the two councilmen. Though they were new to the city council, having been elected the previous November, both had ample street smarts. They shared a concern that this meeting was some kind of setup. But the prospect of meeting the Reverend motivated them to push aside their concerns. Everything that they knew about him indicated he would be an ally to their cause.

"Lia, Roderick," a voice boomed from the loudspeakers. "I am glad that you could join me. Why don't you come down the aisle, and we'll go to my office to chat."

Lia and Roderick looked at one another and nodded. As they walked toward the front of the room, they could detect the faint scent of marijuana. Roderick smiled. Perhaps Rev. Wilkes is secretly a Rastafarian, he thought. As they neared the sanctuary, Jamaal suddenly stood in the choir loft. Lia and Roderick were visibly startled at his abrupt appearance.

Jamaal laughed softly. "I apologize if I alarmed you. I needed to verify your identity before revealing myself. More people than I can count have threatened me, and I find it necessary to be very cautious. Even here. Please, follow me." He stepped down from the choir loft and gestured toward a barely discernible doorway.

Jamaal was silent until the three were seated in his office. As he got comfortable in his chair, he surveyed his two guests. Lia Patel was a diminutive woman with a green and yellow mohawk. She was dressed entirely in black and sported a nose ring. Jamaal suspected she was less than five feet tall and couldn't weigh over ninety pounds. She's too skinny for my taste, Jamaal thought. He reminded himself not to judge a book by its cover. Maybe, he thought, she might be a powerhouse in bed. Her face was contorted in a way that made Jamaal think she must be continually constipated.

Roderick was nearly as tall as Jamaal, but looked like he weighed little more than Lia. He had a scar on his right cheek, and his lips were twisted into a scowl. His head was shaved, and he had studs in both ear lobes. He wore a torn NWA T-shirt and pants that were halfway down his butt. These two are real pieces of work, Jamaal thought. How the hell did they ever get elected to the city council? he asked himself.

"Charles Benton is a weakling," Jamaal finally said. "He has gone soft, both physically and spiritually. He once had a fire in his belly for the same policies we advocate and support. Now his belly is full of caviar and lobster. Today he spends more time worrying about the next election than getting things done. I have lost patience with him.

"For twenty years I have supported Charles in his political ambitions. I have helped raise money for his campaigns. I have given sermons endorsing him, and I have appeared beside him for press conferences and charity events. But my support has not been reciprocated. He has abandoned me when he can do the most good. He is more concerned with appearances than principles. And that is where I think the two of you can help."

Jamaal spent twenty minutes explaining his plan. Lia and Roderick were silent, but nodded each time Jamaal articulated a particular measure to implement. When he finished, Jamaal alternated his gaze between them. They remained silent. Whether they were deep in thought or simply didn't know what to say, Jamaal wasn't sure. "Well?" he finally asked, while holding his palms upward.

Lia and Roderick looked at one another. Roderick nodded, and Lia spoke. "Rev. Wilkes, what you propose is very close to some ideas that Roderick and I have discussed many times. But as the two newest members of the council, we don't have the political clout to pass this. Maybe in time, but not today."

Jamaal took a deep breath. Maybe I was wrong about these two, he thought. "At the risk of being rude, you sound just like the mayor. His favorite excuse is that the time isn't right. For weaklings like the mayor, the time is never right. For those who are bold, as I believe you two are, the time is always right. The bold seize the moment and take action. The weak run and hide."

Roderick stood and balled his fists. Lia grabbed his wrist and directed him back into his seat. "Roderick doesn't enjoy being called a weakling, and neither do I," she said.

Jamaal smiled and nodded. "I understand, and that wasn't my intent. I certainly don't expect you to introduce the ordinance I propose at the next council session. But I think you will be able to do so much sooner than you may realize."

"How is that?" Roderick asked with a tone of hostility.

"I have been working on this plan for more than a year. I have assembled a small army of ministers, activists, tenants, and low-income Houstonians. They don't know my entire plan—just enough to get their support. When the full plan is revealed, I have every reason to believe that they will do anything I command. These people are hurting, and the pandemic is making it worse. They will do almost anything, including busting down some doors, to obtain a remedy. Of course, I am speaking metaphorically. Trust me, if you two get in front of this, you'll get the votes of every renter and low-income person in the city. You'll have a virtual guaranteed victory for any political office you want."

Lia frowned. "Forgive me if I appear daft, but how can you be so certain of that? Your proposal is chalk full of potential problems."

Jamaal grimaced at the grammatical error. "As I mentioned, I have been supporting Charles Benton for twenty years. My support has gone beyond public appearances and sermons. I have shaped his message during each campaign. He started as a councilman, just like you. He then served three terms in the Texas House before moving to the Senate. And now he is the mayor of the nation's fourth largest city. I made that possible. Much of what I did was shape his positions on issues. I told him what policies to advocate for and support. However, he now believes that he knows better than me. Now the puppet thinks he is smarter than his master. Charles knows my plan. I have spoken to him about it multiple times. He professes support for it but refuses to take action. If he won't support what needs to be done, then I will support those who will.

"I am a voice for the most vulnerable citizens in our community. But I am only one voice and can be easily ignored. However, if we join our voices, we can create a choir that can't be ignored."

ALL OF THIS WAS PREDICTABLE

April 2020

Jamaal took a sip of Blue Mountain coffee. Jamaal would have said that the coffee served in Charles' office tasted like mud, but that would be an insult to mud. This office is not only modern, he thought, it projects power, just like its occupant. Power has its privileges, he concluded. Like the world's best coffee. But one has to exercise that power. "I see that your taste in coffee matches your taste in decor," he said as he waved his arm and surveyed the room. With Jamaal's eyes elsewhere, Marta Escobar unbuttoned the top of her blouse to reveal her cleavage. Damn, he thought when he turned back to her. She's making a play at me. Not today, but soon, he told himself.

"Thank you, Reverend. I believe in having the best. Otherwise, what is the point of living? So, how can I help you today?" Escobar asked.

"We are a month into the lockdown, and I think it may be time to put my plan into action." Jamaal took another sip of coffee before placing the mug on the table. "Have you given any more thought to it?"

"Yes, I have. It's a plan with much merit. However, at the risk of sounding like Mayor Benton, because of the plan's ambitiousness, it must be done in stages. I believe we will be ready for the first stage within a few weeks." Escobar took a sip from her own mug.

"Would it be asking too much for you to reveal what these stages are?" Jamaal asked with the smile of a co-conspirator.

"You're an astute man, Reverend. Why don't you venture a guess?"

"First, please call me Jamaal. Reverend is far too formal. Given the context, I think we can skip with the formalities. Don't you agree, Marta?"

Escobar scowled. She didn't like to be addressed by her first name by anyone other than her family and friends, but she would overlook the slight for the time being. "Very well, Jamaal. Care to speculate?"

Jamaal nodded and collected his thoughts. "A month ago, you announced a stay-at-home order and shuttered many businesses. You said that it would last about two weeks to flatten the curve. When that period elapsed and new cases were still increasing, you extended the order for another two weeks. That was nearly two weeks ago. Based on the numbers that I am seeing regarding new cases of COVID, the curve hasn't been flattened. Indeed, cases are increasing even more than two weeks ago. So, I think that you will be extending the stay-at-home order any day now. I suspect that in two more weeks, you will have accomplished what you intended. Then you can begin to implement my plan."

"And what have I intended, Jamaal?"

"Eviction moratoriums and rent freezes, like any dramatic policy, can't be imposed in a vacuum. There must be an emergency or crisis. The pandemic may very well be a public health emergency, but that isn't sufficient. One needs an economic crisis, or at least the appearance of one. An economic crisis makes bold steps such as we have discussed much more palatable because they offer economic relief. However, since the pandemic itself didn't and won't create an economic crisis, one must be manufactured."

Escobar narrowed her eyes as she studied Jamaal's face. I

need to be careful with this guy, she thought. He understands a lot. It would be good to know how much he has figured out. "That's an interesting theory, Jamaal. But what economic crisis am I manufacturing? And why would I do such a thing? My job is to protect the public, not create crises."

Jamaal smiled knowingly. She might think that she is fooling me, but she isn't, he thought. "When you shut down businesses, people lost their job. Unemployment numbers have been skyrocketing ever since. A few weeks without a paycheck would be a struggle for most people, particularly those with a modest income, but four weeks, six weeks.... Six weeks with no income is devastating for most families. They have little savings to sustain them. Yet, they must put food on the table, take the kids to the doctor, pay the rent. They are facing hunger, health problems, and perhaps homelessness. All of this was predictable. How can they live without a livelihood? They can't. They can't unless the government steps in to be their savior. That's where you come in. You can be their savior."

A faint, reluctant smile formed on Escobar's lips. "Continue," she commanded.

"I think that I've hit the high points. I am sure that I don't have all the details correct, but I think I understand the general idea." Jamaal took another sip of coffee. It was cold, but still preferable to what Charles served. "How did I do?"

There is no point in denying it, Escobar thought. I need this guy on my side, and if I lie, he'll never trust me. "Yes," she admitted, "you understand the general idea."

"So," Jamaal said with a smile, "in two weeks my plan will make you a savior." He took another sip of coffee. "Is there anything that I can do to help?"

Escobar thought for a moment. "Actually, there is," she said. "You could rile up your people. Have them email my office. Have them call city council members. They need to make it known how dire their situation is. The more noise that they create, the more the public will support this. After all, fifty million Frenchmen can't be wrong. I am sure that the landlords and billionaire real estate investors will complain. It would be helpful if you can drown them out. Then, the need for renters' protections will be a far-gone conclusion."

I seem to be the only one who knows proper grammar, Jamaal thought to himself. "I think I can arrange that."

"If enough people make enough noise, then I can let the will of the people guide my actions. As a servant of the public, I have a duty to abide by and implement the will of the people. Escobar had repeated those bromides so many times that she was actually starting to believe them.

Jamaal smiled slightly. "Then I will make it my job to shape the will of the people."

I AM A THREAT TO THEIR TYRANNY

April 2020

"**W**hat the hell?" Roger Mason shouted the day after Marta Escobar extended her stay-at-home order. "Two more weeks of lockdown. Comrade Escobar told us it would take two weeks to flatten the curve and then we'd return to normal. It's been a month, and the damn curve hasn't been flattened. And it won't be until we stop this power grab. I warned you people that this would happen. I warned you last fall that electing this communist would be a complete disaster. Now you can see it for yourself."

Mason was broadcasting from the parking lot of the Confederate Grill on San Felipe, just north of the world-famous Galleria Mall. Mark Adams, the restaurant owner, was a big fan of Mason and finally took the talking head's pleas to disregard the stay-at-home order to heart. Adams had closed his business for a month, but if he waited any longer to reopen, there wouldn't be a business. He couldn't afford to keep paying his staff, as well as the upkeep of the building, taxes, insurance, and all the other overhead that accompanied small business ownership.

Adams faced a tough choice, and he decided he would not give up his dream of owning a restaurant without a fight. He had only been open for six months before the pandemic, and the restaurant had developed a loyal following and stellar reviews. It would be one thing to fail because people simply didn't like his restaurant. He could handle that. But he could not handle being driven out of business by government policies.

Adams had developed a plan to keep employees and customers safe. He moved half of his tables to the parking lot and spaced the inside tables at least ten feet apart. Every surface in the restaurant had been thoroughly sanitized, and they would be cleaned each time a table became vacant. Doorknobs and other surfaces that were frequently touched were sanitized every thirty minutes. He had hand sanitizer on every table, in the restrooms, and near the entrance. Adams required his employees to wear masks but made it optional for diners. He wanted to create an environment in which patrons felt safe. Most of his employees were happy to get back to work, but a few refused to wear a mask. Adams reluctantly terminated their employment.

Adams knew he would struggle to break even with the additional costs of regular cleaning and sanitizing. However, breaking even was better than losing money every day the restaurant was closed. He hoped his act of defiance would encourage others to do the same. If enough business owners followed Adams' lead, perhaps the lockdown orders would be rescinded and the city could return to normal.

"I am broadcasting from the Confederate Grill today, and I urge all patriots to come by to support the brave business owner, Mark Adams. He is open today, though with a limited menu. However, he has plenty of beer, wine, bourbon, and just about any other beverage you might desire. I will be here until 1 p.m., so stop by, say hello, and have a cold one with me. We need to show Escobar that we won't tolerate her dictatorial mandates."

For the rest of the show's first segment, Mason continued to taunt and berate Escobar. In between his insults, he pleaded with listeners to visit the restaurant. By the time he began the second hour of the show, all the tables were full and a line had formed in the parking lot. After four weeks of being prohibited from dining in a restaurant, many Houstonians were eager to return to some level of normalcy.

"Welcome back to the show, folks," Mason said to open the second segment. "We are having a tremendous response and I, along with Mark, want to thank every one of you. If we tolerate Escobar's antics, they will continue. Ayn Rand called it the sanction of the victim—the willingness of someone to tolerate an injustice without fighting back. Well, we're fighting back. Let Escobar try to enforce her orders. She can't arrest all of us."

"No, she can't," boomed a loud voice behind Mason. Mason turned to see Sheriff Ricky Alvarez flanked by two deputies on each side of him. "But I can arrest you, Mr. Mason. Please stand and place your hands on the table in front of you."

"How great is this?" Mason shouted into his microphone. "I am being arrested live and on air. This must be a radio first. And it is clearly a violation of my First Amendment right to free speech."

"Mr. Mason, if you refuse to cooperate, we will have no choice but to resort to stronger measures," the sheriff said sternly. "This isn't about freedom of speech. It's about your open defiance of an order that was issued in full compliance with the law. It is my job to enforce the law, and that is what I am here to do. You need to accept that fact and cooperate."

Several diners realized what was happening and moved toward the table where the confrontation was occurring. As the word spread, dozens of patrons congregated around Mason and the sheriff. Mason saw this and stood up. Placing his hands on the table, he exhorted his listeners to back away. "We don't need to start a riot. At least not today. Let the toady sheriff follow his orders. We've delivered a powerful message today, and that is a good start. They are going to arrest me because I am a threat to their tyranny. They don't want me to speak the truth, and they don't want you to hear the truth."

As the deputies took Mason to a squad car, Adams shouted above the din being created by the incredulous crowd. He held up a jar. "I'm putting $100 in this jar to help pay Roger's bail. Anyone who wants to contribute is welcome to do so." He placed the jar on the table that Mason had been using for his broadcast and walked away. "I'm calling my lawyer."

Adams was quickly intercepted by Sheriff Alvarez. "Mr. Adams," he said, "you must shut down your restaurant immediately. If you refuse, we will begin arresting you and your employees. I could arrest you, your staff, and all the diners here, but I'll give you a chance to resolve this without the need to take such actions." The sheriff stared at Adams without emotion.

"That sounds a lot like the threats that terrorists make," Adams replied. "If you don't meet our demands, we will start killing hostages and tossing their bodies out of the door."

"I don't think that it is appropriate to equate the enforcement of a law with the anarchy displayed by terrorists," the sheriff retorted. "Regardless, you must close your restaurant immediately. This is your final warning."

Adams shook his head and quickly weighed his options. If he remained open, he'd be morally responsible for paying bail for his employees. That would surely bankrupt him. He could survive a few more weeks of closure. As undesirable as that was, he was under duress and needed to decide quickly. "Okay, everybody. The Sheriff is ordering us to close. We will bring to-go boxes by your table, and you can take your food with you." Both diners and employees moaned but began preparations to leave.

* * *

Roger Mason was released from jail three hours after his arrest. When he exited the county jail, the press was waiting for him. "What you witnessed today," he shouted to the crowd, "blatantly violated my God-given rights. Escobar can arrest me again and again, but I will not give up the fight. She won't shut me up. I will continue to speak the truth."

DECISIVE ACTION IS NEEDED

April 2020

Marta Escobar was in the press room for her daily briefing with the media. Given the historic nature of the announcement that she was about to make, she was wearing her lucky purple pantsuit. As she approached the podium, she realized she wasn't wearing a mask. Oh well, she thought, do as I say, not as I do. Besides, those damn masks make it difficult to speak clearly. If anyone makes an issue of it, I'll just say that I have received some complaints that my briefings are difficult to understand. Escobar chuckled as she thought of her personal motto: There are two kinds of rules. Those I make, and those I break. And in this instance, I'm doing both.

"Good morning, everyone," she began. "Six weeks ago, we enacted a series of policies designed to slow the spread of the novel coronavirus. Our efforts have been extremely successful. Even though the number of new cases and deaths continues to rise, public health officials assure me that the numbers would be much worse if we had not taken the steps that we did. The hardships that we all have endured have been worth it. Countless lives have been saved. But our work is not done. We need renewed vigilance to defeat this pandemic.

"When I first announced my stay-at-home order, I cautioned

we would face difficult times. I don't think any of us could have predicted just how difficult things would become. Tens of thousands have lost their jobs and unemployment in Harris County is now at an all-time high. Many of those who lost their job had little savings, and they are struggling to put food on the table, pay for health care, and pay the rent. They cannot find gameful employment. Many are feeling desperate, hopeless, and helpless. They wonder how they will continue to survive.

"Our social safety net provides assistance to families needing help with food and health care, but other than housing vouchers, little is done to provide help with housing. However, housing vouchers have a waiting list for years, so they provide no immediate help at this trying time. That eviction filings have set record highs each of the past three weeks is testimony to the fact that our fellow citizens are struggling. And the burden is particularly heavy in communities of color. Given the current state of our economy, the short-term prospects for improvement are not encouraging.

"Over the past two weeks, my office has been besieged with emails and phone calls from desperate renters. They have fallen behind on their rent and don't know what to do. I have received reports from city officials that they, too, have received thousands of phone calls and emails. We have a housing crisis, and it promises to get worse. Decisive action is needed, and it is needed now.

"I have personally contacted both state and federal officials to request emergency housing assistance. To date, my requests have fallen on deaf ears. This leaves me with two alternatives, neither of which is attractive. I could do nothing and simply let thousands of families become homeless and everything that implies. But that alternative is morally reprehensible. Many will find themselves living on the streets, and others will be jammed into overcrowded shelters where social distancing is virtually impossible. If we allow this to happen, new cases of COVID are certain to increase. We cannot sit by idly while our neighbors are tossed from their homes and threatened with exposure to a deadly virus. There, but for the grace of God, go each of us.

"That leaves me with only one viable alternative—take action to stop the evictions and keep families in their home. The public health emergency grants me extraordinary powers, and I will exercise them to protect the residents of Harris County. I have a responsibility to do so, and I will not neglect my duty.

"Towards that end, I am announcing an eviction moratorium for non-payment of rent in Harris County for ninety days. All pending evictions are hereby dismissed, and no new evictions may be filed until this order expires. This order does not absolve renters from their responsibility to pay the rent. But it gives them breathing room and removes the stress of impending homelessness."

Jamaal was standing at the back of the room. He had entered just as Escobar had begun to talk. If she had seen him, she gave no sign. He smiled when she announced the eviction moratorium—one down and six to go, he thought.

"The housing crisis is a public health issue. And just like the coronavirus, it is an issue of life or death. Forcing families into crowded shelters—or worse, the streets—exposes them to unacceptable risks. If we allow that, people will die. This eviction moratorium will allow our most vulnerable families to remain housed. It will keep people safe. This is a vital step in our efforts to fight the pandemic.

"In addition, I am also announcing a ninety-day freeze on rents. No landlord in the county may raise the rent for ninety days. Renters are being hit with increases of fifteen percent or more. This is just compounding their problems. They were already struggling to pay the rent, and such increases make homelessness an actual possibility. Landlords are taking advantage of a public health emergency and that is morally reprehensible. I cannot and will not allow them to prey upon our most vulnerable citizens during an emergency."

Two down, Jamaal thought. Five more and my dream will be a reality, at least for ninety days.

"The public supports these renter protections. A recent

poll found that 60 percent of county residents support such measures. As a servant of the public, it is my responsibility, it is my duty, to listen to the will of the people.

"I would like to announce additional renter protections, but my legal team is still trying to determine what my powers allow. But trust me, I will exercise all powers legally given to me to keep Harris County citizens in their home and safe. I cannot and will not tolerate those who seek to profit from the misfortune of others. If landlords aren't willing to do their part voluntarily, then I will force them to do so. If they don't choose to help those in need, then I won't give them a choice."

Well, Jamaal thought, two out of seven isn't bad. Perhaps in time we'll get the other five provisions.

"The pandemic has wrecked havoc with our economy, and with it, the lives of our most vulnerable neighbors. We must do everything in our power to protect them. That is the promise I made when I was sworn into this office, and I intend to honor that promise. It should go without saying that I intend to grab the bull by the horns. Thank you, and I will see all of you tomorrow morning at the same time."

The media stood in stunned silence. They had heard of such measures being enacted in Seattle, New York, and other bastions of progressive politics. This was unheard of in Houston. They speculated among themselves what other renter protections Escobar was considering. Jamaal listened from a distance, chuckling to himself. If only they knew, he thought. If only they knew.

THIS ISN'T ABOUT ME

April 2020

The reaction to Marta Escobar's latest orders was swift and unsurprising. Renters and their advocates rejoiced, though many complained that her orders didn't go far enough. They wanted more protections to be enacted. Landlords and developers denounced Escobar. As the President of the Houston Landlord Association, Buford Jennings III was at the forefront of the opposition.

A native Houstonian, Jennings was the city's largest landlord, owning over 15,000 housing units. Most of the housing consisted of large apartment complexes, but he also owned single-family homes, townhouses, and duplexes. He began his career in 1990 when he inherited his father's modest real estate portfolio of ten single-family homes and a six-unit apartment building. At the time, he was twenty-three years old and only two years out of college. He had learned much from his father as a part-time employee during college and then full-time after graduation. Within a year of his father's death, Buford had doubled his holdings. Four years later, he had more rental housing units than anyone in the city.

Buford was a stereotypical Texan—big, bold, and brash. He laughed easily and loudly, often at his own expense. Standing 6′4″ and weighing two-hundred-sixty pounds, he was an imposing figure. He wore his white hair shoulder length. Buford said what he thought, often to his later chagrin. He wore a white

Stetson hat, even to church, and was usually seen with an unlit Romeo y Julieta cigar in his hand. Three years prior, his doctor convinced him to stop smoking. Because he liked the feel of the rolled tobacco between his fingers, Buford continued to carry one with him. Besides, as a real estate tycoon, he had a certain image to live up to, and the cigar helped him do that.

Within minutes of Escobar's announcement, Buford was inundated with phone calls from the media wanting to know his thoughts on Escobar's orders. At first, he tried to accommodate the callers, but he quickly realized that he wouldn't be able to get anything else done for days. He told his secretary to tell the media that he would hold a press conference that afternoon. He would make a statement and answer a few questions. But first, he needed to speak to his lawyer.

* * *

At 3 p.m., Buford walked out of his office building to speak to the three dozen members of the press who had assembled in the parking lot. "Good afternoon, and thank you for coming," he said in his Southern drawl. "This morning, County Judge Escobar unilaterally imposed an eviction moratorium and rent freeze on the county's landlords. She did not present her policy to the commissioners court, the democratically elected representatives for the citizens of Harris County. Instead, she acted more like Stalin and Castro and issued a unilateral edict.

"These policies will have a devastating effect on the county's landlords. Most rental property is owned by 'mom and pop' operators, and they have small portfolios. The majority own less than five properties. Many are retired, and they depend on rental income to supplement their Social Security or pension payments. An eviction moratorium will leave them no legal recourse if a tenant quits paying rent and many renters will, knowing that their landlord can't do anything about it. Property owners will have to continue to pay their mortgage, insurance, maintenance, and property taxes with no income. Escobar talks about the hardships that renters face with no income, but she says nothing of the hardships that she is imposing on landlords.

"Judge Escobar said that this moratorium will end in ninety days, but can we trust her? Remember, when she first announced her lockdown, she promised it would last for only two weeks. That was six weeks ago, and we are still in a lockdown. Given her track record, I think it is safe to conclude that she can't be trusted. We can be sure that her latest decrees will last far longer than she says.

"Her order is completely impractical. Central planning never works. Not in Russia, not in China, not in Cuba. And it won't work in America. This country was founded on free enterprise. If Escobar doesn't like the way this country operates, then she should go back to her home country instead of trying to change our system.

"Within twenty-four hours, my attorney will file a lawsuit against Escobar and Harris County. Her dictate is unconstitutional and will not stand. If necessary, I will fight this all the way to the Supreme Court.

"That's all I have to say for now, but I will be happy to answer a few questions."

"Mr. Jennings," said a reporter for a local television station, "you are the city's largest landlord, so this will obviously have a big financial impact on you. Isn't that your real motivation for opposing the moratorium and rent freeze?"

"Young man, this isn't about me. Sure, it will hurt me some, but I can weather this storm. My sole concern is for those who can't. The 'mom and pop' operators I mentioned for one. Many of them are retired and depend on rental income to supplement their Social Security. I am thinking of them, not myself. Escobar said that she is trying to protect the citizens of Harris County, but she is forgetting about many of those citizens—landlords. Of course, there are a lot more renters than landlords, and she is simply coddling those renters to secure their votes. Her orders are politically motivated."

"Evictions are at an all-time high in Harris County," shouted another reporter. "With the economy in shambles, more eviction filings are likely. You appear to support throwing people out of their home amid a pandemic. Aren't you putting profits before people? Isn't that rather heartless?"

"Let me be clear, I am not advocating that landlords file for eviction the moment a tenant is late. Personally, I prefer to work with a tenant when they have financial problems. Evictions can be time-consuming and expensive. But landlords should have the option of eviction. We should be able to run our businesses as we choose. That's what free enterprise is. Good things never happen when the government tells us how to run our business. Nothing good will come from this. It's unconstitutional and impractical."

The same reporter quickly spoke again. "In the past two months, you've filed more evictions than anyone in the county. With that kind of record, how can you claim you work with tenants?"

Buford chuckled. "It looks like you've done your homework, but only a part of it. If you had investigated a little further, you would have discovered that all the evictions my company has filed were against tenants who were four or more months behind on rent. I'll do the math for you. That means that they stopped paying rent before the pandemic even started. So, they can't use the pandemic as an excuse for not paying the rent. We've tried working with those tenants, but they aren't willing to do their part. It takes two to tango, and these tenants don't want to dance. I'll take one more question."

Hands shot up, and Buford pointed to a woman in the front. "In her announcement, Judge Escobar said that she was considering other tenant protections. Given the imbalance of power between tenants and landlords, isn't that a fair thing to do?"

Buford sighed deeply. "I don't know what she has in mind, so I can't really comment on that. But you are right that there is an imbalance of power. The Golden Rule says that he who has the gold rules. Landlords have the gold. They get to set the rules regarding their rental properties. That's capitalism in action.

Thank you all for coming. Good day and God bless." Buford turned and walked back into the building as reporters shouted more questions.

* * *

"That guy needs help," Justin said at the end of Buford Jennings's press conference.

"What he needs," Pratik responded, "is an intellectual bodyguard. That was a rather pathetic defense of his business. His comment about capitalism and the Golden Rule made me cringe. He focused on the impracticality of Escobar's orders but said nothing of their immorality."

"How could he?" Justin asked rhetorically. "He accepts the moral premise underlying the moratorium and rent freeze. He said that his primary concern was for other landlords, not himself."

"I shouldn't be surprised," Pratik replied, "but it is disappointing to see a businessman talk like that."

Justin nodded. "Agreed. With spokesmen like him, it's not surprising that people don't like landlords. So how should we proceed? We could contact him easily enough. After all, he is our landlord. But I think we need a sales pitch. We might get only one chance to convince him."

"Why don't we write an open letter to him and post it on our blog? We can email a copy to him, and a lot of other people will also see it. Even if he doesn't respond favorably, somebody else might."

Justin considered that suggestion for a moment. "I can't think of a better idea. Let's each draft an outline for the open letter and then we'll discuss it further."

"Sounds like a plan," Pratik replied. "Let's meet in two hours."

YOU COULD BE THEIR HERO

April 2020

"**C**harles, to what do I owe the pleasure of you requesting a meeting with me?" Jamaal smiled as he leaned back and placed a foot on the mayor's desk.

"What in the hell are you doing?" Charles shouted.

"I do not know what you are talking about," Jamaal answered with a shrug. "When are you going to update this God-awful office?"

"Don't change the subject, Jamaal. You know damn well what I'm talking about." Charles slammed his fist onto the desk. "You are sneaking around meeting with Marta Escobar, Lia Patel, and Roderick Jackson. Lord knows what you are telling them, but I have a good idea based on what that bitch Escobar announced yesterday—two parts of your proposal. And she hinted that more is to come. Why are you doing this?"

"Charles, I take exception to your use of the word sneaking. Obviously, if I am sneaking around, I am not doing a very good job of it, since you know about my meetings. But who I meet is my business, not yours. Why are you concerned about who I am meeting or what I am doing?"

Charles rose from his chair and pointed a finger at Jamaal. "Listen to me, you son of a...." Like a pouncing cat, Jamaal grabbed Charles' finger and bent it back until it was close to breaking. He released the finger with a satisfied grin on his face. "Shit," Charles screamed, "you nearly broke my damn finger! What is wrong with you?"

"Charles," Jamaal said calmly, "you really should be more hospitable to your guests. Your attitude might give some people the wrong impression. You invited me here and then you began calling me names. How did you expect me to react? Now, where were we?"

"You were about to tell me why you are doing this," Charles said as he tried to shake the pain out of his finger.

Jamaal chuckled. "That's not what I recall. I seem to remember wondering why you are concerned about who I meet. I am still awaiting an answer."

"You are creating a political nightmare for me. The economy is in shambles. If I support you and your proposal at this time, the entire business community will line up against me. I'm going to need them when I run for governor. And those goddamn housing activists are already calling for the city to enact renter protections, including rent control. It's all because of you. Escobar's orders are only temporary, and they know it. They want something more permanent, and they believe it is more likely to happen on the city level. Escobar's orders have riled people up, and the activists demand that the city enact protections," Charles' eyes narrowed. "I know you are behind this."

"Maybe I am, maybe I'm not. Regardless, I gave you first dibs on my proposal. All you did was hem and haw and make excuses. It's not the right time, there is no justification, you can't sell it to voters. Speaking hypothetically, suppose I grew tired of your excuses and inaction. Speaking hypothetically, suppose I presented my proposal to individuals who might actually take action. Would you fault me for that?"

"Yes, I would. We had a deal. You were going to give me time, and then I'd support your proposal when it could be justified."

"I gave you enough goddamn time," Jamaal snarled. "And if

this pandemic isn't justification enough, I don't know what is. Jesus Christ man, half the city is jobless and can't pay their rent. Most of those people voted for you and now you are turning your back on them when they need you most. I can't, in good conscience, continue to support you under those conditions. If this shit continues for much longer, the streets are going to be flooded with the homeless, and many will die. Do you want that to be your legacy?"

Charles shook his head. "You and I both know that these so-called renter protections ultimately hurt renters. Look at San Francisco. Housing is so damn expensive that the middle class can't afford to live there. Landlords convert their apartment buildings to condominiums or upgrade them to escape the rent control laws. Yeah, rent control is a good deal for the few who can find an apartment. But most renters get screwed, and they don't even know why."

Jamaal laughed. "Christ, Charles, you sound like those fucking conservatives. Who was it that said, 'In the long run, we're all dead?' I think it was Keynes. No matter, voters don't care about the long run. All they care about is the immediate moment. And at this moment, they are hurting. At this moment, you could be their hero. You want to be a hero, don't you, Charles?"

"That is very short-sighted, Jamaal. I need to look at the big picture. I need to find a balance between immediate needs and long-term needs. It's not as easy as you think."

"Charles, you are starting to piss me off. I got you what you wanted—power. You said that you wanted to help your community, and now that you have an opportunity, you just sit on your fat ass and make excuses. You are no better than those slimy politicians you used to denounce. In fact, I think that you may have turned into one." Jamaal stood and removed his hat from Charles' desk. "You had your chance. See you around, Chuck."

Charles watched the door close behind Jamaal. That son of a bitch, he thought. He can't be patient, so he's getting everyone riled up and making demands. And I'm caught in the crossfire. Sure, I'd be a hero for the working class if I supported renters' protections. But I'd alienate businessmen and real estate interests. And I will need their money if I'm going to become governor.

THE MAJORITY DOES NOT DETERMINE WHAT IS TRUE

May 2020

Justin and Pratik spent four days writing their open letter. They addressed it to all landlords, rather than addressing it solely to Buford Jennings. The advice that they were offering applied to all landlords, and there was no valid reason to single out Jennings. Initially, they thought they would write a comprehensive argument against the renter protections imposed by Escobar. But they realized that would require a very long letter, and many landlords wouldn't bother to read it. They decided they would limit the letter to twelve hundred words. That was sufficient space to address the essential issues and would be more likely to be read. They could elaborate in the future.

On May 1, they posted their letter:

To all Landlords in Harris County,

Last month, Harris County Judge Marta Escobar proclaimed an eviction moratorium and a rent freeze. Some have argued that these policies impose an undue financial burden on landlords. While this argument is true, and important to make, it does not address the fundamental issue: Escobar's orders are immoral.

Escobar's orders violate the right to property—the freedom to produce and trade. The freedom to produce and trade applies to every value that life requires, including housing. Landlords and developers have a moral right to produce the housing that they believe others desire and then offer that housing on terms they deem appropriate. And renters have the moral right to accept or reject that offer. When the parties can agree to mutually acceptable terms, a trade occurs—money for housing. It is a voluntary trade that benefits all parties.

Both the eviction moratorium and the rent freeze force landlords to trade on terms that they did not voluntarily accept. Landlords must continue to rent to an individual, regardless of the property owner's own judgment and desires. He is forced to accept a rent that he did not voluntarily agree to. Under Escobar's orders, tenants benefit at the expense of landlords. Indeed, when she announced the eviction moratorium and rent freeze, the judge said, "If landlords aren't willing to do their part voluntarily, then I will force them to do so. If they don't choose to help those in need, then I won't give them a choice." She has made it a crime to make choices with which she disagrees.

The judge has attempted to justify this immorality by claiming that she is serving the "public interest." That term is used frequently, but nobody ever bothers to define it. And the reason is: it is impossible to define. It is a nebulous term that can mean anything, which means absolutely nothing. It is simply an attempt to justify forcing some to sacrifice their interests to others. And that is precisely what Escobar's orders will do.

Landlords will be forced to sacrifice their desires and interests for the desires and interests of their tenants. Their own judgment regarding whom to rent to and on what terms is rendered irrelevant. They are forced into involuntary servitude.

In making her announcement, Escobar pointed to a recent poll that found that 60 percent of Harris County residents favor renter protections. She implies that truth and justice are determined by a vote—and an uninformed, informal vote at that. She is wrong. The majority does not determine what is true, what is moral, or what is just. To claim otherwise is to advocate for mob rule. It grants government unlimited powers and holds that the government should act as the majority pleases simply because it is the majority.

A proper government has limited powers. Consider the Constitutions of both Texas and the United States. Both enumerate what powers the government has. Both limit government's powers. And the only proper purpose of government, the only purpose for which that power should be exercised, is the protection of individual rights—the freedom to live as one chooses, so long as one respects the freedom of others to do the same.

Escobar's orders violate this principle. They force individuals—landlords—to act, not as they choose, but as she dictates.

The judge may argue that she is simply protecting the rights of renters. But the rights of some cannot be protected by violating the rights of others. There is no such thing as "renter's rights," just as there is no such thing as "landlords' rights." There are only individual rights, and they apply to all individuals, landlords and tenants alike. To claim otherwise is to imply that renters have rights that are separate and distinct from the rights possessed by landlords. This is a perversion of the concept of rights.

Rights protect the freedom of individuals to act as they judge best. They protect the freedom of landlords to produce and trade housing on terms and conditions that they judge best. Rights protect the freedom of renters to accept or reject the terms and conditions offered by landlords as they—the renters —judge best. Both parties are free to act as they judge best.

Escobar doesn't want individuals to act on their own judgment. She wants them to act only as she permits and dictates.

The judge has claimed that Harris County has a housing crisis. That may be true, but she evades the fact that her orders have made the situation immeasurably worse. In early March, she shut down most of the county's businesses. Even then, it was easy to predict what would happen. When businesses are forced to close, they can't pay their employees. When employees aren't paid, they can't pay their rent. Escobar's lockdown has made the housing crisis worse and created additional problems.

Consider what has happened in the past two months. Escobar exercised unprecedented powers to destroy the local economy by ordering "non-essential" businesses to close. Then, the financial hardships that could have easily been predicted soon exacerbated the housing crisis. Escobar now wants us to believe that further orders and dictates will somehow remedy the problems that her past orders and dictates created.

The judge's lockdown orders, her eviction moratorium, and her rent freeze are immoral. They force individuals to act, not as they deem best, but as she dictates. Her solution to the inevitable problems she has caused by violating rights is to issue a new set of immoral orders that violate rights. She again wants to force individuals to act, not as they deem best, but as she dictates.

If you are the owner of a business, consider how you would react if the judge dictated what you could charge and with whom you could do business. If you are an employee, consider how you would react if the judge dictated the terms and conditions of your employment. Would you resent the judge for usurping your own judgment? This is precisely what she is doing to landlords.

These immoral orders are founded on the premise that individuals must sacrifice for the "public interest." Individuals have certainly sacrificed, but the undefined "public interest" has not been served. Escobar now wants more sacrifice.

The solution to the housing crisis is not more sacrifice. The solution is a restoration of freedom for all businesses, including landlords. Businesses should be free to operate as they think best, taking whatever precautions to protect employees and customers that they choose. Employees and customers should be free to choose which precautions they find acceptable and which they do not. Everyone should be free to act on his own judgment.

For that to occur, we must reject the notion that sacrifice is necessary. We must reject the notion that individuals exist to serve the "public interest." Until that happens, we can only expect the housing crisis to get worse. And with it, more orders and dictates.

Justin Walker and Pratik Shah

NOBODY HAS A RIGHT TO SPREAD LIES

May 2020

"Who the hell are Justin Walker and Pratik Shah?" Marta Escobar demanded. She tossed a hard copy of their open letter onto her desk.

"I'm not sure," Tilde, her assistant, said. "That came in an email last night. I went to the website in the email, and this is the only thing on the site. A Google search found a Justin Walker and Pratik Shah who played football at Ohio State. I don't know if that's them or not."

"Find out what you can. I want to know who these bastards are. How dare they call me immoral!" Escobar shouted. "I won't be intimidated by a couple of stupid football players. I need to get ready for the press briefing in twenty minutes." She waved her hand to dismiss her assistant.

The assistant walked to the door and turned back to her boss. "I think you should get in front of this. The press will ask about it, and it will be much better if you raise the subject."

"Your suggestion is duly noted," Escobar said, without trying to hide her irritation. "Now, leave me alone." When the door was closed, she muttered to herself, "Shit, shit, shit."

* * *

Thirty minutes later, Escobar was standing in the press room. She had quickly changed into her favorite purple pants suit. She was going to need some luck today.

"Good morning, everyone. There were two hundred and thirty-four new COVID cases confirmed yesterday. That is a decrease of two from the previous day. There were two deaths, which is the same as the previous day." Escobar typically spent at least thirty minutes reviewing the latest statistics and information from scientists. But on this day, she had other matters on her mind. She reluctantly admitted to herself that Tilde had made a good point.

Escobar took a sip of water and then took a deep breath. "Thirty minutes ago, I was made aware of an open letter to the county's landlords. If you haven't seen that letter, I am sure that you will soon. It contained some outrageous claims, and I would like to address them because this kind of disinformation that is becoming far too common. And if it continues, people will die.

"The most absurd of these claims is that my orders are immoral. I am a duly elected official in Harris County, and the governor's declaration of a public health emergency gives me certain powers. I have exercised those powers in accordance with the law. To call my actions immoral is beyond the pale. I suppose that they'll be comparing me to Hitler before long. Those who don't have a good argument usually resort to ad hominem attacks." Several of the media chuckled. Comparing political opponents to Hitler had become passé.

"I have a sworn duty to protect the residents of Harris County. I consult with medical scientists multiple times a day to keep abreast of the latest information, as well as what precautions should be taken to protect the public. Those scientists are in unanimous agreement that wearing masks and practicing social distancing will stop the spread of the virus. They also agree that large gatherings pose a serious public health threat, as a single infected individual can pass the virus to countless others.

"My decision to close businesses was not made lightly. I considered the advice of medical professionals and my duty to protect the public. What I have done is highly moral, and I take great offense to anyone who claims otherwise. If my critics had their way, I would have simply let people wander around infecting others and causing who knows how many deaths. They would have me allow businesses to open and permit the virus to spread even faster. That is what would be immoral." Escobar's volume had increased with each sentence. She was close to shouting.

"The letter also implies that my orders are unconstitutional. As I previously said, state law has granted me extraordinary powers during a public health emergency. To claim that following the law is unconstitutional is beyond absurd. I know little about the authors of this outrageous letter, but they appear to be former college football players. That hardly qualifies them to comment on issues of public health. Perhaps they have suffered too many concussions.

"The letter claims that landlords and renters have the same rights. Try telling that to the renter whose landlord raises the rent 25 percent. Tell that to the individual who can't find an apartment because of a past criminal conviction. Tell that to the tenant whose landlord wants to evict him for buying a puppy for his children. Tenants have no choice but to do as their landlord demands, or they will find themselves on the street. Landlords have all the power, and it's time that we created a more equal balance of power. That's what I have done.

"Finally, the letter claims I made the housing crisis worse by protecting the public's health. Apparently, the authors think that I should have simply let thousands of people die. They are putting profits before people, and that is always immoral. The authors are heartless. Undoubtedly, they are being paid handsomely by real estate interests and landlords.

"I am not the one raising rents at an unconscionable rate. I am not the one who threatened to throw families out of their home and into the streets. I am not the one who refuses to rent to someone who got arrested for having a joint twenty years ago. Landlords are doing these things. Landlords are the cause of the housing crisis. And that is why I am asking them to do their part to remedy the situation. That is why I enacted renters' protections, and it is why I will enact more when it is determined that I have the power to do so.

"Housing experts tell me that renter protections have worked well everywhere they have been enacted. They have prevented outrageous rent increases. Renter protections have kept families housed, and in a pandemic, that is particularly important. They have given those with a criminal record a second chance and a new leash on life. That is why we are seeing cities and states across the country enact renter protections. It is time for Harris County to join those enlightened jurisdictions and enter the twenty-first century.

"I ran for this office on the promise that I would protect our most vulnerable citizens. That is what I am doing. Calling that immoral and dictatorial is a disgusting slur. And I will not tolerate such hatred. Nobody has a right to spread lies and misrepresentations." Adopting a German accent, she concluded, "We have ways to make you not talk."

* * *

Justin and Pratik smiled when Escobar ended her tirade. "That was certainly interesting," Pratik said. "Entirely predictable, but interesting."

"I found it humorous," Justin said, "that she said that we would resort to ad hominem attacks, and then she was soon attempting to refute our arguments by saying that we are former football players. I am sure some people will swallow that tripe, but the more astute will recognize that as an ad hominin attack. She certainly gave us a lot of new material."

"Not surprisingly," Pratik said, "she didn't bother to address our point that closing businesses led to people being unable to pay their rent. She just blamed it on landlords. Anyhow, it was great advertising for us. Many people will see her press conference and be made aware of our letter. And the media knows about it too. I suspect we are going to be getting a lot of emails soon."

YOU CAN STOP THIS INJUSTICE

May 2020

Charles hated the weekly "pop-off" sessions that the city council was required to hold. The purpose was to solicit input from the public regarding the city government. It was usually just a parade of angry citizens complaining about one thing or another. Occasionally, some organization would bring dozens of members to council chambers to advocate for their pet cause. When that occurred, the session turned into a repetitive and boring ninety minutes of talking points. The only saving grace, the mayor thought, is these sessions are now virtual. He could turn off his camera when he was bored. Which was most of the time. Maybe there is a silver lining to this pandemic, he thought. He straightened his tie, even though he thought it was stupid to wear a tie to a virtual meeting.

Charles casually looked through the list of scheduled speakers. He cringed when he saw Jamaal's name. What the hell? Charles thought. Don't let him piss you off, Charles reprimanded himself. Jamaal was fifth on the list of thirty-five scheduled speakers. At least he will be out of here soon, the mayor thought.

Charles heard little of what the first four speakers said. He heard something about stray cats, a large pothole on Richmond Avenue, and the lack of COVID testing sites. Charles was focused on the fifth speaker and was trying to determine if he would ask questions. He rarely did it at these sessions. He finally decided that today would not be an exception because it would just give Jamaal more time to talk. And about the last thing he wanted right now was hearing Jamaal talk.

Not that Charles was opposed to Jamaal's proposal. The mayor was ambivalent about renters' protections, as he was with most issues that came before the council. He had learned long ago that the way to succeed in politics was to be pragmatic. Charles picked his battles carefully, and he'd only rock the boat when he was certain that he had sufficient political backing. He had proven himself to be willing to compromise. It had earned him a reputation as being a reasonable man who could work with people on both sides of the aisle. Jamaal strongly disagreed with Charles' "go along to get along" attitude.

The public was given the choice to speak for one, two, or three minutes. When the ninety minutes allotted for the session were filled, no additional speakers would be allowed. Unsurprising to Charles, Jamaal had selected the three-minute option. When Jamaal's name was called, his smiling face appeared on Charles' monitor. Thank God I don't have to be in the room with him, the mayor thought.

"Good morning, councilmen, councilwomen, and Mayor Benton. Today, I want to talk about a crisis that has been looming over our city for years but has finally reached epic proportions. I am referring to our housing crisis.

"In the past ten years, rents have risen over 35 percent while wages have remained stagnant. For low-income Houstonians, this has made it a constant struggle to keep their families housed. Nearly 90 percent of low-income families pay over 40 percent of their income on housing. According to the federal government, a family that pays more than 30 percent of its income on housing is considered cost burdened. Almost all the county's low-income families spend too much on housing, and they must constantly decrease spending on other necessities such as food and health care. This situation is unacceptable.

"The pandemic has made the crisis even worse. Tens of thousands of Houstonians have lost their job through no fault of their own. Low-income families and people of color have suffered the most. Without work, they can no longer afford to pay their rent and face eviction. Fortunately, County Judge Escobar has offered them a temporary reprieve with her eviction moratorium and rent freeze. But that reprieve will not last long, and our most vulnerable citizens will soon face homelessness. But you can act to stop this injustice.

"Housing is a basic human right, just like food, education, and health care. We have a moral responsibility, a duty, to ensure that our fellow citizens have these rights protected. As a society, we protect the rights to food, education, and health care with programs like food stamps, public schools, and Medicaid. We have no such protection for the right to housing. Not on the federal, state, or local level.

"Federal and state officials are turning a blind eye to the most vulnerable among us. If the federal and state governments won't fulfill their responsibilities, then we must take matters into our own hands. We must provide that protection on the local level. Other cities are doing it, and we can do that right here in Houston. We can show the rest of the country, indeed, the entire world, that we recognize our duties to our fellow citizens. We can enact a slate of renter protections that are the most robust in the country.

"Towards that end, I challenge you to introduce, approve, and enact seven policies: rent control, just cause eviction, right to renew, ban the box, the right to counsel, renters' choice, and a living wage. Time does not allow me to elaborate on these policies. But suffice it to say, each of these is necessary to establish a balance of power between renters and landlords. These are necessary to protect the rights of tenants. If we can't take care of our most vulnerable citizens, who will?

"I will be happy to discuss these policies with any of you, either privately or collectively. In the meantime, I trust you will rise to the occasion and meet my challenge."

* * *

Charles had known that it was coming, but that didn't make it any easier to hear. He knew he would soon face a political shitstorm. Housing activists would take up Jamaal's call and assert incredible pressure on the council to enact renter protections. And those two newcomers, Patel and Jackson, will be more than happy to comply, he surmised.

Charles had expected an uneventful second term when he was re-elected in 2019. The economy was doing well, and the city's finances were under control. He wanted to preside over a period of prosperity and then prepare for his run for governor in 2026. He didn't need controversial issues on the table. Sure, if he supported Jamaal's proposal, he'd get the votes of renters and the poor. But businessmen and developers would give their support, and more importantly, their money, to a candidate who was more friendly to their interests.

I need to get in front of this, he realized. But how? Maybe I can express support for renters' protections in principle, but caution prudence. We can't act too quickly or else we may create additional problems. After all, look at what the judge has done. That open letter was right. When you close businesses, people lose their jobs. And when they lose their jobs, they can't pay the rent. He reminded himself that he shouldn't express those last thoughts out loud. Escobar wouldn't be happy if he did.

Shit, shit, shit, he muttered to himself when Jamaal concluded. This pandemic is wrecking my plans. And Jamaal isn't helping.

THIS ISN'T A LIFE-OR-DEATH ISSUE

May 2020

Justin and Pratik walked into the lobby of Buford Jennings' office building. Unlike the man, the building was understated. It was not designed or decorated to impress. It was built to serve a single purpose—running a real estate empire.

Not that the building was poorly designed. The architect had been a disciple of Frank Lloyd Wright, and he adhered religiously to the principle that form follows function. The building was shaped like a "V." One long wing contained a warehouse and offices for the maintenance department. A cafeteria was between those offices and the lobby. The other wing held administrative offices. A conference room separated those offices and the lobby. The warehouse was usually a beehive of activity, with materials and equipment being loaded and unloaded.

Buford had initially objected to the design. He wanted something more traditional—offices in the front and the warehouse in the back. However, the architect had argued that this would subject the administrative offices to considerable noise from the warehouse activities and the constant traffic to and from the warehouse. Buford finally relented. Now, ten years later, he loved the building and was thankful that he had listened to the architect.

The exterior area between the two wings was a beautifully landscaped miniature park. When the weather permitted, employees used the park for their breaks and lunch. As an avid gardener, Buford had been intimately involved in the park's design, as well as the selection of plants. He could frequently be seen tending to his beloved hibiscus, and he often sat in his office looking out at the park. Buford enjoyed gardening because, unlike real estate, success could usually be achieved in a few months.

Buford had reluctantly agreed to meet with Justin and Pratik. He thought he had things under control. But he had been impressed with the open letter the two had written. They obviously have some snap, he had thought. He decided to at least meet the two brainiacs and see what they were like. And then he could resume defending his kingdom.

When Justin and Pratik entered Buford's office, Buford barked, "Good God, you two are just teenagers!" He laughed. "I was expecting a couple of old college professor types."

"Actually," Pratik said, "I'm twenty-one and Justin is twenty."

"Regardless," Buford said while waving his hand dismissively, "you two are still wet behind the ears. What can I do for you?"

"We want you to hire us," Justin said immediately.

"Why would I do that? Hire you for what?"

"We want to be your intellectual bodyguards," Pratik said. He knew the question that was coming next.

"And what the hell is an intellectual bodyguard? I've never heard of such a thing." Buford chuckled, as if the combination of the two words was an oxymoron. He shook his head and frowned.

"A traditional bodyguard protects his client from physical dangers," Justin said. "An intellectual bodyguard protects his client from dangerous ideas, such as those being advocated and implemented by Judge Escobar."

Buford guffawed and slapped his desk. "Damn, you boys are clever. I can see why some, shall we say less informed people, might need your protection, but I was dealing with politicians long before you boys were even in diapers. I don't think that I need a bodyguard, intellectual or otherwise. Buford can take care of himself. Besides, that letter you two wrote is too fancy. I was scratching my head, reading it. We might be a big city, but Houstonians are simple folks. Those fancy words and philosophical mumbo jumbo are going to go right over their heads. You need to keep it simple. That's what I do." He poked himself in the chest to emphasize his point. "I think it works pretty well."

"I respectfully disagree, Mr. Jennings," Pratik said. "Sure, some people may not grasp what we are saying, but we can't write for the least intelligent among us. Our goal is to present a clear, consistent, and rational message without talking down or dumbing down. We want to appeal to the best within people. We want to appeal to their reason."

"But people aren't reasonable. Take the judge, for example." Buford shook his head. "No, that approach will never be successful. It's too philosophical. You'll come across as a pair of intellectual snobs. And that won't go over well, trust me. That kind of talk might do well on a college campus, but not out here in the real world."

"Do you think people will be swayed by your argument that Escobar's policies are economically harmful?" Justin asked. Before Buford could respond, he continued. "People are struggling to pay their rent while you go to your home in Tanglewood every night. Your home is probably worth more than most people make in a lifetime. They will not have any sympathy for you. To them, you're rich, and you can afford to take a financial loss. Purely economic arguments are doomed to failure."

"But most landlords aren't rich," Buford objected. "Those are the people who will be hurt. I am trying to protect them."

"The best way to protect them," Pratik said, "is to protect

yourself. If you fight to protect your rights, you are fighting for the rights of every landlord. Would you find Escobar's orders any more acceptable if they only applied to wealthy landlords?"

"Well, no," Buford admitted. "That wouldn't be fair. Those orders shouldn't apply to anyone."

"Many will say," Pratik continued, "that you are putting profits before people. That implies that you can either help people or you can pursue profits, but you can't do both. That's wrong, you can do both."

"Profits enable you, and motivate you," Justin added, "to provide safe, decent housing for people. That is helping them, but not in the sacrificial manner that Escobar advocates."

"Hold on," Buford interrupted. "What do you mean, sacrificial manner?"

"She wants to force you and other landlords to help tenants at your own expense," Justin replied, "whether or not you choose to. She believes that you have a duty to help tenants, even if it is harmful to you. And if you won't do it voluntarily, then she will force you to do so."

Pratik jumped in again. "Profits are good, and you shouldn't allow others to pretend otherwise. You earn a profit by providing the housing that people want and need. It is a mutually beneficial trade. If you face the issue head on, you'll put Escobar and her cronies on the defensive. They will have to explain why profits are bad, and they can't. You've earned your wealth. Be proud of your profits and defend them as if your life depends on them. Because it does."

"Come on, boys," Buford said condescendingly. "This isn't a life-or-death issue."

"Isn't it?" Justin asked. "How would you feel if everything you've worked for was whisked away from you?"

"I'd certainly be pissed off."

"What else?"

Buford thought a moment before speaking. "I would probably feel empty. I don't know what I'd do if I didn't have my business. It would be devastating if it was taken away. But nobody is trying to take away what I've built."

"Not in one fell swoop," Justin replied. "They aren't trying to take everything today. These renter protections are only the beginning of a hostile takeover. Escobar and her ilk want to take over rental housing. They want the government in control. If you give them an inch today, down the road they will try to get a mile. They need to be stopped. Now."

"You need to take the moral high road," Justin said in conclusion. "Challenge their premises. You'd be surprised how many people will understand and agree with you. Most people are decent and want to do the right thing. They just aren't sure what the right thing is."

Buford thought for a moment. "I like you boys. You say what you think, and it makes sense."

"So," Justin said, "we're not too philosophical for you to understand."

Buford smiled. "No, not at all. Where did you boys learn to be so smart?"

"We both went to Ohio State," Pratik replied, "and got double majors. Mine are in philosophy and business. Justin's are in philosophy and psychology."

"Damn," Buford exclaimed. "You boys really are brainiacs. Look, I really appreciate that you want to help me. But I think that this is going to blow over soon. The moratorium and rent freeze are only for ninety days. When they expire, we'll get back to normal. In the meantime, I will continue to raise hell and pressure Escobar to revoke the orders sooner."

"Okay," Justin said disappointedly. "But don't claim that we didn't warn you."

THEY CREATED
THE CRISIS

May 2020

The pandemic had been a mixed blessing for Roger Mason. His audience was growing by leaps and bounds, but he could no longer visit his favorite bars because Escobar had closed them. He was relegated to drinking Scotch on his back porch or at the homes of friends. Despite the inconveniences, the pandemic gave him a lot to talk about. And if there was anything Roger Mason enjoyed more than talking, he had yet to discover it.

"Ladies and gentlemen," Mason began one morning, "each day I become more and more convinced that this entire COVID thing is a conspiracy among Regressives to strip away our liberties. The Regressives call themselves Progressives, but they aren't advocating progress. Unless you think depending on windmills for power is progress. They tell us that windmills are supposed to power the entire country, but they haven't explained how a windmill will power a car or an airplane. Regressives are so stupid that they probably think that propellers are windmills.

"If you look around the country, the cities and states that are run by Democrats have the tightest lockdowns. Cities and states run by Republicans have much lighter lockdowns, and with at least one state—Wyoming—almost no restrictions."

"To be clear, I am not saying that COVID doesn't exist. It does, and it can cause death. But the seasonal flu causes sixty thousand deaths a year and we don't panic. Regressives, like Comrade Escobar, are using the pandemic to further their political agenda. They want to control your life, and that is precisely what they are doing under the guise of protecting you. The lesson in this is that Democrats want to take away your liberty, while Republicans want to protect freedom.

"They are telling you whether or not you can work. The Regressives are telling you that you can't go to a restaurant, a bar, or a gym. They are telling you that you can't have over six people in your own home. It's your house, dammit!" Mason was shouting now. "They are telling you to wear a face diaper whenever you are in public. They tell you to wash your hands every twenty minutes and disinfect everything you bring into the house. It's an endless string of dictates, mandates, and prohibitions.

"They are making COVID out to be far worse than it actually is. And they are doing so for the purpose of scaring you into willingly sacrificing your liberties. The Regressives want you to believe that giving up your freedom is the path to safety. They are trying to convince you that if you disobey their dictates, you will die. And you will kill others in the process. Don't believe it for a single nanosecond because it isn't true.

"I, for one, don't accept their narrative. Nearly every person who has died from COVID was elderly or had other health problems. These people were about to die with or without COVID. For those in reasonably good health, which is most of us, COVID is no worse than a severe cold. Why should we sacrifice our liberties when the virus poses no risk to us? I know six people who have had COVID, and other than feeling crappy for a few days, they did fine.

"And don't get me started on that guy from the CDC. What's his name? Goldsmith or something like that. He reminds me of Ichabod Crane. He looks like he's having an orgasm every time he talks about COVID. Nobody knew who he was a few months ago, and now you can't watch a news report without seeing his scrawny face. The media are making him out to be a rock star. But what has he actually done during this pandemic?

"Back in January, he said the coronavirus posed no risk to America. A few weeks later he had transformed into Chicken Little, beseeching us with claims that we are all going to die from COVID. And the only way to prevent that was to make everyone wear a rag on their face and put the entire nation under house arrest. That's not medical advice. It's the advice of a tyrant. He's done nothing to slow the spread of the virus. But he has sowed the seeds of fear and panic. And his comrades in arms have been more than happy to cash in on that fear and panic. I don't know if Goldsmith is a good doctor or not, but he has no damn business setting government policy. That is the job of elected officials.

"Remember what another Regressive said during the Great Recession? He said that a crisis is a terrible thing to waste, that it gives you an opportunity to do things that otherwise wouldn't be possible. In a crisis, people are scared, and when people are scared, they will hitch their wagon to any charlatan who promises to pull them to safety. That's what the Regressives are doing. Except they created the crisis that they now promise to rescue us from.

"Think about it. We were doing just fine in January. Then, somebody got sick and Regressives decided it was a public health emergency. First, they instilled so much fear that anyone who had the sniffles rushed to the emergency room. Then, they bombarded us with images of crowded hospitals and health care workers in hazmat suits. Finally, they told us to stay home, work safe, or else. Where were the first lockdowns? I'll tell you where. It was the cities and states that are run by Democrats. California, New York, Seattle, San Francisco, Chicago, Detroit....

"In a certain sense, this sick and twisted strategy is pure genius. For decades the Regressives have been trying to take over the country through the ballot because they know they can't do it with bullets. Their success has been slow and incremental. Americans rarely like sudden, dramatic changes. It's like that adage about the frog. If you throw a frog into a pot of boiling water, he'll jump out. But put him in a pot of cool water and slowly heat it, and he'll be cooked before he has the sense to jump out. That is what the Regressives have been doing for years. They have been slowly heating the water. The pandemic has given them an excuse to turn the heat all the way up.

"Folks, if we allow this to continue much longer, we'll all be cooked. And then it will be too late to jump out of the pot."

NOW IS NOT THE TIME TO QUIBBLE

May 2020

It was eight in the evening and Marta Escobar was sitting at her desk reading the transcript of Roger Mason's program earlier that day. She was sipping her third glass of Patron Extra Anejo as she read. Each sentence made her angrier. "You know how to tell when Roger Mason is lying?" she asked her assistant.

"How?" Tilde responded.

"He's moving his lips. That bastard wouldn't know the truth if it bit him on the ass." Escobar took another sip of tequila. "People are going to die because of his irresponsibility. The sad thing is people believe him. There are people out there who claim that drinking bleach will fight off the virus. And there are many people who believe that nonsense. How stupid do you have to be to drink bleach?"

"Well, if you think about it, maybe that's a good thing," Tilde said with a slight slur in her voice. "The people who believe him are the ones who will probably die. We'll be cleaning up the gene pool." She laughed at her own joke. "I'm just saying."

Escobar joined her laughter. "Tilde, you are so mean. And I love it." She thought for a moment. "I can't try to respond to every idiotic claim that someone makes. Mason alone would keep me busy way into the next millennium. But I can't just ignore his lies either and let people die. And he's not the only one. Those two damn football players, too." Escobar had a sudden thought. "Did you ever watch *The Three Stooges*?"

"What? What is that?"

"Never mind."

"Maybe you can get him pulled off the air," Tilde suggested.

Escobar shook her head. "I don't have that kind of clout. At least, not yet. There may be another way to shut him up. I could issue a prohibition on spreading lies and misrepresentations relating to COVID. Things are confusing enough without him spreading misinformation."

"The First Amendment freaks would freaking freak out," Tilde giggled. "That could be fun to watch."

"Probably so. But what could they do? They could file a lawsuit, perhaps get an injunction. But in the meantime, we could shut these people up." Escobar smiled. "And there is nothing I'd like more than to shut Roger Mason up."

* * *

At exactly 10 a.m. the next morning, Marta Escobar walked to the podium for her daily press briefing. She had a dull headache from the previous night's tequila. It was the fifth night in a row that she had consumed half a bottle. *I am under a tremendous amount of stress,* she rationalized. *I need alcohol to help me relax.* She was thankful that she had hired a driver at the start of the pandemic, or she would have slept on the couch in her office.

"Good morning, ladies and gentlemen," she began. "As you know, we live in dangerous times. The novel coronavirus threatens to become the worst public health emergency in the country's history. We have had to respond to this danger while lacking full and complete knowledge about the virus. While scientists are working around the clock to better understand how the virus spreads and what we can do to mitigate its danger, many among us want to distort and disregard the facts. This poses as much danger as the virus itself does.

"Knowledge is power. It is knowledge that gives us the power to understand and combat the virus. Knowledge gives us the power to bake a cake and the power to save lives. Lies and misrepresentations do the opposite. Lies and misrepresentations destroy lives by forcing people to act in ways that don't serve their best interests. Just as we are working diligently to stop the spread of the coronavirus, we must now work equally hard to stop the spread of false and misleading information.

"Much of what is being said is simply fear-mongering. Right-wing radicals want to scare people when their government attempts to protect them. They claim their rights are being violated while spreading malicious lies and false information. That isn't right. Just as you cannot yell 'fire' in a crowded theater, there is no Constitutional right to lie and deceive the public. There is no Constitutional right to cajole others to engage in risky behavior, such as going out in public without a face mask.

"With that in mind, starting immediately, only medical scientists and doctors may comment publicly on any aspect of the coronavirus and COVID in Harris County. Violators will be subject to fines of $1,000 for each infraction. And after three violations, the offender will be treated to a week's vacation in the Harris County jail." Escobar paused to let her words sink in. The press room was eerily silent as the reporters tried to digest what they had just heard. As the ramifications became clear, several shouted out questions. Escobar raised her hands. "There will be time for questions later. Let me complete my statement first.

"This includes, but is not limited to information about treatments, how the virus spreads, and what precautions are effective. We can't allow quacks to convince people to drink bleach to cure themselves of COVID. People will die if they do so. We are spending an inordinate amount of time refuting the false and misleading statements being made. This is time taken away from the pressing effort to fight COVID.

"You don't ask your mechanic for medical advice. Nor do you ask your doctor for advice regarding automobile repairs.

You rely on the experts in a particular field to provide you with accurate information and guidance. Regarding the pandemic, those experts are doctors and medical scientists. They are the only ones qualified to comment on the pandemic, not talk show hosts and football players.

"My primary job in this public health emergency is to protect the public. That has both a physical and a mental component. The physical component consists of the virus, its spread, the proper precautions, and the most effective treatments for those who contract COVID. The mental component consists of the information that is presented to the public. As the duly elected guardian of the public, I have a responsibility to ensure that the information presented to the public is true and accurate. I take that responsibility seriously.

"Some will claim that this violates the First Amendment. But free speech does not protect liars and fraudsters. Free speech does not protect speech that is harmful to others. You can't shout fire in a crowded theater. You can't claim that your neighbor is a pedophile without proof. And you can't spread lies about a disease. More importantly, now is not the time to quibble over petty issues like the First Amendment.

"Thank you and have a good day." Escobar turned and left the room as the reporters shouted questions at her.

YOU ARE A COWARD AND A TRAITOR

May 2020

Lia Patel and Roderick Jackson sat patiently in Mayor Benton's office while he finished a phone call. Lia dispassionately stared at the wall behind the mayor, while Roderick's eyes roamed the office. This guy sure enjoys having his picture taken with other politicians, Roderick thought. He saw photos of Mayor Benton with Bill Clinton, Barack Obama, Al Gore, John Kerry, and several people he didn't recognize but assumed were prominent Democrats. There was even a picture of Charles Benton with George W. Bush.

The mayor finished his call and looked at his two visitors. "Sorry about that. There always seems to be a fire to put out. I feel like I am running a fire department sometimes," he joked. Lia and Roderick did not respond. "So, what can I do for you two today?" The mayor knew damn well what they wanted, but he would not give that away. Long ago, he had learned to hold his cards close to his chest. Don't let the other guy know what you know. You need to keep him guessing.

"We want to speak to you about the proposal that was made to council by Rev. Wilkes," Lia said. "We agree with him completely and intend to introduce an ordinance to the council in the next week or two. Your support would be appreciated."

Charles stared silently at the two newest members of the city council. Lia met his gaze. Today, her mohawk was purple with a streak of black. Roderick looked at his own lap. He was wearing a Nelson Mandela T-shirt. Sunglasses and a heavy gold chain around his neck completed the gangster look he aspired to. Christ, Charles thought, how the hell did these two get elected to the city council?

"You two are new to politics, so I can't fault you for your naivete," Charles finally said. "Nor can I fault you for falling under the influence of Jamaal. However, progress is not made in giant leaps and bounds. It's made in a series of small steps. The public does not like drastic change, but incremental changes are acceptable. You still wind up at the destination that you sought, but it requires patience."

"What the hell does that mean?" Roderick asked without looking up.

"It means that trying to move the needle too far too fast usually backfires. You need to move the needle slowly."

"And in the meantime," Lia replied, "people go homeless and die. When an opportunity presents itself, we must cease it. Besides, the public accepts drastic change. Look at what Judge Escobar did. She shut down businesses and sent everybody home. That's a drastic change. Sure, there have been a few complaints, but most people have accepted it. The same would be true of renters' protections. Besides, the public is solidly behind such measures. You've seen the poll."

"What the judge did with the lockdown was different. That was about saving lives during a public health emergency. Renter protections are entirely different."

Lia shook her head. "Housing is a public health issue. People without a home are stuffed into crowded shelters where the risk of infection is increased. Or worse, they are forced to sleep on the streets where who knows what dangers they will be exposed to. In either case, their health is threatened. We can protect them. This is a life or death issue."

"Housing may be a public health issue, but that's not obvious to most people." Charles frowned. "Jamaal wants to hit a home run when a series of singles will accomplish the same thing. If we tried to enact everything Jamaal suggests, we'd be attacked from every angle. Landlords, developers, and realtors will fight the renter protections. Small business owners will fight the living wage. We might sell a few of his ideas, but not all of them at once." Charles shook his head. "No, that just won't fly with the public."

"What would you propose, Mayor Benton?" Lia asked.

Charles pondered the question. I've got to give them something, he thought, even if it's crumbs. That should satisfy them for a while. "I could possibly support an increase in the minimum wage. Anyone with half a brain knows that it is impossible to support a family for $7.25 an hour. I would suggest proposing an increase to $15 an hour effective in six months. We'll get a lot of pushback, which is okay. Then we negotiate an agreement to raise the minimum in increments over the next two or three years. We eventually get to the same place, and it will be much more acceptable to the public and small business owners."

"I've heard enough," Roderick finally said. "Jamaal was right. You are a coward and a traitor to your people and the revolution."

"I must not have gotten the memo," the mayor replied. "I was unaware that there is a revolution."

"What Roderick meant to say," Lia explained, "is—"

Roderick jumped to his feet and towered over Lia. "Listen, bitch, you don't speak for me. I have a mind—"

Lia glowered up at Roderick but said nothing. Charles watched the silent communication with interest. After about thirty seconds, Roderick sat down and bowed his head. Apparently, Charles thought, Lia does speak for Roderick.

"As I was saying," Lia continued, "the most vulnerable among us have long suffered under our current system. People of color have suffered the most, and the pandemic has increased the suffering. We must stand together to change the way our system treats those people." Lia paused for a moment. "Thank you for your time for today. We'll consider your suggestion."

THE CITY COUNCIL WON'T HAVE A CHOICE

June 2020

"So, Judge," Jamaal asked, "what are you going to do if the governor allows restaurants and bars to open?"

"I won't do anything," Judge Escobar replied. "He declared a public health emergency in April, and that has given me the powers to deal with it. Until he rescinds that declaration, I keep those powers. He can issue all the executive orders that he wants, but I'm still the boss in Harris County. He's just pandering to the right-wing radicals. It's simply not safe to reopen, and the public's safety is my primary concern. It may be safe in those counties where cows outnumber humans, but not in Harris County." She paused to consider whether she wanted to reveal her biggest concern at the moment. She decided it was worth confiding in Jamal.

"I have more concerns about the hearing tomorrow morning," she said. "Those First Amendment fanatics have sued and are seeking a temporary injunction to prevent me from enforcing my gag order. The judge assigned to the case is a Republican, though he seems a little more sensible than most of them. If he issues an injunction, then Roger Mason and his ilk can continue spewing their lies, misinformation, and hatred. COVID cases are rising nearly every day, and misinformation is going to make it worse."

Jamaal nodded. "I understand your concerns. We are hearing lies and misrepresentations regarding the eviction moratorium and rent freeze too. If your order to silence radicals like Mason stands, perhaps it could be extended to housing issues."

"That would be a little trickier," Escobar replied. "It is easy to identify who is qualified to talk about medical issues, but housing isn't so clear. And a good argument can be made that landlords and developers—those making the most noise—are qualified to speak on housing issues. So, I need to be careful with that one. But they can whine all they want. I will not rescind my order until a judge tells me to."

"Eventually, you will have to. It may be months, or even years, but when the health emergency declaration is withdrawn, your emergency powers end."

"That is why I wanted to meet with you, Jamaal," Escobar said softly. "We must prepare for the day when the moratorium and freeze are lifted. I can't do much on a permanent basis at the county level, but we can make progress at the city level. I would like to see the pressure ramped up on the city council. A series of protests would show council that the people are behind renters' protections."

Jamaal thought for a moment. "I can do that. Would we be able to use county facilities?"

"Of course. You'll have access to every resource I can make available, including county parks and the NRG complex. When do you think you could start?"

"I need at least two weeks. Many people need to be mobilized. We'll probably bus in some people from Austin and San Antonio to inflate the numbers. They have strong tenant unions and have expressed their willingness to help us." Jamaal reconsidered and shook his head. "No, that's not a good idea. We should just depend on locals for the first rally or two. Then, we can bus people in. That way, it will appear that our support is growing.

The people from out-of-town won't be able to attend every rally, and if they are at the first one, but not later, it could look like we are losing support. We want it to look like our support is growing."

Escobar smiled. "Good thinking. Making this look like a growing movement will look good in the media and put more pressure on the city council. What kind of numbers are you thinking of for the first protest?

"Locally, I think we can get about a thousand for the first rally. By the way, I prefer calling it a rally. That has a more positive connotation than protest. And I want these rallies to be positive rather than just a long bitch session. We should focus on why renter protections are good and not on how evil landlords are. Some of that will be unavoidable, but it shouldn't be our focus. Anyhow, we should be able to double or triple that amount by the third rally. These things kind of feed on themselves. When people see others standing up for their rights, they become empowered to do the same. Then, we can probably bus in at least a thousand."

"Those are good numbers," Escobar noted. "Not enough to justify using NRG, though. Perhaps one of the county parks would be good. I'm thinking Boyce-Dorian or El Franco Lee. Both are centrally located and served by Metro. We should keep transportation in mind."

"Good point. We need to be sure people can get to the location. I like Boyce-Dorian," Jamaal said. "It's in the heart of the Fifth Ward and close to EaDo. There are a lot of renters and poor families in those neighborhoods."

"You know," Escobar interjected, "your mention of EaDo gives me an idea. A lot of the city's homeless congregate in EaDo and just on the other side of the freeway. I bet we could round up hundreds of them with the promise of a hot meal."

Jamaal smiled. *This woman knows how to get things done,* he thought. *God, she's hot. I need to get me some of that when this is all over.* "I like how you think. They won't be the most photogenic in attendance, but they are great examples of the housing crisis. I know quite a few of the homeless. A few are surprisingly articulate. It might be worth having some of them speak at a rally. Their stories aren't positive, but I could coach them to put a positive spin on things."

"This is going to be good. I bet the homeless have a lot of great antidotes," Escobar chortled. "First, we build overwhelming public support. With the media's help, of course. They'll eat this up. By the time we are done, the city council won't have a choice. They'll have to enact renter protections."

"That's my plan," Jamaal said. "That's my plan."

AGAINST MY BETTER JUDGMENT

June 2020

The Texas governor strode to the podium on the steps of the state capitol building. It was an unusually warm day, even for June, and the sun was directly overhead. How fitting, he thought. *Some people are going to be happy about what I'm about to announce. But others will certainly give me a lot of heat.*

The governor was in his third term. He had previously served as chairman of the Texas Railroad Commission, which had nothing to do with railroads. It was, however, one of the state's most powerful regulatory bodies as it oversaw oil and gas production, pipelines, and nearly everything else involved in energy production in Texas. Because Texas was the nation's leader in energy production, the Railroad Commission's influence extended far beyond the state. Some called the commission America's OPEC.

Democrats despised the governor because of his perpetual pandering to his Christian base. Opponents called him a hypocrite for advocating freedom of choice in education but opposing freedom of choice for women facing an unwanted pregnancy. The opponents failed to see their own hypocrisy regarding these issues.

The governor wiped the sweat from his brow and looked out at the assembled media. He had let it be known that he'd be making an important announcement, but the governor kept the nature of that statement a closely held secret. Only a few of his closest aides knew exactly what he was about to say.

"Texas has always been unique among the states. We are the only state in the Union to have once been a sovereign nation. Texas is the only state that may operate its own navy. We lead the nation in energy production. Over the past twenty years, we have created more jobs than the rest of the country combined.

"Texans have always been fiercely independent. From the original settlers who ventured into the wilderness with Stephen F. Austin to the brave men who gave their lives at the Alamo to the wildcatters who power our economy, Texans like to take the unbeaten trail. We like to blaze fresh paths and go where others fear to tread. And that is what we will do today."

"This morning, I signed an executive order lifting the statewide mask mandate. I have also allowed all businesses to operate at 50 percent capacity. Texas is the first state to take these bold steps. I hasten to add that, while the statewide mask mandate is lifted, I encourage individuals to continue to wear a face mask while in public. We are still in the midst of a pandemic.

"I think we will see amazing things happen. When individuals are free of the heavy hand of government, they find innovative solutions to problems. Regarding the pandemic, businesses will find new and creative ways to keep employees and customers safe.

"This order does not rescind my declaration of a public health care emergency. The emergency powers granted to city and county officials remain in place so long as they do not conflict with today's order.

"Some will question the wisdom of such measures. After all, we are still months away from vaccines against COVID being available. But I trust my fellow Texans to do the right thing and continue exercising appropriate precautions.

"When Santa Ana laid siege to the Alamo, he offered those inside the mission the opportunity to surrender. Not a single man left. Each was willing to face the difficulties that were before him. They refused to run and hide, and instead, risked their lives to fight for freedom. Today, we are carrying on that proud tradition. We refuse to run and hide from the coronavirus. Instead, we face that challenge head on.

"Davy Crockett, Jim Bowie, William Travis, and all the other valiant warriors at the Alamo have provided inspiration to Texans, indeed, to people around the world, for nearly a century. As the entire world deals with a deadly pandemic, may the bold steps that we are taking today provide that same inspiration across the globe. May God bless Texas."

"Governor," shouted one reporter, "new cases of COVID are increasing daily. It is predicted that we will see a spike in infections in the fall and winter. What will you do if that happens?"

"We will deal with that if it occurs. I can't tell you what we'll do for some hypothetical situation. I must deal with the present. To be honest, I now question the wisdom of ever ordering businesses to close. At the time, so little was known about the virus and how it spreads. Federal public health officials recommended closures and mask mandates. Against my better judgment, I went along with those recommendations. I thought that caution was called for, and given the many unknowns, the safe thing to do was closures and mask mandates. Now that we know more about COVID, I feel it is safe to remove some restrictions and allow Texans to get back to living a normal life."

The governor pointed to a reporter in the front row. "Several candidates for the Democrat nomination for President have said that opening up states at this time is caveman thinking, that it defies the science," the reporter said. "How would you respond to that?"

"To those Democrats who want to control every aspect of your life, any sliver of freedom is old-fashioned," the governor said while laughing. "Let me point out that the science keeps changing. One day we are told that masks aren't necessary, and the next day we're told to double up our masks. And this is coming from the nation's top public health officials. So, the question is: which science should we accept? The so-called experts have been wrong time after time. One more question. Mindy," he said while pointing to his favorite reporter.

"Governor," she said, "most of the state's urban counties have much stronger restrictions than what you had ordered. Does today's order override the county orders?"

"We are going to have to deal with that on a case-by-case basis. The urban areas obviously face challenges that don't exist in King County or Concho County. I certainly don't want to get involved in micromanaging this pandemic, so I am going to allow local officials a little leeway. I will allow local officials to do what they were elected to do. But I'll be watching over their shoulder. That's what I was elected to do."

THE LOCKDOWNS WERE TRIAL BALLOONS

June 2020

"Folks, it's a glorious day in Houston, Texas, and across this great state," Roger Mason said happily. "Two great things happened yesterday. First, the governor opened the state. Texas businesses can now operate at 50 percent capacity. It's not ideal, but at least they can start bringing in some revenue and their employees can work. To celebrate, tonight I will visit my favorite pub—Savile Row. Come by this evening and we will raise a toast.

"The second great thing that happened yesterday was a federal judge issued an injunction preventing Comrade Escobar from enforcing her order for me to shut up. Let's be honest, her order prohibiting commentary on COVID related issues was directed solely at me. I am her biggest critic. If she thinks she can shut me up and silence the criticism, she has another thing coming. And I have an actual judge backing me up.

"Tyrants throughout history have always tried to silence their critics. When the facts aren't on your side, you don't want the facts to be known. And the facts aren't on the side of Comrade Escobar. So, she tried to stop me from sharing the facts with you. But this little thing called the First Amendment got in the way. She has said that I spread lies and misinformation. That is like the pot calling the kettle black.

"Consider her claim that masks prevent the spread of the coronavirus. They don't. The coronavirus is about one-hundred nanometers in diameter. The holes in most face masks are much larger, which means the virus can easily get through the mask. But Escobar hasn't told us this because then people would challenge the wisdom of her mask mandate. So, she keeps the facts hidden and hopes nobody else discovers them. And when someone does and publicizes those facts, Escobar tries to shut them up with unconstitutional orders. The truth will always prevail.

"In other COVID related news, clinical trials of COVID vaccines are scheduled to start next month. One of those vaccines uses a new technology called mRNA. That stands for Messenger RNA. You've probably never heard of it. I hadn't until about two days ago, and I've spent nearly every waking moment reading about it. I'll try to simplify this. Essentially, what mRNA does is genetically modify cells within your body. That sounds like something out of a science fiction horror story, doesn't it? The clinical trials only last a few months, and they focus on safety and efficacy. I don't question the need for the government requiring clinical trials before a medicine can be used. Otherwise, pharmaceutical companies could sell snake oil, or worse. All that Big Pharma cares about is making money, and this pandemic is like a printing press for them.

"But how can a three-month trial determine the long-term effects of genetic mutation? It should be obvious that three months isn't nearly enough time. Hell, ten years may not be enough time. Think about lung cancer. It usually takes decades of smoking before lung cancer develops. The same is true of many diseases. The disease doesn't manifest itself for many years after exposure. What if this vaccine causes cancer in ten or twenty years? What if these mutated cells are passed on to our children? We could create a cancer pandemic in a misguided effort to stop the COVID pandemic. This is scary stuff, and our government is right in the middle of it.

"Mark my words, once the FDA approves the vaccine, we'll start seeing government issue mandates that citizens receive the vaccine. Shutting down businesses, prohibiting large gatherings, and mask mandates were all trial balloons. Government officials wanted to see how much people would tolerate and accept. Folks, I've been saying from day one that the entire pandemic was a ploy to take control of our lives. The vaccine will be just another step toward that goal.

"We'll be told that the vaccine is safe, but how can we be sure? They won't know the long-term effects. By the time that is known, it will be too late. I hate to sound like I'm advocating a conspiracy theory, but this is very suspicious to me. We've been lied to constantly during this pandemic. We've been told that face diapers are effective, that a lockdown would flatten the curve, that washing our hands would prevent infection. None of this is true. Masks aren't effective. The lockdown hasn't flattened the curve. Washing our hands every twenty minutes does nothing except run up our water bill and dry out our skin.

"And how do we know that this vaccine isn't just a cover for the government to inject us with a microchip that can track us? Or worse, maybe it will be some kind of explosive device. Hell, I don't know, but this really concerns me.

"This is the kind of information that Comrade Escobar and her fellow Regressives don't want you to hear. They want to control the information flow. They want you to hear only what they say. Regressives don't want you to hear dissenting opinions or facts that conflict with their narrative. They want you to be mindless sheep who do what you are told.

"For this strategy to be effective, they must scare the hell out of you. They must make COVID look far worse than it is. It's an open secret that the number of deaths is highly inflated. If someone gets shot in the head and tests positive for COVID, then the cause of death is listed as COVID. How stupid is that? And why did the governor of New Jersey send people infected with

COVID to nursing homes? To spread the disease and inflate the death figures. Christ, he sent infected people to places where the residents were at high risk. Either the governor is a complete idiot, or he has more sinister motives. On second thought, maybe it's both.

"Regardless, the Regressives are preparing for another assault on our liberties. Before you line up like cattle to get your vaccine, you should remember what happened at Tuskegee. In the 1930s, the CDC began a syphilis study in Tuskegee, Alabama. The study enrolled poor black men and did not inform them they had syphilis. Nor were they given any treatment to deal with the disease. They were nothing more than lab rats. And that is what the government wants to do with this mRNA vaccine. They want to turn all of us into lab rats. The government did it once, and only a fool would believe that it wouldn't do it again.

"If you think the lockdowns and mask mandates were bad, wait until you see what they do in the future. The lockdowns will pale in comparison. If citizens keep giving the Regressives an inch, soon they will have taken a mile."

JUSTICE DELAYED IS JUSTICE DENIED

June 2020

Charles Benton had a throbbing headache, and he knew it was only going to get worse. The day's agenda for the city council session included a proposed ordinance to enact renter protections. It was authored by Lia Patel and Roderick Jackson. Three other council members had already expressed support for the ordinance.

Charles knew he couldn't support the ordinance the way it was written. Not if he wanted to keep his gubernatorial aspirations alive. Supporting the measure might sit well with urban voters, but statewide elections in Texas were decided by rural and suburban voters. And those voters would not look kindly at someone supporting such progressive policies.

There had been rumors he might face a recall if he didn't support it. Even if he survived a recall election, he would be severely tarnished and his chances at running for governor diminished. *I feel like I'm walking a tightrope with alligators on one side and tigers on the other,* he thought. *Navigating this morass is going to require all my political skills. This is Jamaal's fault,* he muttered to himself as the clerk went through the preliminaries for the meeting. *Sooner or later, I am going to have to deal with him.*

The dreaded moment arrived about sixty minutes into the ninety-minute meeting. The proposed ordinance was read aloud. Charles didn't need to hear it. Jamaal had told him on multiple occasions what such an ordinance should contain. The only surprise was that Patel and Jackson had included a living wage provision. Charles thought that was a strategic mistake and had told the newcomers that in a private meeting. He knew Jamaal was behind it. Charles had previously expressed tepid support for a living wage, both privately and publicly. Jamaal wanted to put the mayor's feet to the fire. Charles might have supported a living wage ordinance, but tying it to renters' protections was going too far. It was the latest attempt by Jamaal to manipulate the mayor.

After the proposed ordinance was read, the floor was opened for questions and comments. The first to speak was the most conservative member of the council. He was a partner in several apartment complexes. "What you two are proposing goes against everything this city, this state, this nation stands for. Houston didn't become the energy capital of the world by embracing socialistic schemes like this. No, Houston has risen to prominence by protecting free enterprise. I can't support anything that violates my free market principles."

"What is this 'ban the box'?" a moderate councilman asked, intentionally trying to shift attention away from the conservative.

"Ban the box means landlords can't ask about an applicant's criminal history on a rental application," Lia Patel replied. "The lack of housing stability is a major cause of recidivism. Those who have served their time in prison have already paid their debt to society. They should not be punished for the rest of their lives for a mistake made in their youth. This gives them a new leash on life and a second chance to turn their lives around. In other cities, ban the box has enabled hundreds to get off the streets and into stable housing."

"So, you want to let child pornographers run wild through

apartment complexes," the conservative shouted. "It's just like you lefties to coddle perverts."

Lia smiled. "No, if they have been released from prison, they have been judged to no longer be a threat. And if they go five years with no further convictions, that judgment is proven to be sound. Who are we to question the decisions of the parole board?"

The moderate councilman had another question. "Okay, and what is just cause eviction?"

"Just cause eviction means that landlords must present a valid reason to force someone out of their home. Far too often, landlords invent reasons to evict a tenant so that they can jack up the rent on a new tenant. One of my constituents was evicted because she was watching her three nieces while their mother was out of the state for work. The landlord said that they were unauthorized occupants of the apartment. Another was evicted because her grandson, who didn't live with her, was arrested for possession of marijuana. That's not fair. That's not a just cause. Our ordinance would stop such abuses of the law and hold landlords accountable for their actions."

"Rent control has never worked," the conservative said with undisguised hostility. "Why should we believe it will work here?"

Again, Patel answered. "We propose a unique style of rent control—Houston-style rent control, if you will. Rather than having a small group of people appointed by the mayor to the rent control board, we propose having an elected board. In most cities, the board consists of seven or nine people. We propose a board of twenty-five. This will allow for the election of people with varying backgrounds and interests. The board will truly represent the people."

"What if only tenant friendly people are elected to the board?" the conservative asked.

"If that is the will of the people, so be it. Too many decisions that impact the lives of Houstonians are made by a small group of people. There are nearly a million renters in Houston. Why should a handful of landlords get to determine how they live, where they live, and what they pay for housing? This ordinance will give the people a voice in how their city operates. That is democracy in action." Lia stared at her fellow council member. "You aren't opposed to democracy, are you?" The conservative just scowled and slapped his hand in the air in response.

Charles usually refrained from participating in the discussion. It was one way to keep his cards close to his chest. But his curiosity was getting uncontrollable. "Why did you include a living wage in an ordinance providing renter protections? It seems to me that these are two separate issues."

"Separate, but inseparable," Patel said. "A person making minimum wage can't support a family. He can't provide adequate food, health care, and housing for his family. What he earns determines what housing is affordable. If he makes more, he can afford more. So what if we keep his rent the same, but he doesn't make more money? He is still struggling, and he will continue to do so until he makes more money. We can give him a significant raise. He won't be able to afford to live in River Oaks, but his life will be immeasurably better."

"We need to strike a balance between the rights of renters and the rights of landlords and business owners," Charles replied. I always want to find a balance, Charles told himself. Early in his political career, he learned that compromise was necessary to accomplish anything. And that meant finding a balance between two extremes. Maybe I can do that with this ordinance. Then I would be the hero. It's going to mean walking that tightrope over alligators and tigers.

Lia Patel shook her head. "Landlords and business owners have all the power. Yes, we need to balance the power between renters, landlords, and businesses. Otherwise, the rights of tenants get trampled. This is the twenty-first century. It is time for us to recognize the rights of renters."

"You propose to raise the minimum wage to $15 an hour in six months," said another of the moderates. She owned a small chain of nail salons. "That seems like too much, too fast."

"Sure, we could raise it in stages over a year, two years, ten years, twenty years. And in the meantime, people are suffering. If $15 an hour is moral and just, and it is, then there is no valid reason to delay. This ordinance is about justice, and justice delayed is justice denied."

YOU ARE THE VICTIMS OF NEGLECT

July 2020

Despite the sweltering heat and humidity—it was a typical July 4th in Houston—Jamaal Wilkes was dressed in his trademark tailored suit and fedora. He looked out at the assembling people, and estimated at least twelve hundred in attendance and more were pouring in. It was much better than he had expected. I shouldn't be surprised, he thought. My network of housing activists is good at mobilizing large numbers of rabble-rousers. He hoped the crowd would control its passions. If a riot broke out, it would not help the cause.

Jamaal had arranged a slate of eight speakers, including a homeless man, a renter with five children, and two housing activists. He would speak first, and Marta Escobar would speak last. He wanted to bookend the other speakers with the two he knew would be most effective. Lia Patel had wanted to speak, but Jamaal thought it best to save her for a later rally.

As Jamaal walked to the podium, the crowd quieted. Jamaal smiled to himself. They know that I'm going to say something important, and they don't want to miss a word. "Good morning, everyone. It is wonderful to see so many people willing to tolerate this heat to stand up for justice. By the time we are done, this heat will be nothing compared to the hellfire we are going to give city council." A roar came from the crowd.

"On this day two-hundred-forty-four years ago, America declared its independence from Great Britain. Today, we are here to proclaim our independence from a broken system. It is a system that relegates many—particularly people of color—to poverty and substandard housing. In the Sermon on the Mount, Jesus proclaimed the Golden Rule: 'Do unto others as you would have them do unto you.' Today, a different Golden Rule dominates our society: Those who have the gold rule. You may have seen that real estate billionaire say as much on television a few months ago." The assembled mass started booing. Jamaal held up his hands to quiet the crowd. "But we will soon do unto them as they have done unto us." Again, the crowd roared its approval.

"Today, many Americans are celebrating freedom. But those of us assembled here today do not share that freedom. We are enslaved by low wages and landlords who put profit before people. We can change that. There is power in numbers, and there are more of us than of them. Across the nation, renters are awakening to this fact. They realize the power that they have but haven't exercised. Our brothers and sisters are scoring victories in city after city, and Houston is next.

"We are here today to call upon the City of Houston, no, to demand that the City of Houston enact several reasonable renter protections. Our demands are simple: Renters should not be subjected to outrageous rent increases. Renters should have the right to renew a lease. Tenants should not be evicted without just cause. Renters facing eviction should be provided with legal representation. Landlords should not be permitted to ask applicants about their criminal history. Hard-working people deserve a wage that can support a family." The crowd roared again.

"Families are broken up when they do not have stable housing. Unstable housing creates an endless cycle of poverty. Unstable housing incentivizes criminal activity. We can put an end to this by ensuring that every Houstonian, no matter his skin color or the size of his bank account, has stable housing.

"Some will argue that these are radical policies. I would ask them: when is justice a radical policy? And these policies are about justice. These policies are about housing justice." Again, the crowd erupted in cheers and clapping.

"The future is created by those who have the strength of their convictions. Today, we are showing the world the strength of our numbers. In the coming months, we must remain true to our principles. For if we do, justice will prevail. Thank you." The crowd began clapping and cheering wildly. They were worked into the emotional frenzy that Jamaal had intended. While that elation would not be sustained for long, many would remember this moment and it would give them strength when victory seemed uncertain. And Jamaal knew it would seem that way at times. That was the nature of politics.

The next six speakers were a continuation of the points that Jamaal had made. This wasn't surprising, since he had written their speeches. He could have spoken for the entire ninety minutes, but he wanted the rally to be inclusive. So, he allowed others to speak, even if the words coming out of their mouths were his. This movement was his baby, and he was going to nurture it to adulthood. Each speech built upon what had been said previously. It was a cohesive package. The exception was Marta Escobar, but Jamaal had no concerns about her. She knew what to say and how to say it. She wasn't the polished speaker he was, but then, few matched Jamaal's oratory skills.

By the time Escobar spoke, the sun was directly overhead. Many tried to escape the heat by moving under the few trees in the park, but nobody was leaving. "I will keep my comments brief," Escobar started. "I am sure that you would like to get out of this heat and enjoy some air conditioning. That is, if your landlord hasn't turned off your power." Many in the crowd moaned in understanding.

"For decades, Harris County has had a housing crisis. My predecessors ignored that crisis. But I don't have to tell you that. You are the victims of years of neglect. The pandemic has only made the crisis worse, and it can no longer be ignored.

"That both state and federal officials aren't heeding our cries for help isn't surprising. Republicans are in control in Washington and Austin, and they never care about the most vulnerable. But here in Harris County, it is different. Some of us in government have heard your cries and responded. I enacted an eviction moratorium to prevent you from being thrown out of your home and into the streets. I enacted a rent freeze to prevent your landlord from gouging you further in these troubling economical times. But these actions are only a temporary reprieve from your suffering. Unfortunately, my powers are limited to temporary measures during a disaster. Someday, that disaster will end, and with it, the protection that I have provided you with.

"However, the city does not have such limitations. The city can enact permanent tenant protections, and we call upon the city to do so immediately. Justice demands it.

"The city is currently considering a slate of renter protections. We must make our voice known to city officials. Contact those officials and express your support for renter protections. We must demand swift action. Justice demands it.

"We cannot allow the naysayers and fear mongers to dissuade us from our mission. We must remain strong in our fight for what is right. Justice demands it. Your presence here today makes me certain that we will prevail in our fight for justice."

All the speakers then gathered on the stage to wave to the assembled crowd and thank them for their support.

YOU BOYS HAVE CATTLE

July 2020

Justin and Pratik attended Jamaal's rally. They were among a small minority wearing a mask. They also wore T-shirts that proclaimed, "I love landlords." Not surprisingly, they drew a considerable number of angry stares and even more angry words. Justin and Pratik attempted to engage many of the protesters in conversation, which the two livestreamed on social media via body cams.

While most of the conversations began civilly, nearly all turned into a screaming rant by the protester. It quickly became obvious that they weren't interested in discussing the issue. They wanted to prove that Justin and Pratik were wrong while denying the intellectual bodyguards an opportunity to state their views. And the protesters appeared to believe that the louder they shouted, the more convincing their argument would be.

One of the more interesting conversations occurred with a young man named Ben. He was about a foot shorter than Pratik. Ben had long, unkempt hair and muttonchop sideburns. He labeled himself a justice warrior. He marched up to Pratik and loudly announced, "You are a pawn of the man."

Pratik smiled. "Just so we are clear, which man are you

referring to?"

Ben twisted his lips and bared his teeth. "You know, the money man. The landlords. They keep raising rents. They don't care about people. All they care about is money, and no matter how much they have, it's never enough. They are robbing their tenants, and it's time that we put a stop to it."

"Have you considered whether the landlord's costs keep increasing?"

"Who cares? That's his problem. Besides, he's got enough money already. How much are you being paid?" Ben snarled. "I bet it's a lot."

"Whether or not we are being paid," Pratik responded calmly, "is irrelevant. How can a landlord maintain his property and pay the bills if the rents he can charge are arbitrarily limited?"

"That's his problem. He's the brilliant businessman. Let him figure it out. Besides, he don't never fix nothing. I know a dude whose AC hasn't worked all summer. That's not fair. Until the pandemic started, he always paid his rent on time. He didn't pay the rent for three freaking months and the landlord refuses to fix his AC."

"So," Pratik said, "this guy hasn't paid the rent for three months, but he expects his landlord to fix his AC. That doesn't seem very fair to me."

Ben stared at Pratik with a scowl. "Fuck you," he shouted before storming off.

Within two hours, the video had over ten thousand views. The following day, they received a phone call from Buford Jennings requesting a meeting in his office.

Buford met them in the lobby of his building. "You boys don't have to wear a mask in here," he said. "I thought you two were against masks."

"We are opposed to mask mandates by government," Pratik said. "We don't oppose private property owners from having such a requirement as a condition of entering the property. It's their property, and they have a right to determine its use."

Buford smiled. "So, what if I said a condition of entering my property is to remove your mask?"

"Then we would leave. We aren't wearing a mask because of Escobar's order," Justin responded. "Pratik's parents have several medical conditions that put them at high risk. We choose to wear a mask to avoid infecting them. To be clear, we aren't anti-mask. We are anti-mask mandates. Given our context, we think that wearing a mask is prudent."

"Very well. Let's go to my office," Buford replied. When they were seated, Buford slid an envelope across his desk. "This is for you two," he said.

Neither Justin nor Pratik moved to pick up the envelope. "What is this?" Pratik asked.

"Open it and see for yourself," the real estate tycoon responded.

Pratik grabbed the envelope and pulled out a piece of paper. As he looked at the paper, his eyes bulged. "Holy shit," he said as he handed the paper to Justin.

Justin was just as stunned as Pratik. Neither said a word as they just stared at one another and allowed the implications of what was on the paper to sink in. It was a check made out to Justice Inc. for $50,000.

"I want to hire you two," Buford said to break the silence. "There is a saying in Texas, 'Big hat but no cattle.' It refers to people who pretend to be wealthy ranchers by wearing a large Stetson and talking big. But they have no cattle. It can also apply to anyone who pretends to be something that he isn't. You boys have cattle. What you two did yesterday proves that. They say that everything is bigger in Texas. Well, you two got the biggest cojones in the state. That took real courage to walk into the lion's den. Anyone who can do that, well, I want them on my side."

"I...I...I don't know what to say," Justin finally stuttered.

Buford laughed. "Just say yes. That check should be enough for six months. We'll see where things stand at the end of the year and go from there."

Justin and Pratik looked at one another and nodded. "Yes,"

they said in unison. Each sat back in his chair and took a deep breath. A dozen thoughts rushed through their minds. Many times, they had discussed a strategy to fight the renter protections. Now that they had a client, they weren't sure where to start.

"Mr. Jennings—," Justin said.

Buford held up his hands. "We're partners. Call me Buford."

"Okay," Justin continued, "Buford, we have several ideas regarding how to fight what is going on. Some will require money, but most will just require time. We have plenty of both now."

"We are getting a late start," Pratik said. "Yesterday's protest made it clear that the renters' protections advocates have been working on this for some time. They must have a network of activists, tenant unions, and other allies. That puts us at a considerable disadvantage. We can overcome that by building our own coalition. That's going to require money, but certainly not $50,000."

Justin laughed. Buford and Pratik turned to him with puzzled looks on their faces. "I just realized the irony of this situation. Everyone is badmouthing landlords, and ours just gave us a huge check."

"I'm your landlord?" Buford asked incredulously.

Pratik smiled shyly. "We didn't think it was important, so we didn't mention it."

"Oh well. I know several of the councilmen who will support us," Buford said. "I could introduce you to them."

"That would be good," Justin replied, "but we don't think that we should focus our efforts on city officials. We certainly need some allies on the council. We can help them better understand the issue and articulate a sound defense of our position. What will be more important is educating the public. It appears the public supports renter protections, and the advocates of those policies are pointing to that fact. If we can change public sentiment, that point goes away. And the pressure on city officials would shift."

"How are you going to do that?" Buford asked. "There's over two million people in this city. Sadly, my dog has more sense than most of them. I mean, they voted for Benton and Escobar, after all." He shook his head.

"I think we should give people more credit," Pratik responded. "Yes, some people they have elected are scoundrels. But far too often, they must choose between two different scoundrels. Voters often don't have viable alternatives. But if we give them a viable alternative to renter protections, I am confident that they will make the right choice."

"I think our first step should be contacting potential allies," Justin added. "We have compiled a list of trade groups that might be receptive. We'll email that list to you when we get home. If you know the officers of any of them, that would be helpful. We'll begin drafting a letter to them. Give us a few days, and we'll be in touch."

* * *

As they drove away from the meeting, Justin and Pratik were lost in their thoughts. Pratik was thrilled that his idea had proven to have merit. They had a client, a very important issue, and a lot of money.

Justin finally spoke. "I'm proud of you, Pratik. You had a dream and pursued it. I was skeptical at first, but I'm glad that I came along for the ride."

"To be honest, I may not have pursued it without you," Pratik said. "I'm not as comfortable in the limelight as you. The important thing is, we're a team."

POLITICS IS THE ART OF COMPROMISE

July 2020

Jamaal was seated at a conference table with three of the four moderate members of the city council. One council member was out of town. Jamaal needed at least two of the moderates to support the tenant protections ordinance. He had asked for the meeting, hoping he could persuade all three who were in attendance.

"I appreciate you taking time out of your busy schedules to meet with me," Jamaal began. "As you know, I am a powerful advocate for renters' rights. The ordinance that is before the council will provide Houstonians with the most robust protections in the nation. I wanted to meet with you to answer your questions and help you better understand the urgency of this matter." The three council members nodded.

"That's a rather radical set of policies," one of them said. "There will be a lot of pushback from the business community and real estate groups. We are already seeing some, and the proposal isn't even a month old. We need to find a balance. This is going too far too fast. Can't you find some middle ground and compromise?"

"There is no compromise between good and evil. There is no balance between justice and injustice," Jamaal replied.

"Renters and poor people have been treated unjustly for decades. Landlords have always had all the power. They can dictate whatever terms and conditions they choose, and tenants have no choice but to accept them or go homeless. That's not fair."

"That seems like an exaggeration to me," the councilman objected. "There are other options besides homelessness."

"Technically, that is true," Jamaal replied. "They can accept one set of dictates from this landlord or a different set of dictates from that landlord. At the end of the day, they must accept somebody's dictates. That doesn't leave the tenant with any viable options." Jamaal thought for a moment. "Consider a robber who sticks a gun in your face and says, 'Your money or your life.' He's given you a choice, but it's not a very attractive choice. That's what tenants are facing."

"Let's talk about this living wage," said the councilwoman who owned nail salons. "I am getting a dozen calls a day from business owners saying that they will have to lay off employees, and a few have said that they will have to close their business or move out of the city. That will help no one. Employees will go from a low wage to no wage."

Jamaal chuckled and waved his hand dismissively. "That's just fear mongering and scare tactics. Business owners always make such dire predictions when their profits are threatened. If those owners really cared about their employees, they'd pay a living wage voluntarily instead of being forced to. It is impossible to support a family at the current minimum wage. To afford a decent two-bedroom apartment, a minimum wage employee would need to work nearly eighty hours a week. That's outrageous. No human being should have to work like that just to provide for his family. Imagine the shame you would feel if you couldn't keep your family housed and fed. That's what tens of thousands of Houstonians feel every single day. Renter protections will restore their dignity and allow them to support their families."

"I understand the need to protect tenants, but if someone is making minimum wage, why are they trying to support a family?" the third councilman asked. "It seems to me maybe someone making minimum wage should refrain from having children until he can properly provide for them."

"People have a right to have children," Jamaal said without trying to hide his irritation. "It is very classist of you to insinuate that they should sacrifice their rights because you object to their choices. It isn't an individual's fault if his employer refuses to pay him a decent wage. He is a victim of the system. To place blame on him is callous." Jamaal looked at his watch. "I'm sorry, but I have another meeting to attend. Thank you again for your time, and please feel free to contact me if you have additional questions. When the time comes, can we count on you to support the ordinance?"

The three council members stared silently at Jamaal with pained looks on their faces. Finally, one spoke. "I'm not ready to commit either way. There is a lot to consider." The other two council members nodded. Jamaal wasn't surprised at the noncommittal attitude. Moderates were seldom willing to stick their neck out. They would probably wait until the vote to decide so that they could see which way the wind was blowing.

* * *

Charles Benton didn't hide his anger. "What the hell do you want, Jamaal?"

Jamaal smiled and placed his hat on the mayor's desk. "Charles, that is hardly the proper way to greet an old friend." Jamaal took a seat. "I know that we've had our differences in recent months, but I'd like to put that behind us. We've done a lot of great things together, and we can do even more great things."

Charles shook his head and slammed his hand down onto his desk. "That bullshit will not work on me. I have grown tired of your deviousness and backstabbing. I don't need or want your help anymore."

Jamaal frowned. "Hear me out. You may find what I have to say interesting and perhaps helpful. If not, so be it."

Charles shrugged. "Go ahead, but make it quick. I have a

council meeting to prepare for."

"Funny that you should mention a council meeting. I just came from a meeting with several council members. They wanted additional information regarding tenant protections. At the beginning of the meeting, they seemed uncertain which way to vote. But by the time I left, they had voiced support for the ordinance the council is considering."

Charles furrowed his brow, wondering who Jamaal had met. It had to be the moderates, Charles thought. The conservatives would never support the ordinance, and the Progressives were certain to. Jamaal would know that he was wasting his time meeting with either of those factions. The four moderates would make the difference. But Jamaal met with only three of them. Then, he remembered Jenkins had gone to San Antonio for a funeral. "Why are you telling me this?"

"I'm giving you an opportunity to save face. At this point, the vote on the ordinance is going to be eight to seven in favor. If Jenkins votes no, and I think she will, your vote will break the tie. However, if you come out in support of the ordinance now, Jenkins would likely vote for passage. That would put the vote at ten to seven. So, it really comes down to you, Charles."

Charles silently stared at Jamaal. "You just don't get it, do you?" he finally said.

"What's that, Charles? What don't I get?"

"How the game is played. Politics is the art of compromise. But you, you rigidly stick to your ideology. If you want to get things done, you must meet the other side halfway. You must be willing to bend."

Jamaal laughed. "The thing is, if you bend enough times, you eventually break. You might know it as metal fatigue. I think of it as mental fatigue. The principle is the same."

IRRESPONSIBLE BUSINESSES SHOULD BE PUNISHED

July 2020

Marta Escobar shook her head as she reviewed the latest COVID numbers. New cases were spiking, and the previous day had seen a record number of confirmed cases in Harris County. "We're never going to beat this thing if those redneck assholes don't do as they are told," she said disgustingly. "Our numbers are approaching those of New York City, and it's four times bigger than Houston. Tougher measures are necessary."

"What do you have in mind?" Tilde asked. They had previously discussed numerous options, but now immediate action was necessary.

"Too many businesses are letting people enter their store without a mask. They need to enforce the mask mandate. I don't have enough police officers to monitor stores effectively. Escobar considered a thought. "I know what I'll do. I'll enlist the citizenry and hit the businesses where it hurts the most. That will get their attention, and they will learn that I am serious."

An hour later, Escobar stood in the press room. "The latest COVID numbers are not encouraging. We had a record number of new cases yesterday. Too many people are flaunting the rules, and the new numbers are a case and point. Too many are going out in public without a mask. And businesses are letting them get away with it. We can't flatten the curve when this is going on. We cannot allow this to continue. Our hospitals will soon be overwhelmed. We won't be able to provide adequate treatment for everyone. Many will be turned away to suffer whatever fate awaits them.

"Actions have consequences. If businesses want to continue their lax enforcement of the mask mandate, then they will pay a price. Today, I am announcing a fine of $1,000 on a business for each individual they allow to enter its premises without a mask. In addition, I am extending the mask mandate to the end of October.

"It should be obvious that we don't have enough police officers to enforce this. There are simply too many stores and businesses. I could order businesses to close again, but at this time, that is not the right approach. Therefore, we are setting up a website for citizens to report businesses for not requiring masks. Citizens can remain anonymous if they choose. However, we are also establishing a bounty of $500 for each reported incident. Responsible citizens should be rewarded when they do the right thing. Irresponsible businesses should be punished when they don't do the right thing. And this measure won't cost taxpayers a penny.

"We are all in this together. However, some people think they are above the law. They are putting their own selfish desires above the public interest. They are putting profits before people. I intend to put a stop to that. It is the only way to stop the spread of COVID.

"At the start of the pandemic four months ago, there was much that we didn't know about the coronavirus. We have learned a great deal since then. And each day we learn more. But the one constant has been the need for the proper precautions —wearing a face mask, social distancing, and avoiding large gatherings. When followed, these have proven to stop the spread of the virus. When they aren't followed, we get numbers like we had yesterday. Each of us should keep this in mind when we hear the latest COVID numbers. If everyone cooperates, we can beat this thing. I will now take a few questions."

"How will this bounty work? What if more than one person reports the same business?" asked one reporter.

"We are still working out some of the details. When an individual reports a violation of the mask mandate, they must also upload a photo. If we get multiple reports for the same violation, then the first to submit a report will receive the bounty. The bounty will be paid as a credit toward the person's property taxes."

The reporter frowned. "But what if someone is a renter? They can't use the credit."

"That's another of the details we are working on," Escobar admitted. "Maybe we'll offer debit cards or something. I don't know, but that's not important now. The entire pandemic has required us to be very fluid. We've had to respond to an ever-changing landscape as new information is gained. I have previously said that we can't be overly rigid in our approach. We must take each day as it comes, reassess where we are, and come up with new tactics. The bounty is an example. We need to encourage businesses to cooperate and enforce the mask mandate. They weren't doing their part, and so we have had to adjust."

"One of the biggest complaints being voiced by the public is the lack of testing sites. What is the county doing to expand the number of testing sites?" asked another reporter.

"We have heard those complaints and are in the process of opening three new sites, including a drive-thru testing site at NRG. These should be operational within three days. These sites will increase our capacity by nearly 30 percent. One more question."

Several reporters shouted questions. Escobar pointed to the reporter from Channel 3. Dammit, Escobar thought, why did I call on her? She's not the friendliest reporter in the room.

"Judge Escobar," the reporter said, "you have had two lawsuits filed against you since the pandemic started. With this extension of the mask mandate and fines for businesses, do you expect more legal actions against you?

Escobar grimaced. "There is always one in every crowd. In this case, there are a handful of people who simply don't want to do their part in the fight against COVID. They would rather cause problems than be a part of the solution. Regardless, my orders, including the mask mandate extension, are legal. Despite the denials from some right-wing radicals, we are still in the middle of a public health emergency. I won't be surprised if those radicals file more lawsuits. They stubbornly cling to their ideology and will never admit that they are wrong. In the end, I'll be vindicated. One more question."

A reporter in the front row shouted, "Rumor has it the governor is about to open the state entirely and allow businesses to operate at full capacity. How does that impact this order?"

Escobar shook her head. "We'll cross that bridge when we get to it." Escobar turned and went to her office just in time to see the governor's press conference.

I TRUSTED TEXANS WITH FREEDOM

July 2020

The governor stood at the podium on the steps of the Texas State Capitol. It was only 10:30 in the morning, but the heat index was already above one-hundred degrees. If it weren't for this damn pandemic, he thought, we could do this some place a bit more comfortable. Of course, if it weren't for the pandemic, this wouldn't even be necessary. With one hand he wiped the sweat from his brow with a handkerchief, and with the other hand he adjusted the microphone.

"Good morning, ladies and gentlemen," he said, "today is a great day for Texas and for freedom. Last month I lifted the statewide mask mandate and allowed restaurants, bars, gyms, and similar businesses to operate at 50 percent capacity. Today, I am rescinding that limitation. Beginning today, all businesses in Texas may operate at full capacity. Texas is open for business. We were the first state to even partially reopen. And now we are the first state to reopen completely.

"Last month, when I announced the partial reopening, my critics warned we would see a dramatic increase in the number of new COVID cases. But that hasn't happened. I will admit that cases are about 10 percent higher than in May, but that increase is isolated to the state's five primary urban areas. In the rest of the state, cases have remained steady or declined slightly. Despite the clamoring of the Chicken Littles, the sky did not fall. I trusted Texans with freedom, and they responded appropriately.

"That's the funny thing about freedom. When people are free, they generally make the right choices. However, when the government issues mandates and prohibitions, they have no choice. If an individual makes an awful choice, only he suffers. However, if a government official makes an awful choice, everyone suffers. Today, I am returning freedom to the people of Texas.

"I am sure that my critics will offer a new set of dire predictions. But I will not waver. My faith in Texans is surpassed only by my faith in God.

"As a part of this executive order, I am rescinding my declaration of a statewide public health emergency. However, because new cases are increasing in the state's urban areas, I am carving out some exceptions for Houston, Dallas-Ft. Worth, San Antonio, Austin, and El Paso. Those metropolitan areas will remain in a state of emergency until we see a decline in new cases for six consecutive weeks. I'll take a few questions."

Hands shot up, and a few reporters shouted questions. The governor held up his hands to quiet the media. Pointing to a reporter from a local television station, he said, "Jill, I think your hand was up first." The governor didn't particularly like Jill, but she often asked stupid questions that were easy to answer. Right now, he wanted easy to answer questions so he could get out of the heat.

"Some people might argue," Jill said, "that you are singling out the big cities because they vote for Democrats. How would you respond to that?"

The governor shook his head. "I'll try to keep this simple. If Corpus Christi got struck by a hurricane, I would have no reason to declare the entire state a disaster area. I would limit my declaration to those areas affected by the storm. It would be pointless to put Amarillo under a disaster declaration. This situation is no different. Some areas of the state are experiencing an increase in the number of new cases, but most of the state isn't. Just as it would be pointless to declare a disaster in Amarillo after a hurricane, it would be pointless to keep the entire state under a public health emergency when most of the state is doing just fine. This has nothing to do with politics or political affiliations. I hope that makes sense." The governor pointed to a young man he didn't recognize.

"Could you clarify what you mean by metropolitan area? Are you talking about just the major cities, or are the suburbs included?"

Another softball, the governor thought. "I am referring to the metropolitan statistical areas used by the Census Bureau. So, for example, the Houston metropolitan area would include Montgomery County, Fort Bend County, and Brazoria County, as well as a few others."

"But," the young reporter interrupted, "cases in Brazoria County are declining. The same is true in most of the other counties adjoining Harris County. It doesn't seem fair to include them. I mean, many areas of those counties are rural. If you are going to exclude rural counties, it seems like it would be fairer to exclude the rural parts of the counties you mentioned."

The governor chuckled. "I didn't hear a question there, but I'll respond. Yes, many parts of counties included in a metropolitan area are rural. And yes, cases are declining in those areas. However, trying to demarcate an emergency declaration along those lines would be virtually impossible. And it would be very confusing. When a natural disaster occurs, the disaster declaration applies to an entire county or counties. From a response perspective, it makes sense to do it that way. The same idea applies to a public health emergency. One more question."

Governor," a reporter shouted before being called upon, "will the county judges keep their emergency powers?"

"Yes," the governor replied. "But I will watch them very closely. I will not tolerate them issuing orders and mandates that effectively nullify my policies. Thank you for coming today." With that, the governor turned from the podium and strode back into the capitol building.

SHE WANTS TO CONTROL US

July 2020

"**G**ood morning, Houston," Roger Mason shouted into his microphone. "Yesterday, the governor opened the state. All businesses can now operate at full capacity. However, Comrade Escobar has kept her emergency powers, and she has been quick to use them. She has extended the mask mandate and threatens fines for businesses that don't abide by her orders.

"In response, beginning today, I will broadcast every day from businesses that have the courage to stand up to Comrade Escobar. Today, I'm at Theater at Home on Westheimer in the heart of Montrose. Please come by to say hello and show your support for Oscar and Sheila Maynard, the owners of Theater at Home.

"The business offers a wide range of home entertainment systems. They offer a turnkey service—sales, installation, and service. This is a great time to get that home entertainment system you've been dreaming of. You're stuck at home and probably binge-watching Greta Garbo movies and reruns of *Dragnet* online. Oscar and Sheila can give you a theater-like experience at home.

"As I mentioned, our not so esteemed Comrade has extended

her order that we wear a face diaper while in public. And, she has announced that businesses that do not enforce the mask mandate will be subject to a fine of $1,000 for each individual who enters their store without a mask.

"This means that a small business must turn away paying customers when they are struggling. And they are struggling because Escobar ordered them to close for nearly two damn months. It wasn't enough to threaten the very existence of small businesses across the county. Now that they may be open, she has come up with a new threat—enforce her orders or get fined out of existence.

"Making matters worse, Comrade Escobar is also attempting to bribe citizens into becoming informants. She admits she doesn't have the personnel to enforce her order, so she is enlisting the citizenry to help her. She is offering a bounty to anyone who reports a business that isn't enforcing her mask mandate. This is straight out of the Soviet Union and the KGB. She wants to turn you against your neighbors. I beg you, don't fall for it.

"Since this is radio, I can't show you the banner that Oscar and Sheila have draped across the front of their store. It reads, 'Freedom Respected Here. No Masks Required.' In the Soviet Union, if you defied the authorities, you disappeared. You were shot, or perhaps worse, sent to the Gulag. Admittedly, Comrade Escobar hasn't gone that far. Yet. But trust me, if we allow her to continue her nonsense, Gulags are in our future. We must resist. And we must start doing so today.

"The easiest way to do this is to quit wearing a rag on your face in public. If masks worked, the damn curve would have been flattened months ago. The fact cases are skyrocketing is evidence that face diapers don't work. Of course, Escobar won't admit this. If she did, it would call into question all the other so-called facts she has told us. She won't admit her errors and allow us to get back to living our lives. She wants to control us, and she will lie to do so.

"Everything Escobar has been telling us has just been a giant propaganda campaign, just like the Soviet Union did. If you repeat a lie enough times, people believe it, even if it defies the facts. Even if it defies what they can see with their own eyes. And that is even more true when you punish anyone who expresses a dissenting point of view. Like they did in the Soviet Union. And like Escobar tried to do with me. But the truth will always prevail in the end.

"George Washington once remarked, 'If the freedom of speech is taken away, then dumb and silent we may be led, like sheep to the slaughter.' We've seen the Comrade try to strangle freedom of speech. And she is doing that to turn us into sheep. Sadly, many are willingly complying.

"You can show your support for brave entrepreneurs like Oscar and Sheila by patronizing their business. And if you aren't in the market for entertainment equipment now, consider making a donation to our defense fund. The funds will be used to fight the Comrade's orders in court, and if necessary, pay any fines that are imposed. We've set up a page on our website for donations. Oscar and Sheila have jump started the fund by donating $10,000. And one of our show sponsors will match all donations made while we are on the air today. He wants to remain anonymous, so I won't mention his Ford dealership on the Gulf Freeway.

"I quoted our first president a few minutes ago. I'd like to close this segment with a quote from one of our greatest presidents, Ronald Reagan. He said, 'Freedom is never more than one generation away from extinction. We didn't pass it to our children in the bloodstream. It must be fought for, protected, and handed on for them to do the same.' Now is the time to fight for and protect our freedom. Only then can we hand it to our children.

"I will continue to fight for freedom and expose the truth. The Regressives stubbornly cling to their ideology and will never admit that they are wrong. In the end, I will be vindicated."

WE SPOKE TO HUNDREDS OF PEOPLE

August 2020

"The last item on the agenda," Mayor Benton announced, "is the renters' protections ordinance. It appears that some compromises have been reached. Rather than review the entire ordinance, let's focus on the provisions that have been changed. I'll turn it over to council member Patel, the chairperson of the committee looking into renters' protections, to explain the changes."

"Thank you, Mayor Benton. Of the seven renter protections that we have proposed," Lia Patel said, "three have been altered. The committee has listened to the concerns of certain parties and tried to find a balance that recognizes the diversity of opinions on these issues.

"In the original ordinance, we proposed a rent increase cap of 3 percent or the rate of inflation, whichever is lower. This seemed to us to be a reasonable return for those investing in real estate. We received considerable feedback on this proposal. After long discussions and negotiations, all parties agreed to a rent cap of 3 percent over the rate of inflation. Further, we had proposed a rent board composed of twenty-five elected representatives. Again, after considerable debate and negotiation, we changed the method for selecting the rent board. Each council member, along with the mayor, will appoint one member. Nine additional members will be elected in a citywide vote." Lia paused to allow for comments or questions.

"If my math is correct," said one of the moderates, "that is twenty-six on the board. How will a tie vote be handled?"

"That will be up to the board to decide that," Lia said. "But I expect there to be no tie votes." The way the rent board would be selected made her confident that the board would be stacked with pro-tenant members.

"Who was involved in these discussions?" asked the most conservative member of the council. He stared caustically at Lia Patel. "If the only people involved in this were a bunch of your radical left-wing cronies, that's hardly fair."

"We heard from members of the various groups that would be affected," Lia responded.

"What the hell does that mean?" the conservative shouted. "You heard from them? Were they involved in negotiations or not?"

"Different people were involved in different discussions," Lia said softly. Across the dais, Roderick was fidgeting anxiously. He wanted to go punch the conservative in the nose. "There wasn't uniform resistance to every provision. We tried to involve those who seemed to have the most concerns about a particular provision."

"I want some names. Was Buford Jennings a part of these negotiations? He is the largest landlord in Houston. To exclude him would be negligent."

"I'm sorry, but I don't recall any names at the moment," Lia said with a shrug. "I'm not very good with names. Besides, we held dozens of hearings around the city and spoke to hundreds of people. It's hard to remember names when you meet so many people."

"You would remember Buford Jennings," the conservative yelled as he jumped to his feet. "This is absolute bullshit."

Mayor Benton pounded his gavel. "The councilman should take his seat and remember to refrain from such outbursts. There may be disagreements, but they should be expressed with civility." The conservative sank back into his seat. He sat silently, scowling at the mayor. "Unless there are further questions, let's move on," the mayor said.

Lia continued when nobody spoke up. "The second provision that was altered is ban the box. We had originally proposed that landlords could not ask about past criminal convictions, nor could they use such convictions in the tenant screening process. Landlords expressed concern that they could unknowingly rent to pedophiles and others who might pose a threat to other residents. We have since changed that provision to allow landlords to ask about felony convictions in the past five years." The conservative made a loud, incoherent noise, but said nothing.

"Why five years?" one moderate asked.

"If someone has avoided a conviction for five years," Lia answered, "statistics show he has likely turned his life around. The recidivism rate declines sharply after four years. We understand and share landlords' concerns about the safety of other renters. We think that this strikes a delicate balance for everyone involved."

"I am suspicious of your statistics," the moderate replied. "It makes little sense that the recidivism rate declines over time. I don't remember the exact numbers, but something like 60 percent of released convicts are arrested within three years, and nearly 80 percent after six years. That's not a decline."

"I meant that a smaller percentage are arrested again after five years," Lia explained. "So, if someone goes five years without being arrested, the chances are pretty good that he has turned his life around. We think those people deserve a chance to improve their lives. One of the primary causes of recidivism is unstable housing. We want to help them overcome that obstacle by giving them an opportunity to find stable housing."

"I'm not sure that I like that," the moderate replied. "It seems like it's coddling criminals."

"Very well, let's move on," the mayor said impatiently. He just wanted to put this entire issue behind him. He had remained uncommitted but knew that he couldn't do that much longer. It looked like the council would vote on the ordinance later in the month.

Lia nodded to the mayor. "The final provision that was changed is the living wage. We originally proposed raising the minimum wage to $15, effective six months from passage. That provision probably received more opposition than all the others combined. Again, we listened to the concerns that were voiced. We agreed to an increase to $12.50 an hour effective in six months. One year later, the minimum will increase to $14 an hour. The following year it will increase by one more dollar. This will give businesses time to adjust."

"I seem to recall you once saying that justice delayed is justice denied," the conservative said rancorously. "Apparently, you were just full of hot air when you said that. Typical loonie Lefty. Say one thing and do another."

"Justice in the end is better than no justice at all," Lia said with a smile. "We tried to be fair, which is more than can be said about those businesses that have refused to pay a living wage. Perhaps you should express your concerns to them, rather than those of us who are helping our most vulnerable neighbors."

"Okay everybody. It's getting late," Mayor Benton said. "I move we adjourn for the day and resume this discussion at our next meeting."

The conservative seconded the motion, and by a vote of eleven to six, the motion passed.

YOU HAD JUST COMMITTED MURDER

August 2020

"Charles, if I didn't know better, I would say that you are stalling," Jamaal said as he took a seat in the mayor's office.

Charles shook his head. "What in the hell are you talking about?"

"You moved to adjourn the last council meeting right in the middle of a discussion about an ordinance of upmost importance to this city. I still don't understand why you won't make a commitment to the ordinance. I have my suspicions, though."

"And what might that be, Jamaal?"

"You want to see how the vote goes down, hoping yours won't matter. Then you can abstain, and nobody gets pissed at you. The more things change...." Jamaal paused for a moment. "You know, Charles, I've been thinking about that night twenty years ago. You know which night I'm talking about, don't you?"

Charles stared blankly. He resisted the urge to punch Jamaal.

"I have been wondering what would happen if the truth about that came out. What if someone whispered in the ear of some young reporter eager to make a name for herself? I wonder what the citizens of Houston would think of you then."

"Are you threatening me, Jamaal? Because if you are, you should remember that you are the one who committed perjury. I was never charged with a crime."

Jamaal nodded. "That is true. But there is no statute of limitations for murder. There is for perjury. You could be tried for your crime, but not I."

"Your reputation will be sullied when people find out that the righteous reverend committed perjury."

"Let's be serious Charles. I was twelve years old and under the control of a father-like figure who coached me on what to say. I will be forgiven, and perhaps even celebrated for finally telling the truth. But you…. Well, that's a different story."

"I didn't coach you," Charles objected.

Jamaal smiled. "No, you didn't coach me, but you and I are the only ones who know that. So, it will be your word against mine. Which one of us do you think they will believe? The man of God, or the tarnished mayor?"

Charles' eyes narrowed. "Why did you do it? Why did you lie to cover for me?"

"Let's look at the evidence. Everyone knew that you and Devon had a love/hate relationship. You were best friends until the two of you started drinking. Then the two of you became mortal enemies. That night, you stormed out of the bar right after an altercation with Devon. You never denied that. The odd thing was that you couldn't remember what you did for the next hour. That's when I came upon you and Devon lying in Miss Betty's yard. You were covered in blood with a knife in your hand. Devon was dead. Even to a twelve-year-old, it was clear what had happened. I was petrified. You had just committed murder, and I was staring at the body."

"I tried to rouse you, but you were still in a blackout. There was no way that I could carry you away, and you were in no condition to walk. You were babbling incoherently and drooling. It wasn't Charles Benton at his best. I stood there trying to figure out what to do. That is when I put together a plan. I took the knife from your hand and stabbed you several times. Though I hated doing it, it was necessary for my plan to work. I wiped the handle to remove my prints and then put it back in your hand. That's the way the police found you when they arrived."

"I told them I was on my way home from playing basketball at the park, which I had been doing, when I heard you and Devon arguing. Hiding in the bushes across the street, I watched as Devon attacked you. I didn't know what to do. There was no way I was going to overpower Devon. I thought he was going to kill you. Somehow, you got the knife away from him. And then you stabbed him over and over. I was paralyzed with fear. I don't know how long I sat in the bushes, but when I finally got to you, you were laying on the ground beside Devon."

"But that doesn't explain why you lied to the police, Jamaal. You weren't in the bushes watching us fight."

"No, I wasn't. I didn't see any of the fight. But it was obvious you had murdered Devon. You were like a father to me, Charles. I had to protect you. If Devon had attacked you first, then you had a good defense. I provided that defense."

Charles hadn't thought about that night in many years. As Jamaal told the story, it seemed like it had happened to someone else. Charles' mind wandered back to that distant memory. And then, he was struck by a realization that had evaded him for over twenty years. "Hearing that story after all these years reminded me of something," he said. "There has always been a part of your story that bothered me, but I couldn't put my finger on it. I haven't thought about it for years. But now I know what it is. The park. When I left the bar, I walked by the park. It was dark."

WE NEED TO CHANGE THE FRAMEWORK

August 2020

Justin and Pratik had sent nearly five hundred emails to prominent landlords, trade groups, and local business owners. So far, only three people had responded, and their interest in the services offered by Justice Inc was tepid at best. Justin was disappointed. He thought that those whose businesses were being threatened would be quick to respond. Pratik, on the other hand, maintained his normal jolly demeanor.

"Justin," Pratik explained, "we must follow the basic principles of marketing. First, we must identify our target market. We've done that. Then we need to make them aware of the service that we offer. We have done that. Finally, we must show how we can solve their problem or bring them value. That takes time. Keep in mind that Buford was resistant at first, but he came around. Besides, thanks to Buford, we don't really need any other clients."

"The video we made at that protest should be demonstration enough," Justin objected. "That's what convinced Buford to hire us. What else can we do?"

Pratik shook his head. "As a general rule, a potential customer must have at least three exposures to a business before he acts. For most of the people we emailed, that was probably their first exposure to us. So, they need at least two more exposures. Also, keep in mind that our email was necessarily short. We couldn't cover everything in a single email. As a last point, we've created an entirely new and unique business. It's going to take people a little time to get their heads around that and get on board. Sure, it would be nice to have more clients, but for now, Buford is enough. And I can give you fifty thousand reasons why."

Justin thought about those comments for a moment and considered his own actions regarding purchasing something new. "I see your point. I saw those ads for the new smart phone at least a dozen times before I bought one. Granted, I didn't really need a new phone. The additional features that it has are certainly nice, but they weren't needed. The people we contacted need us."

"We know that," Pratik replied, "but they don't. The challenge is to make them realize they need us. And the best way to do that is to solve their problem. And we are going to do that with or without their help."

"So, what is their problem?"

"In one sense, they have multiple problems," Pratik said. "They are being attacked by both the city and the county, and those attacks are taking slightly different forms. It doesn't help that many of them accept the same premises as those attacking them. Most lack moral clarity; they don't understand the right to property and its crucial role in their business. I could go on, but you get the point." Justin nodded.

"In a more fundamental sense," Pratik continued, "they have only one problem. And that's the one we need to solve."

"I am thinking out loud here," Justin said, "but I would say that their most fundamental problem is their acceptance of the idea of the 'public interest.' If they rejected that idea, then they would be better able to defend themselves. That's how Escobar has justified her orders, and it underlies that ordinance that city council is considering."

"What about their misunderstanding of property rights?" Pratik retorted. "If they understood that, then they could defend themselves properly. After all, the attacks are focused on violating their right to produce and trade. That is true of what Escobar has done, and it is true of what the city council is considering."

Justin frowned. "That's true. But the 'public interest' rests on the notion that individuals must sacrifice for others, that they must put aside their self-interest in deference to the 'common good.' That is a moral issue, and morality is more fundamental than politics."

"I agree with you, but we are dealing with a political issue. And politically, the right to property is the fundamental issue."

"Yes, but property rights and the 'public interest' cannot coexist," Justin said. "So long as individuals believe they are subordinate to the group, property rights are a second thought." Pratik smiled. "What?" Justin asked.

"Why can't we address both issues? As you said, the two are inseparable. A rational morality—one that rejects sacrifice— naturally and logically leads to property rights. And any defense of property rights must be founded on a rational morality if it is to be successful."

Justin considered that suggestion. "I like that. We defend both property rights while articulating the moral principles that support them."

"I think that property rights should be our primary focus. Most people have a better appreciation of property rights than a rational morality. They will be open to an argument that property rights are sacrosanct. Much more so than rejecting the notion of the 'public interest.' Certainly, we need to address that. But I think it will be easier if we explain the importance of property rights and why these policies violate the right to property. We certainly need to address the underlying moral principles. If we don't, the opposition can continue to frame the debate."

Justin furrowed his brow in thought. Pratik waited patiently.

Finally, Justin spoke. "We're missing the real issue we should address. It's not property rights or moral principles. You just identified it when you said that the opposition is framing the debate. We need to change the framework. That means explaining the importance of starting with the right standard, considering the full context, and examining the pros and cons of alternatives. We need people to think about this entire issue differently. If we do that, everything falls into place. If we don't, then it won't matter what facts or arguments we present. People will process that information improperly. However, if we reframe the issue, they will look at the issue differently."

Pratik was nodding at Justin's last three sentences. "You nailed it. Instead of focusing on changing minds about the issue, we change the way they look at and examine the issue. Our focus should be on method, not content." Pratik was beaming. "I knew I kept you around for a reason," he joked.

"The challenge," Justin noted, "will be to explain all of this without being preachy or moralizing. I remember some of those debates we had with Leftists when we were in college. We were assholes sometimes." Justin and Pratik both laughed at that memory.

"Yeah," Pratik said, "I don't think we changed anyone's mind and just pissed them off even more. Moralizing is not an effective tactic if you are trying to change minds."

"Where do we go from here?"

"Let's start by writing several papers. I'd say let's keep them under twelve hundred words. That's a relatively easy read, and it gives us sufficient space to make a solid argument. I will work on a piece about identifying the proper standard. Why don't you work on explaining the importance of considering the full context? We can address alternatives later."

Justin nodded. "That works for me."

I LIED TO CHARLES

August 2020

Charles returned to his office just before seven in the evening. Fortunately, his staff was gone for the day. He needed quiet and solitude to think about what he had realized earlier in the day.

If the park was dark, then Jamaal could not have been playing basketball like he claimed. He had been candid with Charles about lying to the police. It appeared that he had also lied to Charles. But why would Jamaal lie about playing basketball in the park? He had to be covering up something else.

Perhaps Jamaal and his friends had been smoking pot at the park. They did that occasionally, and it certainly wasn't something to admit to the police. But there was no need to lie to Charles about it. Charles frowned upon Jamaal smoking pot, but Jamaal didn't keep it a secret. Whatever Jamaal did that night, it wasn't playing basketball or smoking pot.

Even to this day, Jamaal insists he was playing basketball. He could have long ago admitted that he had lied about it, and that would have been the end of it. But Jamaal has made no such admission. Not even today. Whatever he was trying to hide that night, Charles thought, he's still trying to hide it. It must be something worse than smoking pot.

Charles reached into a desk drawer and pulled out a bottle of Glenfiddich 18-Year-Old Scotch. He poured himself three fingers and took a sip. Charles could feel himself relaxing as the alcohol's warmth trickled down his throat. Twenty-five years ago, he thought, I could only afford malt liquor. Now, I drink the best whisky money can buy. He smiled at the thought and took another sip.

Charles leaned back and took another sip of the Scotch. He closed his eyes and ran Jamaal's story through his mind. Jamaal said that he found me passed out with a knife in my hand. Devon was lying nearby, dead. It appeared that I had killed Devon. Jamaal knew he couldn't get me away from the scene before the police arrived. So, he fabricated a story that I had killed Devon in an act of self-defense. Jamaal admitted to me he had taken the knife from me and stabbed me several times to make the claim of self-defense more plausible. That was certainly quick thinking on his part.

One question that was never answered is how I got Rohypnol in my system. It explains why I don't remember the altercation with Devon or much else about what happened after I left the bar. I have always assumed that Devon or one of his buddies slipped it into my drink, but that was never proven. Perhaps Devon was trying to dope me up so he could kill me later. The police never pursued that line of inquiry.

If I can figure out what Jamaal is hiding, perhaps I can gain leverage over him. Then I can rid myself of his manipulation. I need something solid. Mere speculation won't suffice. I need to find the truth. Only then will Jamaal take me seriously. But how do I do that?

* * *

It was nearly dark by the time Jamaal returned to his office. Sitting at his desk, he reached into a drawer and withdrew a bottle of Elijah Craig 18-Year-Old Bourbon. He poured himself three fingers and took a sip. Jamaal could feel himself relaxing as the alcohol's warmth trickled down his throat. Not that long ago, he thought, I could only afford cheap wine. Now, I drink the best whiskey money can buy. He smiled at the thought and took another sip.

Jamaal leaned back and took another sip of the bourbon. He closed his eyes and ran Charles's last comment through his mind.

For twenty damn years he didn't remember the park lights, and now he suddenly does. If he remembers that, what else might he remember? If Charles figures out the truth, he will use it against me. Or worse. He might even go to the police. Perhaps he won't remember anything else. In that case, I'd be safe. But I really can't take that chance. I need to be proactive and do something that puts that night in the rearview mirror forever. I thought I had. This is my own damn fault. I'm the one who brought it up today.

I haven't thought about that night for years. It was a crazy night. I had a perfect plan for dealing with Devon. When he got drunk, which was rather often, he would pick fights with Charles. And occasionally, he threatened me. I was tired of his bullying and decided to teach him a lesson. Tino was going to go into the bar and slip a roofie into Devon's beer. I would wait outside for Devon to come out and follow him until the time was right. Then I was going to beat the hell out of him. The Rohypnol would make it easy. But that's not what happened.

I shouldn't have trusted Tino. He was dumber than a rock. Apparently, he put the roofie in Charles' drink instead of Devon's. When Charles stumbled out of the bar a short time later, I thought he was drunk. He was soon out of sight, and I returned my gaze to the door. It wasn't long before Devon came out. He seemed to be in full control of his faculties, but I figured the roofie hadn't fully kicked in yet. I followed him for two blocks, staying in the shadows. He turned the corner onto Westover. I soon heard him shouting. It sounded like he was yelling at Charles. When I turned the corner, he was kicking Charles, who was lying on the ground.

I didn't think, I just acted. I ran the twenty yards between us and leaped into the air. As I left the ground, I leaned my upper body back and pulled my legs in. Just before I collided with Devon, I thrust out my legs. Devon stumbled forward before falling to the ground. He rolled over and produced a knife. Before he could get off the ground, I kicked the knife from his hand. I then kicked him in the head, knocking him unconscious. The rest, as they say, is history.

I am going to have to admit that I lied to Charles all those years ago. He has probably concluded that already, so I won't be telling him anything new. I must give him a plausible reason I lied to him. If it is something that would have been embarrassing back then, Charles will probably buy it. Smoking pot won't do it. He knew that I occasionally smoked pot. He didn't like me smoking it, and he gave me a few lectures about it. But I don't think that excuse will convince him.

What if I tell him I had tried crystal meth that night? It was easy enough to find in the neighborhood back then. Probably still is. I could say that, given his reaction to me smoking pot, I concluded that confiding in him about trying a new drug was not a good idea. Jamaal smiled and drained his glass. As he poured himself another three fingers of bourbon, he thought, yes, I think that story will work.

JUST SAY NO TO FACE MASKS

August 2020

"**W**elcome to a special Saturday morning edition of the Roger Mason Show," the talk show host said excitedly. "I am coming to you today from Eleanor Tinsley Park along Buffalo Bayou. As we prepare to enter the sixth month of Comrade Escobar's mask mandate, we are here today to send a resounding message to her: We won't abide by her dictates." The crowd roared with approval.

"This is our first no mask rally. There are thousands of people here, and I don't see a single face diaper. Free people do not tolerate tyrants, nor do they obey the tyrant's dictates. They stand up for their rights. They just say no to face masks."

"If you want to stand up for your rights, come join us. Nearly a dozen local restaurants are serving food, and starting in an hour, we'll have live music from local bands. Unfortunately, we won't be serving any alcohol as we didn't have time to apply for a permit. This is a very spontaneous gathering. We got the idea Thursday evening, and I called many of our show sponsors to ask for support. We did not know how many would take part, but I am proud to say that nearly all of them are here."

"I know how much all of you love to listen to me talk, but today we're going to do something different. I am going to mingle with the people gathered here and talk with them. We'll talk about how all this nonsense has affected their lives, why they are here, and much more. Escobar and her cronies talk about the will of the people. Today, we're going to hear from the people. So, let's get started with that gentleman holding a sign that says, 'You Voted for This.'"

"Hello sir. What's your name?"

"I'm Cody Rainer."

"Great to meet you, Cody. That's an interesting sign. What's it mean?"

"As you often say, Roger, elections have consequences. If you vote for a fool, you shouldn't be surprised when she does foolish things. That is what's happening. They voted for that fool Escobar and look at the nonsense that she is imposing on us."

Roger smiled and nodded. "How true. What brought you here today?"

"I own a small art gallery in Montrose. Comrade Escobar decided that my business isn't essential, and so I was forced to close for nearly four months. I paid my three employees for four weeks. That's twice as long as the Comrade said we'd be closed. But she didn't rescind her order, and I couldn't afford to continue paying employees with no money coming in. I had to let them go. Fortunately, the governor allowed us to open. But that hasn't stopped Escobar. Now, she wants me to do her dirty work of enforcing her mask mandate or get fined out of existence. We can't allow government officials to tell us how to run our business."

Mason nodded. "That's a story I hear every day. Owning a business isn't easy. You work your ass off to keep the doors open and earn a decent living. And then politicians like Escobar think they know what is best for you."

"You are right, Roger. Until the lockdown, I worked sixty hours a week. I haven't had a vacation in five years, unless you count the lockdown as a vacation. I don't. There was no place to go. And I had no money to go there."

"Thanks for coming out, Cody. He is right. Elections

have consequences. You elect someone like Escobar and the consequences are lockdowns, mask mandates, and attempts to violate the First Amendment."

"Roger," someone near the front of the crowd called out. "I want to talk to you."

Mason saw a man pushing his way toward him. When the man stood five feet from him, Mason could see a bone frog tattoo on the man's arm. "I am sorry for your loss, sir. And thank you for your service. What is it you wanted to talk about?"

"I served in the military for twenty-two years, and I did three tours in Iraq and four in Afghanistan. I fought to protect our freedom. I fought against dictators like Saddam and the Taliban. When I see what is happening right here in Houston, I wonder what I was fighting for. I wonder if it was worth all the sacrifice." The former Navy Seal shook his head in disgust.

"Your efforts weren't in vain," Mason replied. "We still have some freedoms, and a hell of a lot more than the Iraqis under Saddam or the Afghans under the Taliban. Without your efforts, and those of your compatriots, who knows what mayhem they may have visited upon us."

"That may be true, but it's little consolation. I had friends killed in action, and why? So Escobar could sit on her ass and issue orders? I don't think so. It's enough to make me want to go to war with my government. The Founding Fathers did it. Maybe it's our turn."

Mason had often thought that if an armed revolution became necessary, he would lead the charge. But he knew that an armed insurrection would be suicidal. The Founding Fathers may have taken on the most powerful military in the world. But the British soldiers were rank amateurs compared to America's military today.

Mason shook his head. "As much as I sympathize with you, armed revolution isn't the answer. We need to win the battle of ideas by changing hearts and minds, so people quit voting for tyrants like Escobar. We need to win with ballots, not bullets. Since I'm not a male chauvinist pig, let's find a woman to talk to."

He looked around at the people near him for the next person to talk to. He spotted a buxom young woman wearing a T-shirt that proclaimed, "Live Free or Die." *This is much better than sitting in the studio talking on the phone,* Mason thought. *The visuals are much more stimulating.*

"Hello Miss," he said charmingly. "Are you from New Hampshire?" The woman just stared at Mason as if he had just used the dumbest pickup line in history. "Your shirt has the motto of New Hampshire," he said as he pointed at her chest.

The woman looked down, as if she had forgotten what was on her shirt. "Oh, I didn't know that," she finally replied.

"So, what brings you out here today?" Mason asked.

"Well, it's like I am tired of wearing a mask, you know. I wanted to go somewhere I didn't have to wear a mask, you know. So, like a friend told me about this party here, and I thought, why not? I mean, it's better than just sitting around, you know what I mean?"

Mason nodded. *This will not make the highlight reel,* he thought. "Where did you get the shirt?" he asked as he continued staring at her chest.

"Like a friend of mine gave it to me. I don't know where he got it, you know."

Wow, Mason thought, *when God was handing out brains, this woman must have been at the very end of the line. All she got were the leftovers and crumbs at that. At least when people call into the show, they have something they want to talk about. And my producer screens the callers, so I don't have to deal with people like this.* He smiled. "Thanks for coming out to show your support. It's the top of the hour and time for the news and weather."

I SAVED YOUR ASS

August 2020

s Jamaal settled into the chair, he placed his fedora on Mayor Benton's desk. "I appreciate you seeing me on short notice, Charles." The mayor nodded but didn't speak. "As you may have concluded after our last discussion, I wasn't totally forthright with you about that night. I'd like to clear the air."

"Yes," Charles said, "I reached the conclusion that you had lied, not only to the police, but to me as well. Are you going to tell me the truth now?"

"Certainly. I've thought of telling you many times over the years, but it didn't seem to matter anymore."

"Then why does it matter now?"

"It doesn't really matter." Jamaal shrugged his shoulders. "I just don't want you to draw the wrong conclusions, that's all." Jamaal sat back in the chair and placed his hands on his lap. "I wasn't playing basketball that night. But I was in the park." He had practiced what he would say and paused for dramatic effect. Jamaal had learned long ago that using pauses effectively was an important part of persuasive oratory.

"You were smoking pot with your buddies," Charles speculated.

"No, it was worse. I thought we were going to smoke some weed, but the guy who was supposed to bring it couldn't find any. He brought something else, though. Crystal meth." Jamaal tried to look contrite. "I smoked some. I certainly couldn't tell that to the cops, and I didn't think that you'd be thrilled about it. So, I said that I was playing basketball. I bailed you out and saved myself a lot of grief by lying. It was like killing two birds with one lie. If I had told the cops the truth, they may not have believed my story that you were defending yourself. So, I lied, and I did it for you."

Charles thought about this new story. Something about it wasn't sitting right. He finally spoke. "Let me make sure I understand what you are telling me. You were in the park smoking crystal. On your way home, you discovered Devon and me lying on the ground covered in blood. You believed I had murdered Devon, and so you concocted a story about self-defense. To explain why you were out, you lied and said that you had been playing basketball. Do I have it right so far?"

Jamaal felt a rush of adrenaline. "Yes," he said a little too loudly. I can't tell if Charles is buying this, he thought.

"Let me be honest with you, Jamaal, which is something you haven't been with me. You lied to me once. Why shouldn't I think you aren't lying again?"

"Why would I lie about smoking crystal?" Jamaal snorted.

"To cover up something even more sinister."

"Such as?"

Charles shook his head. "That I don't know, and I won't speculate."

"Well, that's an interesting hypothesis, Charles. Maybe you're the one who has been smoking something," Jamaal said with a laugh.

Charles waved his hand. "Let me go on. After finding Devon and me, you quickly fabricated a story. And a very plausible story at that. That showed some quick thinking and ingenuity. But your quick thinking only went so far. You forgot about the lights being out in the park. That makes little sense to me."

Jamaal chuckled and shook his head. "Yes, I came up with a pretty good story on the fly. But it was on the fly. I didn't have time to think about every detail. Jesus Christ, Charles, I was high on crystal meth, but I saved your ass. And now you are criticizing one minor flaw in my story. A flaw, which I should point out, the police didn't notice. They accepted my story. No harm, no foul."

"The police were more concerned with Devon's death. They didn't care where you had been earlier or what you were doing."

"They didn't care," Jamaal said as he slammed his fist onto the desk, "because it didn't fucking matter. You're starting to piss me off. After all I've done for you, you have the audacity to make these unwarranted accusations."

"Calm down, Jamaal," Charles said softly. "I haven't accused you of anything. I'm just thinking out loud. However, your reaction makes me wonder if I'm getting too close to the truth for you."

"I told you the truth," Jamaal snarled. "I was in the park smoking crystal."

Charles wagged a finger at Jamaal. "Fool me once, shame on you. Fool me twice, shame on me. But let's assume for a moment that your story is true. What was it like?"

Jamaal furrowed his brow. "What?"

"What was the high like with the crystal?"

"Why do you care?"

"Humor me."

"Very well. It was intense. Unlike anything I've ever experienced before or since. My skin was tingling and felt like it was trying to crawl off my body. I started sweating profusely and thought that I was going crazy. Just when I thought I was recovering, they made me take another hit. That was even worse. A short time later I snuck away and headed home. It was not a pleasant experience. I will never forget it. Are you happy now?"

Charles smiled. "Happier than you can imagine."

YOU PLAYED THAT WELL

September 2020

s had been the case since June, the city council was meeting in chambers and the public was banned. However, thousands were watching the proceedings online. Today, the council was going to vote on the renters' protections ordinance.

Charles had long known that this day was coming, and he had always dreaded it. However, now that the day had arrived, he felt a strange calmness. In fact, he thought, I have been more relaxed ever since that last meeting with Jamaal. Charles had a plan in place for how he would vote. It would not be popular, but how unpopular would depend on how the council members voted. Charles would vote last, and he may have to break a deadlock. That would require him to take a definitive position on the issue, something that he had religiously avoided to date.

The mayor was only mildly attentive as votes were taken on the approval of several COVID-related contracts. There was no disagreement or discussion, and all passed unanimously. Everyone seemed eager to get to the main event.

Finally, the clerk began reading the renters' protections ordinance. Charles had not been involved in the final negotiations, so he listened more attentively than he normally would. It soon became clear that the ordinance had been significantly watered down. In fact, only two protections remained—rent control and just cause evictions. Even the minimum wage provision had been eliminated. Charles smiled as he realized what this meant. Patel and Jackson had agreed to much weaker measures to secure passage. That meant that they likely had the votes they needed.

After the revised ordinance had been read, the floor was opened for questions and comments from the council members. The most conservative member of the council was the first to speak. "This is still an abhorrent law, but at least you people got a bit of sense and watered it down," he said sarcastically. "Since I wasn't privy to the horse trading that went on, I must assume that you made some back room deals to get the votes you need. I know how these things work. You scratch my back, and I'll scratch yours."

"I resent the implications of that remark," one moderate said. "Are you suggesting that we compromised our principles?"

The conservative laughed. "I wasn't aware that you moderates have any principles to compromise. You wouldn't know a principle if it bit you on the ass." The four moderates scowled at him.

"Let's move this along," the mayor said. He looked around the curved table where the council members sat. They all nodded, apparently knowing the outcome of the upcoming vote.

The clerk began calling the names of the council members to voice their vote. The vote was taken in order of the eleven districts they represented, with the five at-large council members voting last. By the time the clerk reached the at-large members, the vote was 6-5 against passage. The votes of two at-large members were easy to predict. One would vote for, and one would vote against. The last three to vote—all moderates—were up in the air.

After the first moderate voted, the tally was seven for passage and seven against. The next moderate voted for passage. The final moderate, the one who had taken exception to the conservative's comments, could ensure passage or put the issue in the mayor's hands. Though Charles felt certain how the last vote would go, he suddenly felt anxious. What if he had calculated wrong? His vote may matter. Without realizing it, Charles held his breath as the last council member's name was called. When the vote was cast for passage, Charles relaxed.

For Patel and Jackson, it was a bittersweet victory. Their first ordinance—their baby—had made it into law. Granted, it wasn't everything they wanted, but it was a start. They had learned valuable lessons that would serve them well in the future. They didn't get everything that they wanted, but they would in time. Until then, many people would continue to suffer.

All eyes turned to Mayor Benton as his name was called. Finally, they all thought, he would have to take a position. The mayor was reclined in his chair, almost paralyzed as the stress left his body. He looked to the left, and then the right. He turned his gaze to the clerk and said, "Present."

Thirteen of the council members gasped. The conservative chuckled. Patel and Jackson stared at the mayor with daggers in their eyes.

* * *

Jamaal had been watching the council meeting on his laptop and sipping bourbon. When Charles announced his presence, Jamaal smiled and tipped his glass towards the screen. "Well done, Charles," he said aloud. "You're a coward, but you played that well."

HIS NAME IS WARREN HICKS

September 2020

Justin and Pratik had watched the city council meeting in Buford's office. If the ordinance passed, they wanted to immediately begin strategizing.

"Well, boys," Buford said as he shut down his computer. "It looks like we have some work to do. Any ideas?"

"We've been reading about the history of Houston, Justin said, "and we found something that may be useful. In the 1990s, the city council passed a zoning ordinance. Some group—I don't remember the name—led a petition drive to put the matter before voters. Three years later, a referendum was held, and the ordinance was rejected by voters. We might learn something from that. Maybe we can have a referendum."

"Yes," Buford replied, "that zoning nonsense started right before my father passed. He was pissed about it. Said it would ruin the real estate market. He was making plans to fight the ordinance, but he died before he could do anything. While that whole debate was going on, I was busy grieving and trying to take over my father's real estate business. I donated some money to the group that did the petition drive, but that was the extent of my involvement."

"Do you remember the name of that group? Maybe they are

still around," Pratik asked.

Buford shook his head. "I remember the acronym—CPR—but I don't remember what that stood for."

"I remember," Justin exclaimed. "Committee for Property Rights."

"Yes, that's it. If I remember correctly, the group was formed solely for fighting the zoning ordinance. I think it disbanded after the referendum. You might find something in the newspaper's archives."

"That's a good idea," Justin said. "There are a lot of parallels between that zoning debate and what is happening now. It would be great if we could find the people who ran that group and learn what they did. It's only been thirty years, so I would think that some of them are still around. A wise man learns from his mistakes. A really wise man learns from the successes of others. The Committee for Property Rights was successful and overcame a lot of challenges."

"In the meantime," Pratik suggested, "I think we should investigate getting this to a referendum. Houstonians showed the good sense of rejecting zoning thirty years ago, so there is a good chance that they would reject renters' protections as well. But I do not know how to get a referendum on the ballot. Do you?"

Buford shook his head. "Tell you what," he said, "I will call my lawyer, Brad Whitfield, right now. He may not know exactly what is required, but he probably has a good idea." Buford reached for his phone. "I'll put him on speaker so you can hear what he has to say and ask any questions you have." Justin and Pratik nodded.

Once introductions were made, Buford asked, "What do we need to do to get a referendum on these damn renters' protections?"

"There are several requirements," Brad replied, "but two are the most important. First, you must collect signatures from registered voters in the applicable jurisdiction. I think that the required number is 10 percent of the number of people who voted in the last mayor's race, but I could be wrong about that. And you must collect and submit the signatures before the law takes effect. Once the signatures are certified, the ordinance is put on hold until the referendum."

"Any idea how many people voted in the last mayoral election?" Pratik asked.

"No, but I bet it wasn't over 200,000. Mayoral elections usually have a low turnout since they are held in off years for federal and state elections. If I am correct about the numbers, you would need to get at least 20,000 certified signatures. I would plan on getting a lot more than that because many of the signatures will be from people who aren't registered to vote, don't live in Houston, or are disqualified for other reasons."

"If we gathered enough signatures, when would the referendum be held?" Justin asked.

The attorney chuckled. "That's one nice thing about referendum via a petition drive. You can specify when the election will be held. Obviously, sooner would be better than later. But you would need to consider turnout. If that is the only issue on the ballot, turnout will be very low. That could be good or bad, but it should be considered. Also, if the petition drive is successful, the city council will have the choice to repeal the ordinance or wait for the results of the referendum. It's doubtful that they would repeal the ordinance. Those fools never repeal anything. But it is a possibility."

Justin and Pratik looked at one another and shook their heads. "We don't have any other questions now. This has been a big help and gives us a head start."

"Will you draw up the petition, Brad?" Buford asked.

"Sure. Give me a few days. I want to do a little research to make sure it is worded properly. Some of these referendums are worded so poorly that people vote for it while thinking that they are voting against it. We don't want that kind of confusion."

"Oh," Pratik exclaimed, "I have another question. Do you know anything about a group called the Committee for Property Rights that fought against zoning in the 1990s?"

Brad laughed. "My firm wrote the petition that they wound up using. I wasn't directly involved because I was right out of law school. But I met the leader of that group and did more work for them. Warren and I became golfing buddies until I tore up my shoulder about fifteen years ago. From our brief conversation, I get the sense that you two and Warren will get along well."

"It would be great if we could speak with him," Justin said with excitement in his voice.

"I haven't talked to him in years, but I suspect I can track him down. When I do, I'll have him get in touch with you. Just so you know, his name is Warren Hicks."

I DON'T KNOW WHAT TO BELIEVE

September 2020

Jamaal shut down his computer as soon as Charles Benton took his cowardly stance. The ordinance already had enough votes to pass, and Charles' vote wouldn't matter. But he could have taken a stand one way or another. Instead, he did what he had been doing for eighteen months—nothing.

Jamaal knew Charles better than anyone. He knew how much the mayor wanted to be governor. When he first mentioned it over twenty years ago, it was said in jest. He was an obscure, poor black man living in one of Houston's poorest neighborhoods. But he had been a leader in the community for many years. He had been a father figure to many troubled youths, including Jamaal. But he always regarded Jamaal as special, someone who would great things. With Jamaal's help, he soon used his position in the community to catapult himself into politics.

When the neighborhood's state representative decided against running for re-election, Charles threw his hat into the ring. To the surprise of many, he won handily, thanks to Jamaal's ability to raise money and get supporters to the polls. At first, Jamaal was only interested in promoting Charles and his career. But the younger man soon realized that Charles was more interested in getting along than promoting change. That was when Jamaal began to use the secret the two shared as a weapon to manipulate Charles to do what Jamaal considered the right thing. To his credit, Charles acknowledged Jamaal's contributions to his political success, but he did so reluctantly. It often took several heated arguments, and perhaps a threat or two from Jamaal, before Charles would agree to the younger man's strategy.

For some time, Jamaal had sensed that Charles was pushing back. There was nothing overt or explicit that he could point to. It had happened gradually. As he thought about it, Jamaal realized that voting "present" was intended to send a message. Charles would no longer be Jamaal's toady. He had finally grown a backbone.

What happened to make Charles so defiant? Jamaal wondered. If Jamaal told the truth, or at least what Charles believed to be the truth, the mayor would go to jail. Apparently, Charles was willing to take that chance. Or, perhaps, Charles has learned the actual truth. No, Jamaal thought, that couldn't be. There was no evidence, and no witnesses had come forth to contest Jamaal's account. Jamaal was the only witness, and the police had no reason to doubt the young boy's story.

Maybe Charles is bluffing, Jamaal speculated. He wants me to think that he has something on me. "It will not work, old man," Jamaal muttered to himself. "The only way you're going to have anything on me is if I confess. And that will not happen. If you want to play games, you picked the wrong playmate."

Jamaal suddenly remembered Charles' last remark. Jamaal had described the effects of the crystal. When he asked if Charles was happy now, the mayor replied, "Happier than you can imagine."

What the hell did that mean? Jamaal asked himself. Maybe he knows something about crystal and my description wasn't very accurate. I have never smoked the damn stuff, so I had to make up something on the fly. He chuckled at the thought. I'm pretty good at making up things on the fly.

* * *

"What the hell was that all about, Charles?" Andrew, the mayor's chief of staff, asked. They were alone in the mayor's office. "People are already talking. You are going to have a major shitstorm on your hands."

"At the moment," the mayor replied, "I don't really care. Let them talk."

"But why vote present? You've managed to piss off everybody. If you had voted for or against, you would have pissed off the other side. But one side would be happy with you. You just snatched defeat from the jaws of victory."

"I have my reasons for voting the way I did." The mayor stared at his assistant. "If there is nothing else, I would like to be alone for a while." Andrew shook his head as he left the room.

Charles felt a mixture of relief and anxiety. He had openly defied Jamaal for the first time in years. Sure, they had had many heated arguments in private, but nearly every time, Charles wound up doing what Jamaal wanted. But in the process of defying Jamaal, he had, as Andrew so eloquently put it, unleashed a major shitstorm. One day at a time, he told himself. I'll deal with tomorrow and whatever it brings when it gets here.

His thoughts turned back to Jamaal. Charles could tell that he had struck a nerve during his last meeting with Jamaal. But what nerve was it? Charles tried to replay the conversation in his mind. Jamaal first got upset when I mentioned the police didn't notice that the park lights were off. That's a fact, and it shouldn't have upset him. And if the police had noticed, Jamaal's story might have fallen apart. So why would he be upset when I pointed out that they missed that detail?

The lights. God, if only I could remember more about that night. That damn Rohypnol wiped out my memory. The lights. What about the lights upset him?

Charles reached into his desk drawer and pulled out the bottle of Scotch. Though it was early afternoon in Houston, Charles rationalized it was after five in Scotland. He poured himself three fingers and took a sip. Damn, that's good whiskey, he thought. He thought back to the first time he had tried Glenfiddich 18-Year-Old. It was a dinner party held by a lobbyist in Austin. The lobbyist was trying to get several legislators to support a particular bill. I don't even remember what bill it was, and I was going to vote for it, anyway. But it's hard to pass up free food and booze. And that house where the party was. It was set up in the hills outside of Austin with a spectacular view of the city to the east and the Hill Country to the west. When the sun went down, you could actually see stars. They were like twinkling lights in the sky. He took another sip of Scotch as a hint of some distant memory entered his mind. But the memory wouldn't fully form, and so he pushed it from his mind for the moment.

Was there anything else that upset Jamaal? He didn't seem embarrassed when he told me he had smoked crystal. Of course, that was twenty-five years ago, so there really was no reason to still be embarrassed. But he seemed very nonchalant about it. Do I believe he was smoking crystal? I don't know what to believe anymore. Based on the little I know of the drug, his description seemed reasonable. There is no way to know for sure if he is lying. Charles took another sip of his drink. Or maybe there is, he thought.

THEY NEED TO TAKE A LITTLE RESPONSIBILITY

September 2020

Marta Escobar stood at the podium for her daily press briefing. She knew that there would be pushback against what she was about to announce. It didn't matter what she did, somebody would complain. That had been happening since the start of the pandemic, and she had developed a very thick skin in response. That, however, wasn't the primary reason that many of her staff called her "The Lizard Lady" behind her back.

"Good morning, everyone," she said with more exuberance than she felt. "For months, Harris County has been facing two crises. The pandemic, of course, has been our highest priority. We have taken many steps to slow the spread of the coronavirus and treat those who have become infected. Our efforts have been successful, and we are saving lives. However, the second crisis— the homelessness crisis—can no longer be ignored. Indeed, the two crises have intersected and overlapped like a bizarre Venn diagram. In case you don't know what that is, a Venn diagram uses circles to show relationships among things.

"Since the beginning of the pandemic, the number of

homeless in Harris County has increased by nearly 30 percent. There are currently 35,000 people in the county experiencing homelessness. That number would be much higher if I had not imposed an eviction moratorium. Many have lost their jobs because of the pandemic, and they cannot pay their rent. I have enabled them to stay housed and not join the growing hordes of homeless. But I can do more to get our fellow citizens off the street.

"As I speak, there are about 680,000 apartment units in Harris County, and they have a vacancy rate of about 8.5 percent. This means that there are currently about 58,000 empty apartment units in the county. That is almost three times more than the number of homeless people in the county. The solution is as obvious as the day is clear.

"As I said, the two crises have intersected. COVID infections among the homeless are soaring. Three of every four homeless people tested by the county health administration have tested positive for the coronavirus. This is not surprising. The homeless seldom can isolate themselves from others. They have poor diets and are not receiving adequate health care. Many have substance abuse issues, mental health problems, or both. What we see with the county's homeless is a pandemic within a pandemic.

"We cannot allow our most vulnerable citizens to continue to live with the threats posed by life on the streets. Therefore, I am issuing an order that all apartment owners in Harris County begin housing our homeless. This is a simple solution to the problem. The apartment owners have vacant homes. The homeless need a home. I am simply requiring apartment owners to do their part in fighting the pandemic, since they obviously won't do it voluntarily.

"All apartment owners in the county have one week to submit to my office the number of vacant units they own. Representatives from my office, along with volunteers, will be speaking with the homeless and enrolling them in the program. Within two weeks, my office will begin assigning units on a first come, first served basis. Our goal is to have every homeless person in the county living in a safe, decent apartment within six weeks.

"We expect some apartment owners to complain. They will say that we are depriving them of income. But the fact is, the empty units are not producing any income. Housing the homeless will impose no additional costs on them. Such complaints are putting profits before people. Such callous disregard for other human beings is morally depraved. That will not be tolerated on my watch." Escobar looked at the clock on the front wall. "I have time for one or two questions."

'Judge Escobar," shouted one reporter, "giving the homeless housing doesn't address their other needs. They will need food and furniture. Are you going to provide that? And what about pets? Many have dogs for both security and companionship, but many apartments don't allow pets."

Escobar nodded. "That's a good point that we hadn't considered. So, I hereby issue another order. All apartment owners must accept service dogs to live with their human companions."

"What about food? At least when they are on the street, they know ways to get food," the reporter said. "Are you expecting them to go dumpster diving in the apartment complex they get assigned to?"

"We are calling upon food pantries and citizens to donate food. We will set up drop off locations throughout the county. My office will announce those locations within a few days. We will then give apartment owners assigned locations to pick up and deliver food for their residents."

"What about furniture and internet service?" the same reporter asked. "If you really want to help the homeless, you need to do more."

"I can't do everything," Escobar snapped. "I suppose that you'll want me to give them back massages next. We are talking about adults here. They need to take a little responsibility for their own lives. They've been sleeping under a bridge. I don't think that they will complain about sleeping on the floor. At least they will have a roof over their heads." With that, the judge turned and stormed out of the room.

A FRAMEWORK IS A FILTER AND A LENS

September 2020

"Good morning, Houston," Roger Mason crooned into his microphone. "Joining us for the first segment are two very interesting young men, Justin Walker and Pratik Shah. They own a business called Justice Inc and call themselves intellectual bodyguards. I know what the first question on everyone's mind is: what the hell is an intellectual bodyguard?"

Since this was on the radio, Justin and Pratik had each called in on their own cell phones from different rooms in the house. Pratik responded first. "This is Pratik. We are all familiar with the traditional bodyguard. He protects his client from physical threats. An intellectual bodyguard protects his client from intellectual threats."

"Can you give me an example?" Mason asked.

"Sure," Justin replied. "Earlier this month, the Houston City Council passed a so-called renters' protection ordinance. Oh, I'm Justin, by the way. That law threatens the livelihood and well-being of countless property owners around the city. They are outraged and know that they are being treated unfairly. But many don't know how to defend themselves from these kinds of attacks. We provide that defense."

"These are decent, productive people," Pratik added, "who are offering a value that others want and need. Now, they find their own city government is making that more difficult. But, as Justin said, many landlords don't know how to defend themselves. They feel this great sense of injustice regarding the ordinance, but they don't know how to give voice to it convincingly."

"That is an interesting perspective," Mason said. "I have lots of callers who are upset over something, and often rightly so, but they often come across as babbling idiots. They rant and rave and express their outrage, but they don't convince anyone that they have been wronged. Why do you two think you can be their voice?"

"Both Pratik and I have degrees in philosophy," Justin replied. "Many people think that philosophy is some ivory-tower subject that has no application to life. In truth, philosophy is the most fundamental of all the sciences and it is a life-or-death issue. The right philosophy can help you live a happy, flourishing life. The wrong philosophy will lead you to suffering and misery. We have a better understanding of fundamental ideas than most people. I don't say that to degrade anyone, just to point out that we have specialized training. That training allows us to look beyond the slogans and bromides that are often expressed and get to the root premises. I'll let Pratik give an example."

"When city council was discussing the renters' protections ordinance," Pratik said, "we heard a lot about the imbalance of power between landlords and tenants. On the surface, this might seem plausible. After all, landlords set the terms and conditions of a lease. But if we look below the surface, we see that this claim is intellectually dishonest. The interaction between tenant and landlord is voluntary. Neither party must deal with the other. They do so because each has something the other wants. The renter wants a place to live. The landlord wants money. When they can agree to the terms and conditions, then a trade results and both benefit. If they can't agree, each can go his separate way."

"And I should add," Justin said, "what the city is doing is forcing one party—the landlord—to act differently than he would voluntarily choose. The sole purpose of using force is to make people act differently than they choose. A robber threatens you with a gun because you wouldn't voluntarily hand over your wallet. With renters' protections, landlords are being forced to conduct business on terms that they did not agree to. That isn't balancing power. That is giving all the power to renters and their advocates."

"This is a very interesting idea, and I can see where an intellectual bodyguard could be useful," Mason replied. "I have made a living in the marketplace of ideas for years, and you two have a very refreshing approach. You mentioned the renters' protection ordinance. Three days ago, you announced a petition drive to put the issue before voters. What gave you that idea?"

"That was mostly Justin. He is new to Houston and has been trying to learn about the city's history. During his reading, he came across stories about the zoning debate in the 1990s."

"Oh yes. I've heard about that," Mason interjected. "But that was before my time in Houston."

"It was before our time on Earth," Pratik laughed. "We can see some interesting parallels between what happened thirty years ago and what is happening today. Back then, the city council passed a zoning ordinance that was supposedly supported by the public. There was a petition drive to put the issue before voters, and zoning was rejected. Today, city council has passed a renters' protections ordinance that supposedly has the backing of the public."

"And so, just like with zoning," Mason said, "you hope voters overturn the city council's ordinance. You are letting democracy work."

"No, not all," Justin replied. "First, this isn't really a proper issue for voters to decide. Our rights—and this is an issue of property rights—aren't subject to a vote. However, a referendum is the only avenue open to us to defeat this ordinance. It worked in the 1990s, and we hope it will work in the 2020s. Second, we are opposed to democracy. Democracy means unlimited majority rule. It is nothing more than mob rule, a tyranny of the masses. In a democracy, the majority can do whatever it pleases simply because it is the majority."

"It is worth remembering," Pratik interjected, "that America was not founded as a democracy. The Founding Fathers rejected democracy. They established a constitutional republic in which the powers of government are limited. That differs significantly from a democracy. Further, Socrates was put to death in democratic Athens, and Hitler was elected to power in a democratic Germany."

"Before you two go, I want to get your take on Comrade Escobar's latest order. Yesterday, she announced apartments will have to house the homeless in vacant units. Any comments?"

"Oh boy, do we have comments," Pratik said. "But we'd need your entire program to express all of them. So, I'll just say that Escobar is amazingly consistent. She continues to find new, and sometimes creative, ways to violate property rights."

"Okay gentlemen, our time for this hour is up," Mason said. "I am intrigued by what you are saying. I have a lot more questions, and it looks like our listeners do as well. Could you stick around for another hour?"

"I'm game," Pratik said.

"Me too," Justin replied.

When the second hour began, Mason started with a question about framework. "You recently wrote a piece called 'A New Framework for Housing Policy.' I'd like to explore that a bit. What do you mean by framework?"

"A framework is both a filter and a lens," Pratik said. "As a filter, it determines what facts and information we will consider. As a lens, it determines how we evaluate and analyze those facts and information. For example, the framework embraced by Judge Escobar guided her to impose a lockdown, which predictably had dire economic consequences. Her framework starts with the wrong standard of value, fails to consider the full context, and dismisses alternatives.

"Her standard of value was saving lives. This sounds reasonable during a pandemic. However, it's not the government's purpose to save lives. The government's only proper purpose is the protection of individual rights. The judge's standard then led her to impose a lockdown while ignoring the full context, that is, the economic disaster that would ensue. And, at no time has she stated which alternatives she considered and why they were rejected."

"She didn't think that through very well, did she?" Mason interjected. "When businesses are forced to close, people will lose their jobs. And without an income, they can't pay their rent, put food on the table, and pay their bills."

"I assume she thought it through within the guidelines of her framework. Her framework determined what she would consider and how she would evaluate it," Justin said. "When it comes to government policy, the proper standard of value is individual liberty—the freedom of each individual to live as he chooses so long as he respects the freedom of others to do the same. Let's apply this to housing, since that is the issue we are currently addressing. If we embrace individual rights, including property rights, as the standard, then any policy we adopt must protect an individual's right to produce and trade on terms that he voluntarily accepts.

"If we consider the full context—all the relevant and related facts and issues—then we will recognize the fact that individuals are not free to produce and trade housing. Building codes, permits, and land-use regulations are the most obvious examples. These regulations limit how individuals may act, and they add significant costs to the construction of housing. If we truly want to address the affordability of housing, then we must examine how government regulations impact the cost of housing."

"You mentioned considering alternatives," Mason said. "I admit that building codes, the permitting process, and land-use regulations can go too far sometimes, but we need some of these regulations. We don't want poorly built houses falling down on people."

"Roger," Pratik said, "insurance companies have a vested interest in the quality of houses that they insure. They could require an inspection or some type of certification regarding the quality of the construction. Mortgage companies have a similar interest. It's impossible to predict exactly how this would play out because individuals and businesses find creative ways to solve problems."

"Okay, that sounds reasonable," Mason admitted. "But what about the affordability of housing? I'm playing devil's advocate here, but rent control certainly makes housing more affordable. What alternatives are there?"

"We say that the alternative to more controls and regulations is more freedom. The affordable housing crisis, as it's called, is a supply shortage," Justin said. "There aren't enough affordable housing units available for low- and moderate-income households. Instead of imposing a price cap on the existing housing supply, the alternative is to increase the supply. That would moderate rents and probably lead to lower rents. And one way to increase the supply of affordable housing is by removing the regulations that drive up the cost of building new housing."

"Sadly, our time is up," Mason announced. "It's been a pleasure speaking with both of you. This has been fun and informative. To my listeners, we will post information for signing the petition on our website. I urge you to sign it."

YOU MOVED THE GOALPOSTS

September 2020

"I want to congratulate the two of you for your first legislative victory," Jamaal said to Lia Patel and Roderick Jackson. They were seated in Lia's office.

"We had to make a lot of concessions to get it passed," Lia replied. "I'm not happy about that. We should have passed the ordinance as you originally wrote it."

Jamaal waved his hand dismissively. "I wouldn't fret over it. Young legislators often try to hit a home run the first time they get to bat. But a series of singles can score just as many runs. To mix my metaphors, you moved the goal posts, and that is a victory in and of itself."

"What do you mean?" Roderick asked with an unmistakable tone of anger. Whenever Roderick spoke, which was seldom, he sounded angry. He normally just scowled and made faces.

"Prior to the passage of the ordinance, there were no renter protections in the city. Now there are two protections. Two powerful protections, I might add. So, you have established the precedent. It is just a matter of expanding on what has already been done. It may take several more attempts, but if you can move the goal posts each time, you will eventually get everything you wanted at the beginning."

"You're sounding like that wimp mayor of ours," Roderick snarled. "I didn't want to cave, but Lia insisted on it. And if that petition drive works, voters may overturn our ordinance." He cast an unfriendly glance at his colleague.

"I am just recognizing the reality of how politics is played. As that great philosopher, Mick Jagger, once said, 'You can't always get what you want. But if you try, sometimes you will find that you get what you need.' You needed to move the goal posts, and that is exactly what you did. Instead of sulking, you should plan your next step."

Roderick silently stared at Jamaal. Lia carefully considered Jamaal's words. "What should our next step be?" she finally asked.

Jamaal smiled. "That's what I wanted to talk to you about. I strongly suspect that the petition drive is going to be successful. We can't do anything about that other than prepare to present our case to the public. You two are going to need to be front and center on this. But that can wait a little longer until we are certain that there will be a referendum. In the meantime, I suggest you move the goal posts again, and—"

"I am tired of your goddamn sports analogies," Roderick interrupted. "Why don't you talk like a normal person?"

Jamaal chuckled. "Roderick, if I didn't know better, I'd say that you have some anger issues. And, by the way, it's not an analogy. It's a metaphor."

"Fuck you," Roderick shouted.

Lia glared at Roderick. He shook his head but remained quiet.

"As I was saying," Jamaal continued, "you should introduce a new ordinance that contains the renter protections that you removed."

"That's just stupid, man," Roderick shouted. "There is no way that will pass."

Jamaal smiled. "Probably not. But you can again make a few concessions and get one or two passed. To use a different metaphor, then you rinse and repeat."

Lia looked skeptical. "I am afraid that I must agree with

Roderick. I don't see how we could get it passed. And even if we did, those two idiots will probably start another petition drive."

"Let them," Jamaal said. "Hell, let them start ten petition drives. That can benefit us. First, they will need to spend a lot of time collecting signatures. Their efforts will be divided, and that is good for us. Second, voters will grow unhappy with them because the petitions will interfere with the legislative process. That needs to be a point that we stress. The council was democratically elected and should be allowed to do its job. Most voters will agree, particularly if they are presented with a series of referendums."

"Maybe so," Lia replied, "but won't we look like fools if we try to pass provisions we removed a month ago?"

Jamaal shook his head. "I know Roderick will hate this, but does a football team quit trying to score after getting a touchdown? No. It keeps trying to score every time it gets the ball. And it does that until it wins the game. You just scored a touchdown. Now, it's time to score another and another and another until you win the game."

Lia scowled. "I still don't know. You said that voters might get pissed off at the guys behind the petition drive. But might they also get pissed at us for passing another ordinance so soon?"

"I don't think that's likely. The council was elected to serve the people. That is what you are doing. These kids are the ones trying to usurp the will of the people. If we spin it that way, they will become public enemy number one." Jamaal thought for a moment. "It's an issue of divide and conquer. If we give them a bunch of ordinances to fight, they will be overwhelmed. If they want to play in the big leagues, let's show them how the pros do it."

EMPOWERING THE DISEMPOWERED

October 2020

"You have accomplished a lot in the past seven months," Jamaal said. He was sitting in Marta Escobar's office, sipping Blue Mountain coffee. It was my idea, though, he thought to himself. "But much work still needs to be done."

What an insolent prick, Marta thought. He acts as if he is the only one who understands what we are trying to accomplish. I'd love to order him out of my office, but he has been useful. "Yes, I know," she finally said. "I have been taking baby steps, trying to minimize the pushback."

"Well, that doesn't seem to work well. You've had what, four lawsuits filed against you?"

"It's only three, and none have any merit."

"That's one lawsuit every other month since you took office. That must be some kind of record for a county judge," Jamaal said sarcastically. "I guess it is appropriate that you'll be spending a lot of time in a courtroom, since you are a judge. Kinda, sorta."

"If you are trying to woo me with kind words, it isn't working," Escobar snorted. "There will always be people who resist positive change. I can't do anything about that. Besides, I will rarely be in court. That is what I have lawyers and staff for. I have more important things to do with my time."

Jamaal frowned. "If you ask me, and I am well aware that you haven't, I'd say that you should ignore the pushback. In fact, I'd say that you should try to create more pushback."

Marta stared at him like he had just predicted that the Houston Texans would win the Super Bowl this season. She shook her head. "Why would I even consider doing such a thing? I have enough problems as it is. I don't need to be creating more headaches for myself."

"I'm not suggesting that you create more problems for yourself. What I am suggesting is that you create more problems for your opponents, particularly those two kids. I think they are going to prove to be our biggest nemesis. Give them more than they can handle. Give them so many battles to fight that they won't know which side is up. They may be smart, but they only have twenty-four hours in a day."

Escobar nodded. "I agree about those boys. They came out of nowhere to lead this damn petition drive. That involves the city, but I won't be surprised if they make a move against me. They seem young enough and naïve enough to try something like that. Do you know anything about them?"

"No, but I have a few people doing a little investigating. Anyhow, baby steps give them time to regroup and mount an attack. But what if you overwhelm them? If you keep enacting more and more renter protections, they can't keep up. Their resources will be spread thin. The same people who are opposed to you are also opposed to what the city is doing. The more battles that they must fight, the more likely they are to fail. Let's get everything on the table. If they want to clear the table, then let them try."

Marta considered Jamaal's suggestion. "That might have some merit," she said. "In fact, I was considering announcing a right to counsel order, as well as a county-wide minimum wage."

"That's a good start, but I don't think that I'd do them at the same time. Announce them a couple of weeks apart. And then, every two weeks or so, add another. They will try to stomp out one fire while you are starting another."

"Why do I think that you have had a similar discussion with some members of the city council?" Escobar asked with a sly smile.

"I don't know why you think that, but I have. It's a two-pronged approach. If both the county and the city enact renters' protections, there is simply no way for the opposition to overturn everything. If we give renters a taste of freedom from their landlords, they won't give up that freedom without a fight. Those resistant to change might have a success or two, but at the end of the day, we'll be much closer to our goal than we were just six months ago."

"And what is your goal, Jamaal?"

Jamaal furrowed his brow. The answer seemed obvious to him. "Empowering the disempowered. Righting the wrongs that have been perpetuated against certain segments of our population since the day the Pilgrims landed here. Women, Blacks, Hispanics, Asians, gays—all have been and continue to be subjected to demeaning treatment. What I really want, what has driven me for over twenty years, is justice. All the groups I mentioned have been treated unjustly. My ancestors were held as slaves. Women couldn't vote until about one-hundred years ago. Asians were locked up in concentration camps during World War II. Your people have been stuffed into barrios and forced to live in deplorable conditions. Gays have been subjected to beatings and worse. I could go on, but you know the history."

My God, Escobar thought, this guy is a true believer. I knew they existed, and I've met a few. Most people saying similar things have some end game they are pursuing. He seems to have no alterior motive. He just wants to help people. Sure, I want to help people too. But that is just the means to my ends.

"These groups have fought long battles to achieve justice. But one group hasn't done that. One group has continued to be abused by the system. That group is renters, and particularly renters of color. The landed, mostly white, elite class has used housing as a hammer to enrich themselves while beating the most vulnerable into submission." Jamaal's voice was rising, and his inflection sounded much like a Sunday sermon. "I say enough. I say that it is time for renters to take control from the elites. And that time is now."

THEY WILL LIE TO US

October 2020

"**F**olks," Roger Mason intoned, "I sure hope you remember the lesson I gave you about the COVID mRNA vaccine because the day of reckoning is fast approaching. The FDA has released the vaccine for general use. Shipments are on the way as I speak, and within a few days we will be beseeched with pleas to get jabbed. For those who don't remember what I told you about the vaccine, I'll give you a refresher lesson.

"This new vaccine is called mRNA. That stands for Messenger RNA. RNA has an important role in controlling how our cells function, including genetic expression and protein synthesis. To make a very complex subject simple, the mRNA vaccine alters our genetic makeup. The purported purpose is to alter our cells so that they can fight off the coronavirus.

"That might sound like a good thing, but there is a lot more to the story. This technology has barely been tested. The clinical trials had about forty thousand participants, but half of those got a placebo. There are, what, three hundred and forty million people living in this country. That means that they tested this new drug on a tiny fraction of 1 percent of the population. I am not a scientist, but that does not seem like a sufficient sample size.

"But the scarier part is that the trials lasted less than a month. Any long-term effects of this vaccine are impossible to determine. Yet, the FDA has declared it safe. How can they possibly know that it is safe? Well, they can't. Just because nobody has exhibited problems within a few weeks of getting the vaccine doesn't mean that they won't have problems a month, a year, or decades from now. Hell, people must smoke two packs of unfiltered cigarettes for decades before they get lung cancer. How can the FDA possibly know what the long-term effects of this vaccine will be? They don't, and they don't care. Yet, they want us to believe that it is safe because they tested it on a few thousand people. And how do we know if the clinical trial actually used the mRNA vaccine? We don't. It could have been sugar water, or even last year's flu vaccine.

"There have been a lot of stupid and ridiculous things happening during this pandemic, but this has to be near the top of the list. This vaccine could kill more people than the coronavirus ever thought possible.

"This is going to be the largest PR campaign since the recall of the New Coke. We'll probably be shown videos of politicians and egghead celebrities getting jabbed. Those who get their medical advice from the Kardashians will believe that the vaccine is safe. And how will we even know if these politicians and celebrities are getting the real vaccine or a placebo? We won't, but we'll be beat over the head with all the virtue signaling. They will probably even come up with some stupid sticker that you can wear to show the world what a good person you are by being vaccinated.

"I don't know what lies they will tell us, but trust me, they will lie to us. They have been lying to us since day one. They lied when they told us that if we don't wear a face diaper, we will kill people. The government lied when they told us that the lockdown was only for two weeks to flatten the curve. They will lie to us when they tell us that the vaccine is safe. They will say anything to convince people to get vaccinated, and that gets us to the heart of the matter. Why will they be so adamant about us getting the vaccine? What is their motivation?"

"They will claim that they simply want to save lives. That's a steaming bowl of Barbara Streisand. This vaccine got rushed to market in record time. It usually takes years, and often a decade, to go through trials and get FDA approval. This vaccine took less than seven months from development to approval. The reason, as it usually is, is money. Big Pharma is going to rake in billions of dollars, and I am sure that some government officials will find a bit of that money makes its way into their Swiss bank accounts. Big Pharma doesn't care if the vaccine is safe, and neither does the FDA. All they care about is money."

"Government is supposed to protect us and keep us safe. It has failed miserably during this pandemic. The government put us all under house arrest and destroyed businesses and lives. It forces us to wear a rag on our face every time we leave home. And what good has it done? None. New cases are increasing every day. More people are dying every day. They haven't stopped the damn virus from spreading, but they sure have made our lives miserable."

"If you don't think that this is all about control, then you haven't been paying attention. Every time Comrade Escobar opens her mouth, it's to impose new controls and restrictions. Her favorite words are 'You must' and 'You can't.' You must wear a rag on your face. You must stay home. We aren't allowed to hug our friends. You must, you can't, you must, you can't. And if you don't obey the orders, you will be fined. Don't be surprised if they threaten to fine you for not getting vaccinated. They will threaten you to toe the line, or else."

"Before we end this segment, I'd like to share one piece of good news. You may remember Justin Walker and Pratik Shah, the two young men who are leading the petition drive to overturn the city's renters' protections. I just received an email from Pratik stating that they will submit sixty-five thousand signatures to the city tomorrow. They needed about twenty thousand valid signatures, so that should be more than enough to send the issue to the voters in a referendum next April."

IT'S OUR JOB TO LEAD

November 2020

Charles Benton shook his head in dismay as the clerk read a proposed ordinance authored by Lia Patel and Roderick Jackson. The bill was a rehash of the original renters' protection ordinance that just a few months previously had been rejected by the council. To gain support and passage, Lia and Roderick had to dramatically alter their original ordinance. The new ordinance contained all the provisions that had been removed from the original prior to passage. What the hell are these kids thinking? Charles asked himself. They are letting Jamaal drive the boat because this clearly has Jamaal's fingerprints all over it. And he seems intent on steering them right into the rocks.

After the clerk finished reading, the council's most conservative member slapped the dais. "What the hell are you two trying to prove? You tried to jam the same thing down our throats three months ago, and you got shot down. You'll get shot down again. This is the kind of childish behavior that we get when those kinds of people are in a position of power."

One moderate spoke up. "This may be a first for me, but I must agree with him. You two are trying to go too far too fast. I said that before. While I empathize with your intentions, you need to have a little more patience. People need some time to adjust to the changes we've already made. If you keep throwing fresh changes at the people, eventually they will rebel. Look at the hornets' nest you've already stirred up."

"And I might add," another moderate said, "there will be a referendum to overturn the renters' protections we already passed. Do we really want to invite another referendum? We need to let the people speak before we do anything additional. Let's find out what voters want before we consider more protections."

Half the council members turned their attention to Lia Patel. The other half turned to look at Roderick Jackson. The two council members sat on opposite ends of the curved dais. Lia and Roderick had sat quietly, listening to the banter of the other council members. Lia smiled, while Roderick remained stone faced. "Well?" the conservative said. "What do you have to say for yourself?"

"Perhaps this will pass and perhaps it won't. That's what the process is for, to discuss, iron out differences, and then draft a law that everyone can live with. As far as a referendum is concerned, I welcome it. It is an opportunity for voters to vindicate us and show the right-wing extremists what a progressive city Houston truly is."

"Why not wait until after the referendum to consider more measures?" asked one moderate. "If the voters approve the renter protections, that will be our cue to move forward with more. And if they don't, then that will also be a cue. We should allow the electorate to speak. After all, we serve the people of Houston."

Lia shook her head. "The electorate spoke when they elected us. It's our job to lead, not follow."

The moderate frowned. "I'm just saying that maybe we shouldn't be so extreme. Landlords and small business owners are already creating an uproar."

"And in the meantime, tens of thousands are suffering," Lia replied. "We can't put every issue before the voters. If we did, we'd get nothing done. We are supposed to be the city's leaders. It's time for us to act like it. And that means taking bold steps. Everything that I am hearing on the streets shows overwhelming support for renters' protections."

"You're probably only talking to your commie friends," the conservative snipped.

"I have an idea," said another moderate. "Why don't we review the reasons we rejected these protections before? Maybe that can save us some time."

"We rejected them," the conservative snarled, "because they are anti-American. Can't you people see that? Look at Venezuela. Chavez has run that country into the ground with his commie ideas, and now these two want to do the same right here in Houston. I can't believe any of you would even consider voting for this nonsense."

"One man's nonsense," Roderick barked, "is another man's justice." He rarely spoke during council meetings. "White bigots like you thought it was nonsense to free the slaves. Your type wouldn't even let women vote or gays to marry. I'm getting really tired of that man," he said while pointing at the conservative. "If he knew what's good for him, he'd shut up."

Charles banged his gavel. "Gentlemen, let's remain civil. We can disagree without resorting to name calling or threats. I agree. Let's discuss the reasons these protections were removed from the previous ordinance."

For the next forty-five minutes, the council members had a lively discussion. Several of those who had voted against the ordinance voiced varying degrees of animosity toward any form of renter protections. The moderates who voted for passage agreed that the complete slate of renters' protections was too radical for a single ordinance. They urged a more gradual approach. By the end of the meeting, it appeared no minds had been changed. That's okay, Lia thought. We have time to remedy that problem. The important thing is that we have renters' protections back on the table.

THIS WILL MAKE
THEIR HEADS SPIN

November 2020

A week ago, Marta Escobar had announced that she would no longer hold daily press briefings. She told the press that it was curtailing the time she had to deal with the myriad problems associated with the pandemic. The truth, however, was that she had long ago grown tired of giving a daily briefing to the media. It was a complete waste of her time. And the worst part of it was answering the inane questions that the reporters inevitably asked. If they would just stop and think for a moment, they could answer their own questions. But that would be asking too much. I suppose it's true, she had thought, that those who can become county judge, and those who can't become journalists.

The reporters were not happy with her announcement. They were going to have to do some work to get news to report. Since March, all they had to do was attend her briefing, turn on a voice recorder, and they had enough material to last the rest of the day.

Instead of a daily briefing, she would issue a daily written statement. She could write it at her leisure. In fact, she wasn't planning to even write most of the statements. She'd have her assistants do the writing, and she would review it before it was released. That's why she had a staff—to do the things that she didn't enjoy doing. And other than issuing orders, there wasn't much that she enjoyed doing.

She chuckled as she read today's statement. This will shake things up, she thought. I must give Jamaal credit. He has the city and the county pursuing similar goals, and that is making it very difficult for those far-right radicals to mount much opposition. Sure, they will have a referendum in a few months, but the city is already considering more renters' protections. And this, she thought while shaking the papers in her hand, this will make their heads spin.

The statement read:

> *The pandemic has created unprecedented challenges for all of us. Each of us has had to make many sacrifices. Throughout this ordeal, my sole concern has been saving lives. While my efforts have been successful in that regard, many of our most vulnerable neighbors are falling behind.*
>
> *Our economy is in shambles and unemployment is still too high. Despite a rent freeze, tenants are paying too much of their wages just to stay housed. They cannot afford adequate food, transportation, and health care when they must pay 50 percent or more of their wages for housing.*
>
> *My eviction moratorium applied only to cases filed for non-payment of rent. Despite that moratorium, we are seeing record numbers of evictions being filed. Landlords are inventing lease violations and other excuses for evicting tenants. This is an injustice, and we cannot allow it to continue. Renters should not be evicted because they purchase a puppy for their children. A single mother should not be evicted because she is caring for her sister's baby. A grandmother should not be evicted because her grandson, who doesn't even live with her, was arrested for selling drugs three blocks away.*
>
> *Harris County is at a breaking point. We already have record numbers of homeless people on our streets. Given the economy and the heartless actions of landlords, that number*

could easily double or triple in a matter of months. I cannot simply stand by and watch so many of our most vulnerable citizens be subjected to demeaning and inhuman conditions.

Six weeks ago, I announced a plan to use vacant apartments in the county to house our homeless. To date, that program has helped remove nearly 2,000 people from the streets. However, much work remains to be done, and today we start that work.

As of today, all tenants facing an eviction will be provided with free legal representation. Renters face an unfair disadvantage when they go to the eviction court. Nearly 90 percent of landlords show up with an attorney, while only 10 percent of renters do. Tenants don't know their rights, and they often fail to even show up in court because they don't know the process. This gives landlords an unfair advantage. The right to counsel will correct this power imbalance and give renters a fighting chance.

In jurisdictions with the right to counsel law, evictions declined by over 80 percent. This is a case and point that most evictions are unjust. Today, we are taking steps to stop this injustice in Harris County.

Further, I am announcing an immediate increase in the minimum wage to $12.50 in Harris County. This will mean an additional $200 a week for a minimum wage employee working a forty-hour week. That is money that many families desperately need for food, health care, housing, and other necessities.

These measures alone will not remedy all the challenges that we face. But they will help our most vulnerable citizens remain housed. It will allow them to live with dignity.

Marta Escobar smiled when she finished reading the briefing. Jamaal was right. The more that they could throw at the enemies of progress, the easier it will be to overwhelm them.

I CALL IT CONTEXT BRIDGING

November 2020

Justin didn't recognize the number when his phone rang. He hesitated for a moment, but answered. "Hello, Justin," said a gravelly voice. "This is Warren Hicks, and I understand you would like to speak with me."

"Thank you for calling, Mr. Hicks," Justin replied excitedly. "My partner and I are fighting these renters' protections laws and see some parallels to the fight against zoning in the 1990s. We thought you might offer us some guidance and advice."

"Yes," Warren said, "I've been following your work, and I am impressed. You seem to understand the actual issues and articulate them well. I'd be more than happy to meet with you and your partner. I don't get out much these days because of health concerns about the pandemic. If you'd like, you could come to my house in Missouri City. I would ask that you both wear a mask."

"That would be great!" Justin exclaimed. "No problem with the mask. We always wear a mask when indoors around others. When would you like us to come by?"

"Any time that is good for you."

Justin did not know where Missouri City was located, so he looked it up on his map application. "We are about thirty minutes away," Justin said. "We need to get a few things together, but we could be there in about an hour."

"That works for me. See you then."

* * *

Fifty-five minutes later Justin and Pratik pulled into Warren Hicks' driveway. Neither of the young men had ever been to Quail Valley, and they marveled at how quiet and peaceful the neighborhood was. Two golf courses meandered through the neighborhood, creating an environment much different from anything they had seen in Houston.

When Warren answered the door, Pratik said, "This is a really cool neighborhood. I don't play golf, but it must be fun living on a golf course."

Warren smiled. Most visitors enjoyed the serenity of Quail Valley. "I moved here about twenty years ago," he said as he led them through the house to his back patio. He walked slowly and with a slight limp. Justin estimated Warren was in his late sixties or early seventies. He was a little shorter than Justin and seemed underweight. Other than eyebrows, there wasn't a single strand of hair on Warren's head.

"I saw the direction Houston was heading and didn't like it," Warren continued. "Even though zoning was shot down by the voters, city council kept passing ordinances that would have been a part of the zoning regulations. It was a backdoor approach to zoning, and I had no desire to fight each of the ordinances. A few of the people who fought zoning with me attempted to stop the historic preservation ordinance, but they weren't successful. Please, have a seat." Warren gestured to the patio furniture situated to look out at the fairway for the seventh hole. A pitcher of iced tea, a bowl of sliced lemons, and three glasses were on the table. As they took their seats, Warren said, "You can take your masks off out here. I need to be cautious indoors." Justin and Pratik nodded in understanding.

"Would you care for a glass of iced tea?" Warren asked as he sat. "I brew it myself, and the lemons came from that tree in the corner." Both Pratik and Justin nodded. Warren continued to talk as he poured the tea. "It's unsweetened. I could never understand why Southerners ruin excellent tea by putting sugar in it. All that is necessary is good tea leaves and a hint of lemon. Anyhow, I doubt you came here to discuss the virtues of iced tea. How can I help?"

"We see a lot of parallels between what happened with zoning in the 1990s and what is happening today," Justin said. "City council tried to ram a zoning ordinance down the throats of Houstonians, claiming overwhelming support. Renters' protections advocates claim that Houstonians want renters' protections and the city council is trying to ram it down the citizens' throats." Warren nodded but said nothing.

"That's the political similarity," Pratik said. "But in the 1990s zoning advocates claimed that land-use regulations would protect property rights. Today, housing activists claim laws are needed to protect renters' rights. In both instances, the concept of rights is being perverted. I don't know if the zoning advocates claimed it was a matter of justice, but housing advocates certainly are. Both the pro-zoners and the housing activists are collectivists, and their standard of value is the group. For zoning, it was neighborhoods. For the housing activists, it's renters. These are the moral similarities." Warren nodded again but remained silent.

Justin continued. "We know we need to address these moral issues, but we don't want to appear moralizing. But to return to what I said, how did you overcome those claims of overwhelming support for zoning?"

Warren smiled. "Yes, it can be a challenge to attack others' moral premises yet avoid the appearance that you are asserting moral superiority. Of course, if I read you two correctly, you are morally superior, that is, you embrace a superior morality. We can talk about that later, but first let me answer your question. This might surprise you, but we spent little effort trying to overcome the claims that a vast majority of Houstonians wanted zoning. We addressed it occasionally, but we didn't give it a lot of attention. We had a lot more to say about the moral premise underlying that claim."

"That individuals should be subservient to the group," Pratik interjected.

"Exactly," Warren responded. "We explicitly identified and then rejected that moral premise. The pro-zoners didn't expect anyone to challenge them on moral grounds. We caught them off guard, and they rarely even attempted to address our arguments. Instead, they focused more on two other groups that were opposing the proposed zoning ordinance. One group wasn't opposed to zoning per se, just that version of it. They spent a lot of money on billboards and media ads, but nobody really took them seriously. The other group focused mostly on practical arguments against zoning—economics, corruption, things like that. They got more attention than my group. Other than helping with the petition, our efforts were primarily philosophical."

"Our client thinks we are too philosophical," Justin said. "We disagree with him, and we aren't going to dumb down our message. Did you get resistance? Were people willing and able to discuss the deeper moral and philosophical issues?"

Warren nodded. "Yes, that was a challenge. Most people don't give a lot of thought to philosophical issues. Most have a very mixed bag of premises, some good and some bad, as I'm sure you know. We tried to appeal to the good premises. And I think we were effective. One thing we did was use concrete examples that were easy to understand. Then we'd explain the moral issues involved. For example, zoning advocates claimed that deed restrictions, which many neighborhoods in Houston have, were simply one form of zoning. We explained that there is a fundamental difference between zoning and deed restrictions. The former are mandatory and coerced. The latter are voluntary and contractual. People could understand that difference. We did the same thing with many of the arguments the zoning advocates raised."

"How did you do that without alienating people?" Pratik

asked. "Justin and I seem to turn people off when we raise the issue of altruism. We tend to sound like we are saying, 'I'm right, and you are an idiot.'"

"Been there, done that," Warren said. "When I was younger, I would browbeat anyone who would listen. It wasn't effective, and I doubt I changed anyone's mind. But it takes time to learn to control our passion and communicate effectively. It took many years to discover a better approach. I call it context bridging. If we are trying to persuade others, we must recognize the difference between their context and ours. Context bridging is the process of closing that difference, of bringing their context closer to ours. When we do that, it is much easier for the other person to see, and perhaps, agree with, our point."

"How did you bridge the context?" Justin asked.

"By reframing the issue." Justin and Pratik looked at one another and smiled.

"What?" Warren asked.

"We've concluded that we need to reframe the debate over renters' protections," Justin said. "But we aren't sure how to do that."

"Yes, that too took me a while to figure out. I finally realized that the most effective approach is to find a common value with my audience. Too often, a political debate focuses on a particular policy rather than the goal that is sought. Let me give you an example. Housing activists argue for rent control, and you argue against them. What goal are they seeking? What goal are you seeking? I would say that both sides want to enable individuals to get affordable housing. If we establish that as our common goal, then the discussion shifts to the best way to achieve that common goal. We can now work together rather than arguing about a particular policy."

The three spent the next three hours discussing strategy. The sun was setting, and it was obvious that Warren was getting tired. "Warren, we've taken enough of your time. You have been extremely helpful."

"It's been my pleasure," Warren replied. "You two give me

hope for the future. And please, call me anytime you have questions or want to run something by me. I wish I could join you in this fight, but as you probably noticed, I don't have the energy that I did when I was younger."

A CLEAR CHOICE
BETWEEN GOOD
AND EVIL

November 2020

"I think it's a conspiracy," Buford Jennings said. "It can't be a coincidence that Escobar is announcing new orders at the same time the city council is considering more of these damn renter protections. Both the city and the county are doing something very similar, and I find that suspicious."

"If there is a conspiracy, which I think will be very difficult to prove," Justin said, "I'm not sure that it matters."

"Of course it matters," Buford bellowed. "If we have all the local government officials working in cahoots, well, that's got to be illegal. If we can prove that, then all this nonsense would go away, and I can get back to my actual job."

Pratik shook his head. "Obviously, I am not a lawyer, so I don't know what the law is. But it isn't unprecedented for city and county officials to work together. I was only ten, but I remember the Houston mayor and the county judge appearing on television together all the time after Hurricane Ike. They were coordinating efforts, and I don't recall anyone complaining. Granted, this would be a different kind of coordinating, but I'm not sure it's worth worrying about."

"I agree with Pratik," Justin said. "We need to focus on the issues. If we try to prove a conspiracy, we could go down a rabbit hole with no escape. It will just distract us, as well as voters. We could waste a lot of valuable time and accomplish nothing."

Buford frowned. "I don't agree with you two. But you seem to know what you are doing. At least for now, we'll do it your way. You got enough signatures for a referendum, and that alone is impressive. So, I will defer to you two. At least for now. We have about five months before the vote. What do you propose to do?"

"Pratik and I have been discussing this for weeks. We have decided on two primary modes of attack. One, we will continue to write blog posts and use social media to get our message out. Two, we will contact civic associations and other community groups and offer to speak to them. Warren Hicks suggested that. He spoke to a lot of civic groups during the zoning debate in the 1990s, and it seemed to be effective. Speaking to people face-to-face is far more convincing than a blog post because we can address their specific concerns. And, as we learn about their concerns, we have additional material for our blog."

"How are you going to handle all the different issues?" Buford asked. "There is what, five or six renter protections, and I expect the city to raise the minimum wage. If you try to address all of those, the message will be spread very thin."

"Right now, we plan to address the individual protections, as well as the minimum wage," Pratik replied. "But when we do, we will focus on a few core principles. Principles such as rights and justice will be prominent in all of our writing and talks. This will allow us to deliver a consistent message across multiple issues."

Buford furrowed his brow. "I don't understand."

"Let's say I am writing a piece about the minimum wage," Justin said. "I can address the fact that minimum wage laws violate the right to produce and trade as one deems best. If someone decides that working for $5 an hour is in his best interest, there is no rational reason he shouldn't be free to do so. Further, minimum wage laws are an injustice. They grant some workers a wage that they haven't earned, and deny others a wage that they would be eager to accept."

"To further the example," Pratik said, "let's say I am writing about the eviction moratorium. This too violates the right to produce and trade on terms one judges best. The moratorium forces landlords to continue renting to someone, regardless of the property owner's own judgment and desires. That's an injustice. And if the tenant doesn't pay the rent, the landlord suffers the additional injustice of being deprived of the money that is rightfully his."

"As a last example," Justin added, "let's say we are addressing the right to counsel. This is an injustice because it forces landlords to pay a portion of the fees of those fighting against them. Some of the landlords' tax dollars will pay for his tenant's attorney. That too violates the landlords' rights, as they are forced to surrender their money for a purpose that they may not agree with."

"So," Pratik concluded, "you can see how we can apply the same basic principles to these different issues. This will allow us to have a very consistent message, no matter what the particular issue or topic. I'm sure that we will bring in other principles, but even then, they will integrate with everything else we are saying."

"I think that you boys are going to be talking over everyone's head," Buford said. "Most voters aren't as smart as you two. You need to talk to them in a way that they can understand. All this talk of rights and justice is fine, but it's going to make people's heads spin."

"We agree we should speak in a way that they can understand," Pratik said. "But that doesn't mean that we should talk down to them. Most people can follow a logical argument, particularly if you use examples they can understand. That is a big reason we want to speak to groups face-to-face. We can learn what their concerns are, as well as get feedback on which messaging works well and which doesn't."

"Housing activists are talking about rights and justice," Justin said with irritation in his voice. "They have a perverted view of those concepts, but we must address that. If we let them talk about rights and justice and we say nothing, it will imply that they have rights and justice on their side. We need to identify why they are wrong and then present a more rational position."

"Most people aren't rational," Buford objected. "My god, they elected that tramp Escobar for Christ's sakes."

Justin shook his head in dismay. They had had this conversation multiple times in the past. "As we've said before, if you give someone a choice between two things that are bad, can you really fault him for choosing one? No. If someone is forced to choose between ingesting arsenic or cyanide, it's not accurate to say that he chose to poison himself."

"I see your point. I've voted for people that I couldn't stand, but they were the lesser of two evils." Buford seemed to understand.

Justin nodded. "Look, back in the 1980s, Houstonians voted for the people who wound up enacting the zoning ordinance. But when voters saw what the politicians did, they rebelled and overturned the council. The election for city council members may well have been a choice between two evils. But the zoning referendum was a choice between good and evil. When there is a clear choice between good and evil, we are confident that people will choose the good once again."

"Our goal," Pratik said, "is to clarify that respecting property rights is good, and renters protections are evil. We want to give voters a very clear understanding of the two options, just like what was done in the 1990s with zoning."

I RISKED GOING TO JAIL

November 2020

"Jamaal, you've been strangely quiet," Mayor Benton said as the Reverend took a seat. "With a referendum on your pet project coming up in a few months, I'd think you'd be talking to anyone and everyone."

Jamaal smiled. "That's where you and I differ, Charles. I do my best work behind the scenes. Instead of giving speeches and writing articles, I recruit others to the cause. If I can recruit two or three people a week, my influence increases exponentially."

"Very well," Charles replied. "But I didn't ask you here to talk about politics. I want to talk about that night."

Jamaal frowned and shook his head. "How many damn times do we need to talk about it? Frankly, I am tired of the topic. I put it behind me long ago, and I suggest you do the same."

Charles stared at Jamaal. "I've done a little research since we last spoke. You claimed you smoked some crystal meth that night. The effects typically last at least four hours, and include agitation, unfocused thinking, and paranoia. Those effects contradict what you claim happened. You say that you came up with the story that I killed Devon in self-defense, but that kind of quick thinking is unlikely for someone under the influence of crystal."

Jamaal jumped from his chair and glowered down at the mayor with balled fists. "Are you calling me a liar, Charles?"

Charles motioned for Jamaal to return to his seat. "No. I am just pointing out an inconsistency in your story. I hoped perhaps you can resolve that inconsistency."

The two men silently stared at one another. He'll either come clean with the truth, or tell another lie, Charles thought. I must come up with something, Jamaal thought, and it needs to be plausible. Maybe I should just stick to my story and be more adamant about it. I cannot tell him the truth.

"What can I say?" Jamaal finally said. "Drugs affect different people in different ways. Perhaps the shock of what I saw sobered me up. I don't know. All I can do is tell you the truth. You can choose to believe it or not."

"Okay, let's talk about the lights," Charles said. "You said that you found Devon and I lying in Miss Betty's yard. She always kept her front porch light on at night. But you said that the yard was dark when you discovered us. That means that her light wasn't on, just like the park lights."

"What the hell is it with the lights?" Jamaal shouted. "I don't remember if her light was on or off. If I said that the yard was dark, then it must have been off. What does it matter?"

"Maybe it doesn't matter. Maybe it does," Charles said philosophically. "Since I can't remember much about that night, I must rely on your testimony. And you have already proven to be less than candid. So, when I detect some inconsistencies, I must ask myself why."

"Damn Charles, that was twenty-some years ago. My memory of that night isn't much better than yours."

"Well Jamaal, a month ago you seemed to remember that night very clearly. Now you claim you don't remember much. Another inconsistency. How many is that now? Three? Four? When someone is called on a lie, they can either confess or tell another lie to cover the first. And if he gets called on the second lie, he must tell another. At some point, the liar can't distinguish between fact and fiction. His story fills with inconsistencies until it finally collapses." Charles shrugged and raised his hands. "I'm just saying…."

Jamaal felt his heart racing. I don't think that Charles has figured out what happened, he thought, but he is getting dangerously close to doing so. "What are you getting at?" Jamaal asked angrily.

"I am saying that your story has more and more inconsistencies. I find that very suspicious."

"Charles, I know that we've had our differences over the years. But I have always been there for you. Hell, that night I was more than there for you. I kept your sorry ass out of prison. And I risked going to jail myself to do it. I think you should keep that in mind before you make accusations. Besides, we both have more important things to worry about."

Charles shook his head and wagged a finger at Jamaal. "Let's consider a few facts. Of the three people involved that night, one is dead—Devon. One can't remember anything because he was drugged—me. And the third person, the only one not stabbed that night—you—has admitted to lying to the police and to me." Charles let his words sink in.

Jamaal stood up and grabbed his hat from the desk. "I don't know what game you are playing, but I will not participate. If you think I did something nefarious that night, prove it. You can't, because there is no evidence." With that, Jamaal walked out of Charles' office, slamming the door behind him.

I'LL SHOW THEM
HOW THE PROS DO IT

November 2020

"**S**heriff, it's good to see you again," Marta Escobar said. "I am glad that you had time to meet with me. We have a very troubling problem that requires your help."

The sheriff raised an eyebrow. It was highly unusual for the county judge to get involved in criminal matters. "And what would that be?"

"There are a couple of young men—Justin Walker and Pratik Shah—who are creating a lot of turmoil throughout the county. They seem to think that they can do whatever they please, regardless of the will of the people. They seem to think that it's appropriate to say whatever pops into their little heads, whether or not it's true."

"Have they committed a crime?" the sheriff asked.

Escobar shook her head. "None that I know of. But that's not the point. They are being very disruptive, and they are doing so in a way that is immoral. I don't need you to arrest them. I just want these two people to know that they are being watched. If you see them doing something illegal and can arrest them, then that would be the icing on the cake. We are in the midst of a pandemic and these two are impeding my efforts to save lives.

Along with that idiot on the radio, they are making it hard to convince people to cooperate."

"You have a funny way of winning hearts and minds."

"I don't give a damn about hearts and minds," Escobar snapped. "I want laws, and I want them obeyed without question."

The sheriff frowned. "So, you are asking me to tail two individuals who have committed no crime? I might be wrong, but it seems to me that this is purely political. I'm not sure if I want to get involved in that. This sounds just like that fiasco with the radio guy. That blew up in your face, and I suspect that this will, too."

"Let me remind you, sheriff," Escobar said sternly, "who controls the funding for your department. Many people are calling for the police to be defunded, and I can say that I am sympathetic to that point of view. The way I see it, we can work together, or you can deal with the consequences."

Good Lord, the sheriff thought, this woman really is a bitch. I'd heard rumors, but I wasn't sure if I believed them. It seems to be true. "I don't like this at all. This looks like a train wreck in the making. You said that we have a problem. How is this my problem?"

Escobar grimaced. "Financially, you are my subordinate, and you should do as I say. I am not asking you to do anything illegal. There is nothing wrong with tailing two suspicious individuals. The police do it all the time. They know who the bad guys are, and they monitor them. I'm telling you, these two characters are bad guys. If you keep an eye on them, you'll discover that soon enough. And if they turn out to be the fine, upstanding citizens they pretend to be, then no harm, no foul."

"I still don't see how this is my problem," the sheriff repeated. "Why are you using me to further your political agenda?"

"Because I can! Funding!" Escobar shouted. "Your problem is funding. I can do something about that, just in case you forgot that fact. If you want me to scratch your back, then you need to scratch mine."

"And how long do you want this surveillance to last? We are already short staffed. This will be a strain."

Escobar shrugged. "Sheriff, that's why you get the big bucks —to make the tough decisions. I want this to last as long as it needs to last. Maybe longer. What do you say? Are you on board?"

The sheriff took a deep breath as he struggled to control his anger. This woman was trying to manipulate him, and he wasn't the slightest bit pleased about it. "What the h.... What does that mean? It should last as long as it needs to last and maybe longer?"

"It means that they need to be tailed until I tell you to stop. That may be next week, or it may not be until the damn referendum these two are responsible for. Hell, it may not be until sometime in the next decade." Escobar shook a finger at the sheriff. "I am running out of time and patience. I need a decision. Now."

Well, it isn't illegal, the sheriff thought. I can't allow our budget to get cut. That would be a disaster. He nodded. "Okay," he said softly. "I'll do it."

Escobar smiled. "I knew I could count on you. Let me outline what I have in mind. I don't think 24/7 surveillance is necessary. I just want them to know that we are monitoring them. And make it appear random, but consistent. For example, park across the street from their house at random times. If you see them leave the house, follow them occasionally, but not always. If they go to a store, sometimes follow them there and back. Mix it up so they never know when they will be watched. That is far more unnerving than constant surveillance. Don't you think?"

That's what this is about, the sheriff thought. She wants to intimidate these two young men. "What is the purpose of this?"

"Ideally, they would drop their support for the referendum. At a minimum, I don't want them engaged in additional activism. I want them on edge. If they want to play in the big leagues, I'll show them how the pros do it."

THERE WASN'T A PROPER BALANCE

December 2020

Charles Benton was tired. He was tired of the pandemic. He was tired of the petty squabbles between city councilmen. Charles was tired of running the nation's fourth largest city. But most of all, he was tired of wondering about the Rev. Jamaal Wilkes.

Jamaal had a secret, something that he refused to divulge to Charles. The mayor could not fathom what it might be, but he knew it would be the key to cutting the strings that Jamaal had around his neck. Charles was sitting in the council chambers but barely listening to the discussion going on. He was trying to figure out what he could do to discover Jamaal's secret. Charles sensed he was getting close to discovering the truth. Jamaal had ended his attempts at manipulation, and that told the mayor that the reverend was getting nervous.

A series of seemingly random ideas popped into his head. He quickly dismissed most of them. But one idea kept recurring. Jamaal had given one story to the police and another to Charles regarding the events of the night in question. But Charles' only knowledge of Jamaal's account to the police was Jamaal himself. What if he had told the police something different from he claimed to have told the police? Maybe there is something in the police record that will provide a clue. The more that Charles considered this idea, the more he liked it.

"The next item on the agenda," the clerk announced, "is the renters' protections ordinance." That got the mayor's attention, and he turned his focus to the immediate proceedings. As the clerk read the final version of the ordinance, Charles realized it was exactly as it had originally been written. That was highly unusual. Charles looked at Lia Patel. She was looking at the mayor with a sly smile. Charles then turned to look at Roderick Jackson. He was glaring at the mayor with a snarl. Both seem confident of passage, Charles thought. These two are learning the game quickly.

There was a brief discussion after the ordinance was read. The conservative made his normal snide comments, and the other council members largely ignored him. When he had entered the chambers, Charles planned to vote "present" once again. He had experienced much less heat after the first vote than he had expected, and he thought abstaining again would be a safe position to take.

But as he sat listening to the few comments being made, he realized he should toss aside his plan. If this was a parade, he wanted to get in front of it. When there were no further comments on the ordinance, Charles spoke up.

"I would like to make a few observations before we vote. As you all know, I abstained the last time we voted on renters' protections. This is a very complex issue involving many parties. I had concerns, and justifiably so, that there wasn't a proper balance between the interests of those parties. Rather than make a choice that I would later regret, I abstained. The ordinance was already approved, and my vote wouldn't have made a difference.

"In the weeks since that vote, I have studied the issue more carefully. I have spoken to colleagues in cities that have enacted renter protections. What I discovered eased the concerns that I had previously had. The renters' protections that were passed and are being considered here are less stringent than those in many cities. It would appear that Council Members Patel and

Jackson have struck the balance that I thought necessary."

Charles rarely spoke at council meetings. When he did, he usually had everyone's undivided attention. Today was no different. The conservative stared at the mayor with narrowed eyes and pursed lips. Lia Patel stared at the mayor with pity in her eyes. Roderick Jackson stared at the mayor while shaking his head. The other members of the council had looks of confusion.

"And so, it is time that we put our political differences aside and work together for the common good. It is time for Houston to enter the twenty-first century, and this ordinance is a significant step towards doing so."

With that, a vote was taken, and the ordinance passed by a 11-6 margin. Charles Benton voted for the ordinance.

HOW DID YOU KNOW MY NAME?

December 2020

Justin and Pratik spent the evening talking to the Sunnyside Civic Association. It was the fifth time in the past two weeks that they had met with a civic group to discuss the upcoming referendum, but their first in a low-income neighborhood. As they had done with the previous meetings, instead of delivering a lecture, Justin and Pratik asked questions to guide the conversation. They wanted the people who would vote in the referendum to be engaged, and the two young men wanted to identify what confusions and concerns those voters had. They wanted to eliminate the confusions and respond to the concerns.

Each meeting began with several questions. Pratik would ask how many people were renters. Usually, about half the audience raised their hands. Tonight, nearly 75 percent indicated they were renters. Justin would then ask how many renters hoped to someday own a house. Nearly every hand was raised. They used this to segue into a discussion of property rights.

"The right to property," Pratik would say, "means the freedom to produce, trade, and use material values—property. It means that you can build something and sell it or keep it for your own personal purposes. It means that you can offer goods and services to others, who are free to buy your products or not. Property rights mean developers can build the housing they think is appropriate and then sell or rent it. It means that you can buy or rent the housing that you desire and can afford. Both you and the developer are exercising your right to property."

"Property rights might seem like an ivory tower topic," Justin would say, "but if you are like most people, almost all your waking hours are spent producing, trading, or using material values. The issue of property rights is everywhere. But the freedom to produce, trade, and use property can be violated in many ways. Can you think of a few?"

At each meeting, someone quickly said that a robber or burglar violates property rights. And then, the audience would be stumped. Justin and Pratik would then prod the attendees with a question: Have you, or someone you know, been stopped from starting a business? Each time, several people shouted "YES." The two young men would then slowly draw out how this violated the right to produce and trade. They would then ask if anyone could see a similarity to renters' protections. Most of the time, someone did, though they often expressed it crudely.

The conversation would then shift to the referendum and the issues involved. At each meeting, they showed that renters' protections were founded on the wrong standard of value. Those measures asserted the group possesses rights. In truth, only individuals—all individuals—possess rights. And that includes landlords and tenants alike.

The audiences were generally receptive to the message being delivered by the intellectual bodyguards. As Justin and Pratik expected, there was a great deal of confusion about the meaning of the right to property. Most of those in attendance believed that some restrictions on property use were necessary, though they admitted that those restrictions often went "too far"—a term that was used often but never defined.

While there was often disagreement, the conversation was always civil. Justin and Pratik were uncertain how many minds they changed, but they were certain that they had given the attendees a new way to look at the issue. And that was their primary intent.

"Pratik," Justin said as he drove home, "there's a police car following us again. I can't tell if it's a sheriff or constable." After each of their meetings with a civic group, they were followed by a law enforcement vehicle. On multiple occasions, they had seen either a sheriff's deputy or a constable deputy parked across the street from their home.

"Perhaps," Pratik had quipped more than once, "they are protecting us from the crazy progressives."

"I'd sure like to find out what is going on," Justin said. "It feels like we are being stalked."

"I have an idea," Pratik replied. "Take a right at the next light, but don't use your turn signal."

As they approached the light, it turned green. Justin turned right, and as Pratik had suggested, didn't use his turn signal. The police car turned as well, and its lights came on almost immediately. "This will be interesting," Justin said as he pulled to the side of the street.

Both young men lowered their windows as the officer approached their car. Justin also lowered the back windows to give the officer a clear view of the interior. Justin lightly gripped the steering wheel, and Pratik placed his hands on the dashboard.

When the officer was standing outside his window, Justin turned. "Good evening, officer," he said.

"Good evening, Mr. Walker. Please give me your driver's license and proof of insurance," the officer said. With the two documents in hand, he returned to his squad car.

"Justin," Pratik said, "he knew your name before he saw your driver's license. If we were back in Ohio, I might understand that he recognizes you, but this is kind of scary."

"I know. Maybe we can get to the bottom of this and find out what is going on."

The officer returned a few minutes later. "Do you know why I pulled you over?" he asked.

"I didn't use my turn signal. Pratik was navigating, and he told me to turn right at the last minute. I didn't have time to turn the signal on."

"Yes," the officer replied. "I'm going to have to issue a citation for the infraction." He handed the driver's license, proof of insurance, and a citation to Justin. You are scheduled to appear in court on January 4. Or you can pay the fine ahead of time. Information is on the back of the citation. Have a good day."

The officer started to turn. "Officer," Justin said, "I have a question."

"Yes."

"How did you know my name?"

"Oh, it wasn't hard to figure out. Sunnyside is my patrol, so I keep up on local happenings. I heard that you two were going to speak to the civic association tonight. This is a rough neighborhood, and I decided I'd keep an eye out for you in case there were problems after the meeting. You two don't fit the demographics for the neighborhood, if you know what I mean. So, you were easy to spot."

Justin thought for a moment. It seemed plausible, but something didn't sound right about that story. However, he decided this wasn't the time to push the issue any further. He just nodded. "Okay. Thanks, officer."

As they pulled away, Pratik was the first to speak. "I'm not buying it. It sounds plausible but come on. He didn't have to greet you by name. I think he was trying to send a message."

"I agree," Justin replied. "We seem to have police cars near us all the time. They are parked across the street. The police follow us to the store. They follow us home. But this is the first time that we've been pulled over. And for something very minor."

"I think he wanted to let us know that what's been going on isn't random. This has involved both deputies from the sheriff and the constable, so this has to be coming from higher up. The question is who? And why?"

Justin laughed. "That's two questions. But seriously, what is the hierarchy for the sheriff and constable? Do they report to anybody?"

Pratik shook his head. "I don't know the answer to that, but it's worth looking into. Wait. Escobar. She is the top person in the county government. The sheriff is part of the county government, but I'm not sure about constables."

"Other than attacking some of her policies, we have done nothing aimed at her. The referendum pertains to a city ordinance, so I can't see why she would care."

Pratik nodded. "Me neither, but she lusts for power and politics can make strange bedfellows."

HEARTLESS RACISTS

January 2021

The Houston News Journal, the city's only daily newspaper, began the year with a series of articles examining the plight of renters with a focus on low-income households. Long on emotional content, the stories were unsurprisingly short on substantive context.

The first article featured Juanita and Hector Garcia. The young immigrant couple paid over 50 percent of their income for housing. Speaking through an interpreter, Juanita explained that they constantly struggled to feed their four children and pay for health care. Hector worked for a landscaping company and made $8.50 an hour. Juanita, who was pregnant, cleaned offices at night and brought in $250 per week.

"Something needs to be done," Juanita complained. "We can't go on living like this. We came to Texas because of the opportunity to make a better life for our family. But this isn't better than what we had in Monterrey. We were told that these new laws would provide some relief, but now we aren't sure. We don't want to return to Mexico, but we can't continue living like this. Somebody needs to help us."

The story examined how renter protections and an increase in the minimum wage would benefit the family. The former would stabilize their housing costs while the latter could increase their household income by about $900 a month. Combined, the two measures would vastly improve the family's financial situation.

What the story didn't explain was why this couple was attempting to raise five children while making such a low wage. Food, clothing, and health care for the children consumed nearly half of their monthly income. The choices made by the couple were a primary cause of their financial problems, but pointing out this would have diminished the emotional impact of the article. Nor would such facts have been considered politically correct.

Another story focused on allegedly negligent landlords. Shanna Griggs complained her landlord refused to replace the air conditioner compressor. Instead, he installed three window units in the two-bedroom house Griggs rented. During July and August, on many days, the three units struggled to keep the house below eighty degrees. One of her three children had asthma and the high temperatures within the house caused frequent respiratory problems.

The story went on for nearly three thousand words detailing the landlord's unwillingness to replace the faulty compressor. The article claimed that the cost of the three units was more than a new compressor, so the landlord couldn't claim that it was a matter of money. In truth, the window units cost about 10 percent of the price for a new compressor, but the paper counted on few people knowing that fact. It was mentioned in passing that Griggs hadn't paid the rent since February 2020. Nor did the article mention any attempt to contact the landlord for his side of the story. The tenant's story was sufficient for the paper's purpose.

The *News Journal* had yet to take an official editorial position on the upcoming referendum. But there was no mistaking the paper's support for renters' protections and an increase in the minimum wage. The series of articles focused on the difficulties faced by low-income households because of the pandemic. Virtually nothing was said about the difficulties faced by landlords and small business owners. Nor was it mentioned that Escobar's lockdown had started a cascade of problems that were rippling through the county.

The articles provided Justin and Pratik with an abundance of material for their blog and social media accounts. However, they simply didn't have enough time to address every claim that was made. Instead, they focused their efforts on identifying the full context and pointing out that most of the individuals who were highlighted had made many decisions that led to their current financial problems. Many of the responses to their posts called the two heartless racists. Justin and Pratik care to address every claim made about them, but they agreed they should write something about the claims of racism. Pratik pointed out that suggesting that people make more rational decisions wasn't racist. It was simply sound advice. However, that didn't stop the claims of bigotry.

The Baker Institute at Rice University released a poll regarding the referendum during the first week of the month. Nearly 65 percent of those polled expressed support for renters' protections. It was discouraging news for the two intellectual bodyguards, but they took the news in stride.

"Polls can be very skewed," Pratik had said. "How questions are worded can have an enormous impact on the answers that are given. Let's not give too much credence to that poll. The only poll that counts is the one in April."

"Yes," Justin had replied. "I remember reading that days before the referendum on zoning a poll was released that found that zoning would be approved by about 55 percent of the voters. What happened on election day was considerably different."

Pratik considered that point for a moment. "That is something that we should address," he said. "That could help undermine the impact of the poll. And I am sure that there will be more polls in the months leading up to the referendum that will show similar results. Many people are influenced by polls. They want to be on the winning side. If we get in front of this, we might use it to our advantage."

"How do we do that?"

Pratik thought for a moment. "I'm not sure. Let's call Warren and see what he thinks."

NO WONDER THE LEFT KEEPS WINNING

January 2021

The Texas governor was determined that his state lead the way regarding pandemic policies. He would show the country, indeed the world, what Texas stood for. He was willing to take bold steps, because that is what presidential candidates were supposed to do, and the governor was being mentioned as a potential candidate in 2024.

"Today, Texas takes another step toward freedom," he said to the assembled media. "This morning, I signed an executive order prohibiting so-called vaccine passports. This order applies to all government institutions, as well as private businesses. Texans should not have to choose between getting a vaccine and going to the grocery store. Texans should be free to live as they choose. This order allows them to do so.

"Vaccine passports require individuals to present proof that they have received the COVID vaccine before entering a building. Such requirements mean that those who do not get the vaccine cannot engage in the activities that life requires. They cannot go to the grocery store, the doctor's office, or a home improvement store. It may even mean that they lose their job.

"Forcing individuals to get a vaccine or lose their job goes against our sense of fairness. Texans should not be forced to make such choices. My order protects the freedom of everyone to make his own decisions regarding his health care, including vaccination. It protects each individual's right to keep his medical history private. We will not allow our citizens to be denied services simply because they have not been jabbed in the arm.

"Vaccine passports create two classes of citizens—those who can take part in society and those who can't. An individual should not be forced to reveal his medical history to be employed or visit a store. Texans should be free to go where they want with no restrictions and without the need to 'show their papers'.

"Other states allow vaccine passports, and that is their prerogative. But we do things differently in Texas. We don't like being told what to do. We don't allow the federal government to dictate how we conduct our affairs. And we won't tolerate businesses dictating how individuals conduct their affairs.

"Like many things that my administration has done during this pandemic, this is a bold step. We will continue to take bold steps and go against the crowd. We will say no to the government issuing dictates and yes to freedom. While much of the world has lost its mind and attacked freedom, Texas has stood tall in defense of freedom.

"I hasten to add that I highly encourage Texans to get vaccinated. But individuals have vastly different circumstances. They should be free to make such decisions in consultation with their doctor, not by some mandate imposed by the government or a business. We must protect each individual's freedom to act as he thinks best.

"Many will criticize this executive order. But let me remind everyone that I was also criticized when I opened the state and allowed businesses to operate at full capacity. The critics said that I was inviting a disaster, that COVID cases and deaths would soar. But guess what? That hasn't happened. New cases and deaths are slightly above the national average, but that is hardly the catastrophe that was predicted. My critics were wrong before and they will be wrong this time. Freedom is never wrong.

"Since the pandemic began nearly a year ago, many have talked about a new normal. What they meant was that we should become accustomed to unprecedented government controls and restrictions. But that is not normal. Not in America, and certainly not in Texas. Freedom, not government control, is normal.

"My order does not prevent government or private entities from implementing COVID-related policies to protect the public health, so long as those policies comply with state and federal law. We are, after all, still in the midst of a pandemic. It is neither my intention nor my desire to impede prudent and medically sound policies.

"Texas has been leading the way as we show the other states in the Union the responsible way to deal with a pandemic. We will continue to do so. God bless Texas."

*　*　*

"Interesting," Justin said after the governor finished speaking. "The governor says that individuals should be free to act as they think best, and then he promptly issues an order that prohibits business owners from acting as they think best."

Pratik nodded. "That's typical of Republicans. They talk about freedom, but then they support policies that are anti-freedom. No wonder the Left keeps winning policy debates."

SOMEONE LEFT-HANDED

January 2021

Charles Benton had waited nearly three weeks to receive the police report for Devon Little's death from the police chief. At the time of Devon's death, the police did not have the same technological capabilities as they did today. Instead of a quick search on a computer, somebody had to go to the basement and dig through boxes. As was the department's policy, when an old file was pulled, the contents were then entered into the computer system.

Years ago, some had argued that all the old records should be digitized to enable easy access. But the police chief at the time pointed out that such a task would take years and be enormously expensive. Besides, he said, we will need information on only a tiny fraction of those cases. If we ever access an old record, we will enter it into the system then. To enter all old cases would be a waste of taxpayer money and provide no benefits.

It was after seven in the evening before Charles finally had time to open the file the police chief had emailed. As an additional favor, the chief had also included the coroner's report in the email. The police report was only six pages long. It described what the responding officers found at the scene, along with descriptions of the three individuals present.

The description of Charles was not flattering:

Charles Benton was found lying on the ground clutching a knife. He was muttering incoherently and unable to stand without assistance. He appeared to be under the influence of drugs or alcohol. He had suffered two knife wounds, which were examined and treated by paramedics. One wound was on his right forearm. The second wound was on his on his chest that went diagonally from his right shoulder to the left of his navel. Neither wound was life threatening. Once Mr. Benton's condition was stabilized, he was transported to Southmore Hospital for testing and observation.

A later note in the record stated that Charles had tested positive for Rohypnol. He gradually recovered from the effects of the drug and was released from the hospital the following day. It was also noted that after interviewing Jamaal Wilkes, officers concluded Charles had killed Devon in self-defense. No charges were filed, and the case was closed.

Most of the report comprised the officers' interview with Jamaal. Jamaal's story in the police report was essentially the same as the story he had related to Charles, with only a few minor differences. Charles was perplexed. He had hoped that he would discover a major discrepancy, and it would be the key to figuring out Jamaal's secret. He felt like he had reached a dead end and started to close the file.

On a lark, he looked at the coroner's report. Charles had never read such a report before and quickly concluded that it was not the most exciting prose ever written. It was filled with medical terms, descriptions of Devon's body, and all the other details a coroner must discover when conducting an autopsy. Charles found it curious that, in addition to a dozen stab wounds, Devon also had a diagonal cut from his right shoulder to the left side of his navel. The upper portion of the cut did not penetrate deeply into the body because of the protection afforded by the rib cage and sternum. However, when the blade reached the bottom of the sternum it penetrated the liver approximately two inches. The damage to the liver caused Devon to bleed out.

As he read this description, Charles placed his right hand on his right shoulder and moved it diagonally down his chest. He was trying to envision what he had done that night. He hoped that reenacting the motion of cutting Devon would spur a long-forgotten memory. But nothing was happening. Being right-handed made the movement awkward. Frustrated, Charles stood and opened his closet door. A full-length mirror was mounted on the inside of the door. Charles faced the mirror and repeated the diagonal motion with his left hand.

Charles stood staring at the mirror with his left hand resting on his abdomen. An idea was trying to form in his mind, but it wasn't making itself known. Charles repeated the motion a second and then a third time. And that is when Charles realized the knife cuts on both Devon and him were made by a left-handed person. Both he and Devon were right-handed. However, Charles knew someone left-handed, someone who was at the scene that night.

A ROSE BY ANY OTHER NAME

January 2021

The last weekend of the month, the city held a two-day convention in the George R. Brown Convention Center downtown. The stated purpose of the event was to inform voters of the issues surrounding the upcoming referendum. However, in truth, the convention was a city-sponsored sales pitch to convince voters to approve renters' protections.

Though he had no official ties to the city government, the Rev. Jamaal Wilkes organized the event. He had convinced Lia Patel and Roderick Jackson to use whatever influence they could exert to get approval to use the city-owned convention center. That had proven to be a simple task. The council members who had voted for the renter protections were eager to convince voters to rubber stamp their efforts. If voters rejected the renters' protections, they very well might reject the council members in the next election.

Jamaal used three of the center's theaters for a series of speakers. Each speaker would be given forty-five minutes to present their case. They would give their talk three times, which would allow attendees to move from one theater to another. There were to be three speakers in the morning and three in the afternoon each day.

The exhibit halls would contain booths manned by nearly every housing advocacy group in the county, along with several from Austin and San Antonio. Those taking part received financial support for the booth fee, printed materials, and other resources. The source of the funds wasn't revealed, and nobody, including the *News Journal's* reporters, bothered to ask. If anyone had bothered to investigate, it would have been discovered that the mayor's office was using a discretionary fund to pay the expenses for the housing activists. Jamaal found it humorous that Charles had stalled for years but now seemed to be totally behind renters' protections.

Jamaal also moved nearly all of downtown's homeless population to one of the exhibit halls. He wanted the men and women to recreate life on the streets. Visitors to the convention could then wander through the homeless camp to get a sense of what unhoused individuals experienced. He arranged with Marta Escobar to provide plainclothes security guards to monitor the activities within the camp. He did not want the homeless to create a public relations nightmare through inappropriate actions. Besides the restrooms available inside the convention center, Jamaal arranged for dozens of portable toilets to be placed behind curtains. There were certain aspects of life on the street that he preferred to keep hidden.

When reporters asked city officials why they were allowing a convention to be held during a pandemic, they said that housing is a public health issue. They judged the public health threats posed by homelessness to be more serious than the public health threat posed by COVID. The reporters accepted that claim without a second thought.

Jamaal had given no thought to including opponents of the renters' protections, nor had he expected any to be interested in doing so. He was taken aback when he learned that Justin and Pratik wanted to have a booth. He quickly nixed the idea, but was later told by Lia Patel they could not deny space to anyone who could pay the booth fee. Jamaal responded and established a fee of $5,000 for a standard ten-foot square booth. He thought, incorrectly, that the two young men could not afford such an exorbitant price. Instead, Justin and Pratik contracted for three adjoining booths.

Buford Jennings had immediately agreed to pay for the booths and anything else his intellectual bodyguards needed. This was their chance to make a big impression. Warren Hicks, one leader of the 1990s fight against zoning, agreed to recruit people to help man the booth.

Justin and Pratik spent two grueling days answering questions, shrugging off insults, and distributing literature. As they had expected, many of the attendees were hostile. Some said that opponents of renters' protections shouldn't be allowed to vote or express their opinions in public. Justin and Pratik knew they would never change the minds of such people. They were at the convention to talk to those who were undecided.

One housing activist picked up their paper on rent control. He began reading as he walked away. He hadn't gone far before he turned around and stormed up to Justin and Pratik. "You are doing nothing but spreading lies!" he shouted. "You should be ashamed of yourself. There will not be a rent control board. It's a rent advisory council."

Pratik smiled and asked if he could see the offending piece of paper. When the activist handed it over, Pratik crossed out the words rent control board and wrote rent advisory council. Handing the paper back to the activist, Pratik said, "There, that should make you happy. I have corrected my lie."

The activist looked at what Pratik had done and crumbled up the paper. He threw the wad at Pratik and yelled, "You are still a liar." A crowd had formed to see what the commotion was about. The activist turned and pushed two older women out of his way. As one fell to the floor, he stomped off.

"Interesting," Pratik said. "He was so hung up on the name of the agency that he couldn't understand the principles we are addressing. Too bad we didn't record that."

Justin smiled and held up his phone. "But we did, my friend, we did. I'm going to write a short commentary about this and then upload it to our social media accounts. Viewers will see how unprincipled and rude the housing activists are. The name of the agency regulating rents isn't important and doesn't change our point. A rose by any other name is still a rose. An immoral and unjust regulatory agency remains immoral and unjust no matter what it is called."

Another activist argued that Justin and Pratik couldn't predict that rent control would be bad in Houston. "Sure," she admitted, "they have gone a little overboard in New York and San Francisco, but that is New York and San Francisco. We are going to have Houston-style rent control."

"And what is Houston-style rent control?" Justin asked. He remembered that thirty-years prior, zoning advocates had talked about Houston-style zoning.

"Instead of having the entire rent advisory council appointed by the mayor," she replied, "our city council members will each appoint one person to the board, and the rest will be democratically elected."

"Changing the way," Justin said, "that the advisory board is selected doesn't change the fact that certain principles underlie rent control, no matter which adjectives you put in front of it."

"But our rent control will come from the democratic process," she objected.

"Rent control forces landlords to rent their properties on terms that they would not voluntarily choose," Pratik said. "And that is true whether the controlling agency is appointed or elected. That is irrelevant. What is relevant is the fact that property owners will be forced to operate their businesses as others dictate, not as they would choose. That is unjust."

The activist smiled. "I guess we'll just have to agree to disagree." She started to walk away but suddenly turned around. "You guys are kind of cute. We could put aside our differences for a while and have some fun. Some girlfriends are coming to my place at seven, and it would be nice if you two joined us."

Justin and Pratik looked at one another and both winked.

Turning to the girl, they shook their heads and lied in unison, "We're gay." Though untrue, they had used that line many times before to reject unwanted propositions.

YOU THOUGHT I SUPPLIED AN ALIBI FOR YOU

February 2021

It was a Friday evening, and the Rev. Jamaal Wilkes was working on Sunday's sermon. The words normally came easily and eloquently, but tonight an ominous feeling was paralyzing his mind. He was reaching for the bottle of bourbon in his desk drawer when his office door opened. Charles Benton walked in and closed the door behind him.

"Good evening, Charles," Jamaal said with more enthusiasm than he felt. "To what do I owe this pleasure?"

Charles took a seat without being prompted. "We haven't spoken in some time, and I thought it would be good to catch up."

"I was just about to enjoy a little bourbon," Jamaal said. "Would you care to join me?"

"Certainly." Charles remained silent while Jamaal poured three fingers into two tumblers. His hand was shaking slightly as he slid one tumbler to the mayor and took a sip of his own drink. Charles didn't reach for the glass but simply stared at the minister.

"Well, this is a wonderful conversation we are having. Was

there something in particular that you wanted to discuss?" Jamaal asked.

"Actually, there is." Charles picked up the glass in front of him and drained the contents. He needed the liquid courage that the alcohol would provide. "I've learned some things about that night. Some things that I believe you will find interesting."

Jamaal drained his own glass and picked up the bottle. He held it to Charles but was waved off. "I'm all ears," he said as he poured himself another three fingers.

"I don't know why it didn't occur to me before, but this was a clue that everyone overlooked. Including the police, I might add. I can't fault them for that oversight, because they had the testimony of an eyewitness."

Jamaal shifted in his chair but remained silent. Charles felt his heart pounding in his chest and took a deep breath to calm himself. "I think I will take a little more of the fine bourbon," he said. Jamaal slid the bottle to the mayor, who poured himself two fingers.

"You told the police that you came upon Devon and me fighting. Devon had a knife that I somehow took from him. I proceeded to stab him to death. Your story had credibility because, as you said, I had also suffered several stab wounds. You later confided in me that you had stabbed me to bolster your story. How am I doing so far?"

Jamaal nodded and took a sip of his drink.

"Your story coincided with all the evidence at the scene. So, the police had little reason to question it or look for other explanations. After all, it was just another sad instance of one black man killing another. Devon's death was ruled an act of self-defense, and no charges were filed against me. But I have been punished ever since." Charles took a sip of bourbon.

"You led me to believe that you had saved me from prison, that I had attacked Devon and killed him. You have used that to manipulate and control me. Your plan has worked well." Charles finished his bourbon and slammed the glass onto the desk. "Until today."

Now, Jamaal could feel his own heart pounding in his chest. This son of a bitch has figured it out. But he can't prove it. There was no evidence at the scene.

"I don't know all the details about what happened that night," Charles said calmly. "For example, I don't know how I got Rohypnol in my system. I don't know if Devon attacked me, or if I attacked him. But I know I didn't stab him to death. You did. And then you tried to make it look like I was the killer. You wanted me to have a lifelong debt to you, and you nearly succeeded. But tonight, I say, this shit will be no more."

Jamaal had barely spoken since Charles entered his office. "I suppose I shouldn't be upset that you finally figured out the truth. I got twenty years out of that story, and I've done fairly well. Of course, I helped your career too, so it wasn't a completely one-sided deal."

"Why?" Charles shouted. "Why in the hell would you do such a thing? You framed me and then provided me with an alibi. How sick and twisted is that? Why did you kill Devon?"

"I had no intention of killing him," Jamaal said without thinking. The bourbon had gone to his head. "Tino was supposed to slip the roofie into Devon's beer, but that shit head put it in yours. I had planned to follow Devon when he left the bar and beat the hell out of him. The roofie would make it easy to do. I was tired of him treating me like a dog. I figured that if I beat the hell out of him, he might show me a little respect. When I saw you stumble out of the bar, it never occurred to me that Tino had fucked up. When Devon came out, I followed him. He saw you before I did, lying in Miss Betty's yard. He started shouting at you, telling you to stand up and fight like a man. By the time I could see the two of you, he had kicked you at least once. I yelled at him to stop, and he turned to face me. He pulled out a knife."

"When he realized it was me, he relaxed. 'Get out of here, you little pussy,' he said, 'or I'll kick the shit out of you too.' I snapped and ran at him in several long strides and then jumped into the air. I had planned to kick him in the head, but he raised his arm, and I connected with his right arm. The knife flew out of his hand and landed beside me. He charged me as I picked up the knife. I slashed at him several times, to no avail. I finally connected, and then again. He fell to the ground, and I pounced on him. I stabbed him over and over. As I lay there panting, I realized I would be in great trouble. You, however, could have an alibi supplied by me."

"The irony of this is that for all these years, you thought I supplied an alibi for you. In fact, you've been supplying an alibi for me."

Charles stood. "I never want to see you again. You disgust me." Charles walked out of the room and didn't bother closing the door. When he exited the front of the church, four police officers entered. The police chief was waiting for Charles. "We got it all. Jamaal will be charged with Devon Little's murder. I was skeptical about wiring you, but you were right."

WHAT ABOUT A DEBATE?

February 2021

"It's not looking good, boys," Buford Jennings said. "The most recent poll shows 62 percent supporting renters' protections. Granted, we gained three points from the last poll, but we need to make a lot more progress than that. What do you plan to do?"

"We understand your concern about the poll numbers," Justin said. "We would like to have seen a bigger move, but we still have nine weeks before the vote. That means we need to improve just over one percentage point per week." Justin wasn't as optimistic as he was trying to sound.

"We have made a lot of progress in the past three months. We have been giving at least ten talks a week. To date, we've met with almost eighty different groups since we submitted the petitions. The *News Journal* is ignoring us, but a few of the talk radio shows have had us on and we are getting at least five emails a day from independent journalists and bloggers from around the city. And the followers on our social media accounts are approaching one-hundred thousand. We are getting the word out."

"That's all great, but apparently the word that you are getting out isn't working," Buford objected. "I told you two a long time ago that you are too intellectual for the average person. You need to dumb it down."

Warren Hicks had been silent, but he spoke up. He spoke in a soft yet compelling manner that demanded attention. "Buford," Warren replied, "when we were fighting against zoning, we didn't dumb it down. We presented many of the same principles that Justin and Pratik are addressing, and we did it similarly. It worked back then, and we are confident that it will work again today. Dumbing down the message means distorting the message, and distorting one's message is never an effective strategy."

"Times have changed," Buford snorted. "Back then, nobody would have even considered renters' protections. Now, the city council is handing them out like cheap candy. I don't see how the zoning debate is relevant today. Different times. Different people. Different issues."

"Same principles," Warren replied. "You hired Justice Inc to do a job, and I think you are getting your money's worth. I have spent considerable time talking with them and mentoring them. I must admit that I didn't develop the understanding and ability to articulate ideas well until I was much older than they are. Also, during the debate over zoning, polls routinely showed that 60 percent or more the voters supported zoning. The polls were wrong then, and I don't give the current polls a lot of credibility."

Buford shook his head in frustration. He felt like they were ganging up on him. Suddenly, his eyes lit up. "What about a debate?"

"That is an interesting idea, but who would we debate?" Warren asked.

"I don't know. There are all kinds of idiots on the other side. I'm sure one or two of them are stupid enough to debate you."

"I know almost nothing about debating," Pratik said. "I watched some of the presidential debates last year and found them to be absolutely useless. It would have to be Justin."

"Keep in mind the number of candidates who took part in those debates," Warren explained. "Sometimes there were eight or nine. Each candidate gets little time to speak and develop a policy. So, they snipe at one another and try to give good sound bites. But we don't have to do it that way."

"What do you mean?" Buford asked. Justin and Pratik turned to Warren.

"The structure of a debate has a lot to do with its effectiveness in educating voters. For example, one way to structure a debate is to allow each side a set time for an opening statement. Then, each side gets a set time for rebuttals. And you can have any number of rebuttals. Or, after opening statements, the two sides are asked questions from the audience. Or, you can have a moderator ask the questions. All of these can be effective, but not necessarily equally."

"Which do you think would be best?" Pratik asked.

Warren thought for a moment. "I see ways in which any of them might be best. Doing an opening statement and then rebuttals allows more time to speak. Plus, we know the other sides' positions much better than they know ours. So, it could be easy to keep them on their heels. Of course, that could happen to us too, but I doubt it. Taking questions from the audience would allow us to address the specific concerns of voters. It would be more like a dialogue than a lecture. Having the moderator ask the questions would allow us to pre-screen them. That would allow us to prepare, but it provides the same benefit to the other side. I need to give more thought to this."

"This could be the difference between winning and losing," Buford said gleefully. "Nearly everyone in Houston will have a chance to hear your message, not just the few dozen who show up at a civic club meeting."

"If we are going to make this happen, we'll need to move fast," Justin said. "I'm not sure that I'm up for a debate. Let me think about this overnight, and we can talk again tomorrow."

* * *

"I'm willing to do a debate," Justin said the next day. "However, we need to find a high-profile opponent. Otherwise, it would be like the Astros playing a local high school team. The Astros would certainly win, but they wouldn't impress anyone in doing so."

"Jamaal Wilkes is probably out of the question since he got arrested," Pratik said. "I doubt that any of the council members would debate you. What about Escobar? She's certainly high profile, and she seems to love being on television. Many people would tune in just to see what crazy things she might say."

Justin winced. The mere thought of trying to respond to Escobar's incoherent statements made his head hurt. But Pratik had a valid point. "Do you think she would do it?"

Pratik smiled. "We won't know until we ask. I will contact her office as soon as we are done here."

I WILL WIPE THE FLOOR WITH THIS KID

February 2021

"I think you are making a huge mistake," Tilde said. "There is nothing to be gained by doing this."

"If I want your opinion," Marta Escobar retorted, "I will ask for it. I don't, so I didn't. But since you think that I'm making a mistake, why don't you tell me why?"

"There is no upside. And there is lots of potential downsides. What if Jamaal gets convicted? How will it look for the county judge to have supported a murderer?"

"We don't know that he is guilty," Escobar objected. "And even if he did it, he was only a child at the time. In my book, he has redeemed himself with his work since."

"A lot of voters won't see it that way. They will see it as more evidence that you are soft on crime."

Escobar waved her hand dismissively. "Those people will never vote for me, no matter what I do. Many people idolize Rev. Wilkes. Supporting him at a time like this will endear me to them."

"But what if he is convicted?"

"That's even better. I can say that I don't know what troubles he experienced in his youth, but I know what kind of man he has become. If anyone deserves a second chance, it is the Rev.

Wilkes. I can say that he has fought tirelessly for the poor, the downtrodden, people of color, yada, yada, yada. My base will love it. And don't forget, I am up for re-election next year. His followers will love it too. There is no downside."

"Is that all you care about? Getting re-elected?"

"Yes. What else do politicians care about? They say whatever they need to say to get elected. Then, once they are in office, they spend most of their time running for re-election. When you have built your base, you run for a higher office. Rinse and repeat. I didn't invent this game we call our political system. But I sure as hell am going to play it with conviction. And that means doing whatever it takes, including saying things I don't really mean."

"I didn't know you were so cynical," the assistant said.

"That's not cynicism. That is realism. I'm just recognizing the reality of modern politics. I don't know what your problem is. You seem to enjoy the perks of being around power."

"What does that have to do with it?"

"Some people are cut out to be leaders. Other people—like you—don't have what it takes. But they can be very useful. Many like being around those who do have what it takes because there are a lot of benefits to being associated with people with power. And there is nothing wrong with that. We need people like you."

The assistant furrowed her brow in bewilderment. "Should I take that as an insult or a compliment?"

Escobar smiled. "Take it any way you want. So, do you still think that I am making a mistake?"

The assistant shrugged. "I don't know. You make some good points. But my gut tells me that this is a mistake. Oh, before I forget, one of those boys behind the petition drive called this afternoon. He is proposing a debate between you and his partner —that Justin kid. I almost told him no on the spot, but then I thought I should at least tell you first."

Escobar's mouth was agape. "You're shitting me. Why would they do that? I am a county official. The referendum is a city issue. It makes no sense."

"He didn't think that the fact that you are a county official really mattered. You know the arguments in favor of renters' protections as well as anyone, and they want to debate the best."

"I'll do it," Escobar said enthusiastically.

Now the assistant's mouth was agape. "Seriously? Again, there is no upside."

Escobar shook her head. "Tilde, that is why you will never amount to anything. You can't see opportunities when they are biting you in the ass. We can make this a high-profile event. I will get the vote of every renter and poor person, as well as the people of color vote. This is a golden opportunity. I will wipe the floor with this kid and become the county's champion for the underdog in the process."

"He may not be such a pushover. He seems very articulate and sure of himself."

"So? I'll simply point out that helping renters is the moral thing to do. He can articulate all he wants, but he can't talk himself out of that rabbit hole. I have the moral high ground and nothing he says will change that fact. Did he say when they want to do this?"

"No. He said we can discuss dates and venues. Do you have any preferences?"

Escobar thought for a moment. "The referendum is in eight weeks. A week or two before the vote would be good. The debate will be fresh in everyone's mind, so victory in the referendum will be assured. As far as the venue is concerned, it should be large. I bet Jamaal could get a lot of his people in the audience to cheer for me. NRG is obviously too big, but the convention center there might be good."

The assistant was looking at the calendar on her phone. How about the last Saturday in March? That will be ten days before the referendum."

"Perfect. That is way more time than I will need to prepare. This is going to be fun." Tilde frowned. She wasn't as optimistic as her boss.

THE MORAL HIGH GROUND

February 2021

The second half of February was a flurry of activity as both sides of the referendum prepared their final push before the April vote.

The *News Journal* began another series of articles in support of renters' protections. Each day, the feature story highlighted how renter protections would benefit a particular family. Nearly every story featured Black and Hispanic families. In the interest of diversity, the paper included one story about an Asian family and one about a white family.

* * *

Much to the surprise of Buford, Warren, Justin, and Pratik, Marta Escobar accepted the offer to debate. The two sides spent nearly a week negotiating the details of the debate, including format, location, and length. Escobar wanted a town hall style debate, in which audience members would ask questions and both parties would then answer. Warren did not like this format. He suspected Escobar would stack the audience with individuals favorable to the renters' protections. The questions would be loaded, and Justin would spend most of his time pointing out fallacies, rather than making substantive statements.

Justin suggested having a moderator ask questions. Each side would then have a set time to respond. They would then have a shorter period to offer a rebuttal. They would alternate answering first. Justin and Escobar would each submit twenty questions, and the moderator would randomly select the questions to be asked. They would begin the debate with each giving a five-minute introduction to their position. The debate would end with each giving a five-minute summary. Justin also suggested Roger Mason to moderate.

Given Mason's hostility towards Escobar, at first, she was adamantly opposed to that idea. It was pointed out that Mason would not be speaking. He would merely ask questions and keep time. If he were the moderator, he would promote the debate on his program, and that would help increase the viewing audience. This last point finally swayed Escobar to agree. She wanted to maximize her exposure. Like Escobar, Mason was always looking for ways to increase his exposure, and he quickly agreed to moderate the debate.

Escobar suggested the Toyota Center for the debate. It could hold eighteen thousand people, which gave Justin pause. Such a turnout seemed ridiculously optimistic to Justin, given that the debate would be live streamed on social media. Escobar had already indicated that she might suspend the mask mandate for the event. Justin concluded she intended to bring in her supporters to fill the arena. He agreed to the venue, with one stipulation—each side would get nine thousand tickets to distribute as they chose. Escobar reluctantly accepted the counterproposal.

Justin preferred a longer debate, which he believed would work to his advantage. He would have more time to point out flaws and fallacies in Escobar's arguments. The longer the debate, the more time he would have to refute her claims and assertions. She, too, wanted a longer debate, as this would give her more time in front of the camera. They agreed to two hours, with the stipulation that upon agreement of both sides, the debate would be extended thirty minutes.

With the details agreed to, the two sides began preparing for the debate on March 27.

* * *

Jamaal Wilkes was out of jail on bail, awaiting trial later in the year. He was maintaining a low public profile, but worked diligently behind the scenes in opposition to the referendum. He was also arranging for nine thousand renters and their advocates to attend the debate. Escobar had given him all the tickets allotted for her.

Marta Escobar, Lia Patel, and Roderick Jackson all issued statements of support for Jamaal. They cited his years of good work as evidence that a mistake in his youth should be forgiven. They neglected to mention the fact that the mistake, as they called it, was a premeditated act of violence.

* * *

As soon as Escobar agreed to the debate, Justin and Pratik began preparing. They printed out copies of every statement, press briefing, or speech that Escobar had made since she first declared her candidacy for county judge. Justin wanted a comprehensive understanding of her worldview. It would enable him to better anticipate her comments and respond appropriately.

While Justin reviewed Escobar's public statements, Pratik began drafting the twenty questions that they would submit to Mason. They wanted to cover a wide range of concrete issues, but wanted the questions formulated to allow Justin to expose the moral premises underlying each side's position. Justin knew that he could state Escobar's premises, but it would be more effective if she would state them, even if only implicitly. Justin could then use her words to explain those premises more explicitly. In doing so, he would seize the moral high ground.

* * *

For her part, Marta Escobar did nothing to prepare for the

debate. She believed she had the moral high ground, and all she had to do was state why renters' protections are moral. There would be no debating about that fact. And she had two pages of statistics detailing the dire situation that low-income households were facing to prove her point. As far as she was concerned, that was game, set, and match.

I HAVE AN ACE
UP MY SLEEVE

March 2021

"What if those kids show up at the convention?" Charles Benton asked Marta Escobar. They were sitting in the mayor's office shortly after announcing a renters' protections convention being co-sponsored by the city and the county. The event was scheduled for the same day as the debate.

"That would be great," Escobar answered. "Let them wear themselves out before the debate. It really doesn't matter. I am going to wipe the floor with him."

"You sound very confident," Charles replied. "How is your preparation going? I used to spend an insane amount of time preparing for a debate."

Escobar waved her hand. "I'm not doing anything. What is there to prepare? The arguments I will make are straightforward. I've been doing it for nearly a year. I could probably do it in my sleep."

Charles frowned. "These kids seem pretty sharp. I wouldn't sell them short. They have come up with some novel arguments. God, I wish they were on our side of this."

"I have morality on my side, and that will trump anything that he can say." Escobar thought for a moment. "Landlords are putting profits before people. That is outrageously immoral. At a time like this, everyone needs to do their fair share. But landlords don't want to do their part. All they care about is making money. Voters will not be happy about that. That Walker kid will have to defend greed, and he can't do it."

"Why are you doing this debate? What's in it for you?"

"Charles, you know how the game is played. You are always positioning yourself for the next office. This is going to give me tremendous exposure and make me a champion to the poor and people of color. I'll have their vote from now until the day I die. And I'd like to see the referendum defeated. I don't like the idea of two young kids getting away with disrupting the democratic process."

"Isn't the referendum a part of that process?"

"Come on Charles," Escobar snorted. "We're alone here and you don't need to lay a snow job on me. That might work on the voters, but we are elected to do a job. These kids are interfering with our ability to do that."

The mayor silently stared at the judge. "I still think that you are underestimating them."

"Perhaps so," Escobar said with a sly smile, "but I have an ace up my sleeve. It would look bad for their side if they didn't even show up for the debate, wouldn't it?"

* * *

"I told you there was a conspiracy," Buford Jennings said. "Those bastards have been planning this for some time."

"Maybe so," Pratik said, "but we can't do anything about it."

"We could sue them and file for an injunction to stop the convention," Buford replied. "We can't let them get away with this."

"When life hands you lemons," Justin retorted, "make lemonade. Yes, the timing is suspicious. Maybe we can use it to our advantage. We could have a booth and get a lot of literature handed out. Combined with the debate, a ton of people can hear our message."

Pratik shook his head. "You can't man the booth. You have the debate to worry about."

Justin frowned. "The convention center is less than two blocks from the Toyota Center. I could work the booth until late afternoon and then walk over to the Toyota Center."

"No, Justin," Warren said as he shook his head. "You need to rest that day. A two-hour debate will be grueling, and you need to be at your best. I can get people to man the booth. I got help the last time."

"You're right, Warren," Justin conceded reluctantly. "We will need to order more literature. We have some things left from the last convention, but not enough. If we had more time, we could incorporate some of our latest writings. I'd love to get Pratik's piece titled 'The Creed of Sacrifice' into more hands. But we only have two weeks."

"I could have it formatted and submitted this afternoon," Pratik said. "We already have a template for our literature, so formatting will be easy. We should be fine. I think we should also print Warren's pieces 'Celebrate the Producers' and 'The Morality of Profits.' Can you think of anything else?"

Justin thought for a moment and then shook his head. "No, that should be enough. We don't want to overwhelm people with information, and I think those are our most powerful pieces." Warren nodded in agreement.

Pratik nodded. "Okay, I will get working on it immediately. And you, my friend, need to get back to your preparation."

NOW WHAT AM I GOING TO DO?

March 2021

The big day had finally arrived. At 6:30 P.M. the debate that might shape Houston's future would occur. It had dominated the news for the previous two weeks. In a superficial attempt to appear objective, a few news outlets had even contacted Justice Inc for comments. Anything said by Justin or Pratik was heavily edited, and the media reported nothing of substance.

All the tickets for the event had been distributed. Jamaal had given more than a thousand tickets to homeless people camping near the Toyota Center. As an enticement to attend, he had also given them vouchers for food and beverages inside the arena. Combined with two nights free room and board at the convention center, Rev. Wilkes was a hero to these homeless men and women. The remaining tickets were given to housing activists and tenants' unions.

As Justin and Pratik had expected, Roger Mason promoted the debate on his show. Within an hour of his first mention of the debate, over two thousand listeners requested tickets. When Justin and Pratik learned of this, they let Mason handle the distribution of their tickets. It would be one less thing for them to worry about.

The Friday night before the debate, Justin and Pratik stayed at the Four Seasons Hotel in downtown Houston. It was only three blocks from the Toyota Center and four blocks from the convention center. Pratik and Warren had reluctantly agreed that Justin could help man their booth in the morning. Justin would return to their hotel room after lunch to rest and do any final preparation for the debate. Warren Hicks had come through with eight volunteers to help man the booth. It promised to be an exciting day.

An hour before the convention opened at nine Saturday morning, a line three blocks long had formed. As exhibitors, Justin and Pratik could enter the building through the back. By some stroke of luck, they had been given a booth near the entrance. When the doors opened, the first sight many visitors saw was the large Justice Inc banner. Many recognized Justin and Pratik and more than a few shouted profanities and insults. But a surprising number came to the booth to talk to the two intellectual bodyguards, pick up literature and make friendly comments.

The volunteers recruited by Warren Hicks insisted they could man the booth for the afternoon until the convention closed at six that evening. After more than three hours on their feet, Justin and Pratik welcomed the chance for a leisurely lunch and some quiet time in their hotel room. Just after three in the afternoon, Pratik received a call from one volunteer. A constable had come to the booth looking for Justin. The volunteers told the police officer they didn't know where Justin was. As the constable walked away, he immediately made a phone call. While the volunteers couldn't hear what he was saying, it was clear that he was very agitated.

Ten minutes later, Marta Escobar received a phone call from a sergeant in the Precinct One constable's office. Justin Walker was not at the convention center, and nobody seemed to know where he was. "What the hell?" Escobar shouted. "Wasn't he there earlier?"

"Yes," the sergeant said.

"Why didn't you detain him then?" Escobar demanded.

"We were told to wait until three."

"How did he slip away? Weren't you keeping an eye on him? This is fucking ridiculous."

"Our instructions were to confirm his presence in the morning. We did that. When an officer went to detain him at three, he was no longer present. We could detain him once he arrives at the Toyota Center," the sergeant suggested.

Escobar considered that for a moment. "No, that will look suspicious. Plus, the press will be there. I gave explicit instructions and you people have fucked up my plan. I knew that I should have defunded you when I had a chance." She disconnected the call and threw her phone against the wall. "Shit, shit, shit," she muttered. "Now what am I going to do?"

Escobar had planned to have Justin detained and questioned about alleged vandalism of pro-renters' protections signs. The allegations were merely a pretense to prevent Justin from attending the debate. Now, Escobar had to go with Plan B. Unfortunately for her, she had no Plan B.

WE ARE OUR BROTHER'S KEEPERS

March 2021

Justin and Pratik entered the Toyota Center just before five. They were directed to the floor of the arena and spotted Roger Mason. He was talking to several television reporters. "How long do you think he can refrain from insulting Escobar?" Pratik joked.

"He won't make it through the introductions," Justin predicted.

The next ninety minutes were spent testing microphones, lighting, and reviewing the rules of the debate. The doors to the arena opened an hour before the debate would begin. By the time Roger Mason started the introductions, there were very few empty seats.

Just before Justin walked onto the stage, Warren Hicks pulled him aside. "Justin, are you nervous?" The younger man nodded. Warren smiled. "Good. I'd be concerned if you weren't. Nervousness is normal. It can be a good thing if you don't let it overwhelm you. It can help you stay focused on what is important. You'll do well."

Roger Mason sat in the middle of the stage. Justin sat ten feet to his right, and Escobar sat ten feet to the left. Five television cameras were spaced in front of the stage. Justin was surprised at the intensity of the lights. He could feel a few beads of sweat forming on his brow. He wasn't sure if it was from the heat of the lamps or his nervousness. Each of the debaters would speak at their own podium, which was slightly angled to allow them to look at their opponent, as well as the audience, as they spoke.

"Good evening, ladies and gentlemen," Mason began. "In ten days, Houstonians will be asked to decide the future of our city. Will we head into the cesspool of socialism, or will we retain our liberty?" Justin looked over at Pratik, who was sitting in the front row. Pratik nodded and smiled. Mason hadn't explicitly named Escobar, but the target of his insult was clear to everyone.

"Tonight, we will hear arguments for both sides of the upcoming referendum to repeal the city's renters' protections. In opposition to the referendum is Harris County Judge Marta Escobar. Supporting the referendum is Mr. Justin Walker. The format for tonight's debate is: Each side will make a five-minute introductory statement. In a coin flip, Ms. Escobar will go first. Following the introductory statements, each side will be given two minutes for rebuttal. I will then ask a question that both debaters will have four minutes to answer. We will continue with this format until our time is up. Prior to this evening, both sides submitted twenty questions. I will select the questions randomly and we will alternate who answers first. We will conclude with five-minute closing statements from each side. If, at the end of two hours, both sides agree to continue, we will extend the debate for thirty minutes. Otherwise, we will move on to the closing statements. With those formalities out of the way, let's have some fun. The floor is yours, Ms. Escobar."

Marta Escobar stood and walked to her podium. She was dressed in her lucky purple business suit. "An event like this does not happen magically. Many people worked behind the scenes to make this debate possible, and I would be remiss if I failed to thank them. Of course, I can't thank everyone, or we would be here all night. However, a few deserve special mention. First and foremost, I'd like to thank my assistant, Tilde Garcia. She worked late many nights while we were negotiating the details of tonight's debate, and her tireless efforts enabled me to focus my efforts on leading the county government.

"As you know, we have been in the midst of a pandemic for a year. We are winning the fight against COVID, but much work still needs to be done. I beseech each and every one of you to continue to do your part and take the recommended precautions. You can be a part of the solution, or you can be a part of the problem." She turned and stared at Mason as she uttered the last sentence.

"I'd also like to thank the fine staff here at the Toyota Center for making all the arrangements. When we called to inquire about using the arena, they were quick to volunteer the facility at no charge. They even agreed to discount the prices for food and beverages. That is the kind of corporate spirit that is so desperately needed in these troubling times.

Escobar took a sip of water and looked at the timer that showed she still had a little over three minutes. Christ, she thought, five minutes is a long time to talk. She usually just talked until she said what she had to say, and she was seldom concerned about the time. "Mayor Charles Benton deserves a special thank you for suggesting this debate. He thought it important for voters to hear both sides of this issue in order to make an informed decision. I will admit that I was hesitant at first, because I am a county official. But he pointed out that I am also a Houstonian and have been a leading voice for renters' protections. I am honored that he thought I would be the best representative for the city's ordinance.

"Finally, I would like to thank Mr. Walker for graciously agreeing to this debate. It must be difficult for such a young man to stand before so many people to debate serious issues. We will all understand if he appears nervous and stumbles on his words. I remember my first public appearance as a candidate for the office I now hold. My nerves were so worked up I forgot what I was going to say, and I had note cards in front of me." Escobar laughed nervously. "I wound up telling a joke that nobody found funny.

"Mr. Mason said that this referendum is about the future of Houston. I agree. However, I don't agree that the choice we face is between socialism and liberty. The choice is between compassion and greed. Do we want to help our most vulnerable citizens, or do we want greedy corporate landlords to reap outrageous profits while tens of thousands are homeless? The decision we make will add to the number of homeless people or keep people housed. We must decide whether we want to enable families to live with dignity, or do we want to allow them to suffer?

"This is a moral issue. We are our brother's keepers. We have a moral duty to help those less fortunate. In ten days, when you enter the voting booth, you will face the choice of voting for need or voting for greed. I trust you will make the right choice. Thank you."

Mason looked at the timer. "You still have seventy-five seconds, judge." Escobar waved him off and sat down.

A CHOICE BETWEEN SLAVERY AND FREEDOM

March 2021

Roger Mason turned to Justin. "Mr. Walker, would you like to make your opening statement?"

Justin nodded, stood, and took two steps to his podium. "In the Declaration of Independence, Thomas Jefferson wrote that all individuals are endowed with certain unalienable rights, including life, liberty, and the pursuit of happiness. We have heard these words many times since childhood, but what do they mean? How do they apply to the issues before us tonight?

"The right to life means the freedom to live as one chooses. The right to liberty means the freedom to act as one thinks best. The right to the pursuit of happiness means the freedom to choose both the ends and the means to achieve satisfaction, joy, and happiness. These rights are exercised through another right —the right to property. The right to property means the freedom to produce, trade, and use material values, such as smartphones, televisions, automobiles, computer repairs, and housing.

"Consider for a moment how much of your waking time is devoted to producing, trading, or using material values? If you are like most people, you spend almost all your time doing one of these things. When you go to work, you produce material values. When you go to the grocery store or the mall, you are trading for values. When you surf the Internet or watch a movie, you are using values. The rights to life, liberty, and the pursuit of happiness mean the freedom to produce, trade, and use the values that sustain and enhance our lives.

"The right to property, like all rights, imposes a negative demand on others. They must refrain from using physical coercion to interfere with our actions. Each individual has a moral right to act as he judges best, but he cannot force others to act against their own judgment. Regarding property, an individual has a right to produce whatever values he chooses and others must respect his freedom to do so. He has a right to sell those values to willing buyers, but he cannot force anyone to buy his products or services. He has a right to use those values if he chooses, as well as use the values that he obtains through trade. We cannot exercise the rights to life, liberty, and the pursuit of happiness without the right to property.

"These rights apply to all individuals, black and white, male and female, gay and heterosexual. They apply to tenants and landlords. They apply to every individual in this building, to every individual watching on television or the Internet, to every individual. Everyone has a right to produce, trade, and use values without physical interference from others. Protecting this right must be the standard by which we judge every government policy, including renters' protections.

"When a robber sticks a gun in your face and demands your money, he is using force to deprive you of your property. He is violating your right to use and trade your money as you judge best. The same is true of any law that compels individuals to produce, use, or trade values in a manner that they did not voluntarily choose.

"The so-called renters' protections passed or considered by the city violate the property rights of landlords and developers. Rent control, for example, forces landlords to accept a rent that they would not voluntarily agree to. The landlord is denied the right to trade on terms that he finds acceptable. Ban the box forces landlords to ignore information that might help them make wise decisions regarding tenants. Again, the landlord is forced to act in a manner he would not voluntarily choose. And this is true of all these so-called renters' protections. All of them force landlords to act contrary to their own judgment.

"In violating property rights, renters' protections deny landlords the right to life, liberty, and the pursuit of happiness. Landlords are denied the right to live as they choose, to take the actions they think necessary to achieve their happiness. Instead, they are forced to act as others deem best.

"Other people do not always make decisions with which we agree. When that occurs, we can attempt to persuade them to act differently. Or we can force them to act differently. Persuasion or force—these are the two alternatives. The advocates of renters' protections do not attempt to persuade landlords to act differently. They resort to the coercive power of government to force landlords to act as they—housing activists and tenants— think best. The landlord is forced to produce and trade a value— housing—on terms that he did not choose or agree to.

"An individual who is forced to produce and trade on terms he does not voluntarily accept is nothing more than a slave. Whether the terms of production and trade are dictated by a slave master with a whip or a politician with a pen doesn't change that fact.

"I seldom agree with Judge Escobar, but I agree with her that it is desirable for low-income households to afford safe, decent housing. The affordable housing crisis is a supply shortage. There isn't enough affordable housing. The solution to a supply shortage isn't price controls and other regulations. The solution is to restore freedom to the producers.

"In ten days, you will have a choice between slavery and freedom. You will have the choice to vote to protect the freedom of individuals to produce and trade as they think best or to vote to force them to act as the city council demands. Thank you."

Justin returned to his chair just as the timer sounded.

RIGHTS PERTAIN TO FREEDOM OF ACTION

March 2021

Much of the audience erupted in boos and shouts of derision. An equally large portion of the audience clapped and shouted encouragement. The din continued for nearly a minute before Roger Mason acted. "Ladies and gentlemen, I must ask you to refrain from such outbursts," Mason's voice boomed through the overhead speakers. "We are here to have a civil dialogue, and if you cannot respect that fact, I must ask you to leave." The audience was suddenly silent. "Very well," Mason said, "Judge Escobar, you have two minutes for rebuttal."

Escobar walked to her podium. "I'm not sure where to begin. I didn't know that it was possible to make so many outrageous statements in only five minutes. Mr. Walker talked a lot about rights. I'd like to talk about rights too. I'd like to talk about the rights that Mr. Walker failed to mention.

"The first of these rights is the right to safe, decent housing. We live in the richest country is the history of the human race, and yet nearly half of our citizens struggle to stay housed. Too many people spend half of their income on housing. That is not acceptable. It is a moral outrage.

"The private sector obviously has no interest in providing

affordable housing for low-income households, particularly if those households include people of color. If the private sector won't do it, then the government must step in.

"The second right that Mr. Walker failed to mention is the right to a living wage. He said that requiring landlords to provide decent housing at an affordable rate is slavery. What about all those people working for minimum wage? They are wage slaves. It is impossible to raise a family on minimum wage.

"Of course, Mr. Walker doesn't care about the poor or people of color. He only cares about protecting the profits of his greedy corporate sponsors. He is putting profits before people. We must put people first, and if that means some landlords lose a little of their profits, so be it." Escobar turned and walked to her seat with fifteen seconds remaining on her timer.

Mason said nothing to Escobar this time. Instead, he turned to Justin and said, "Mr. Walker, your rebuttal, please."

Justin stood and walked to his podium. "If we are going to make the best decisions regarding renters' protections, then we must consider the full context, all the relevant information and facts. There is no such thing as a right to housing or a right to a living wage. Rights pertain to freedom of action. There is a right to produce housing or trade with others to obtain housing, but there is no right to force others to provide that housing. There is a right to improve one's skills to obtain a higher wage, but there is no right to force an employer to pay a specific wage.

"Advocating for the right to some value means the annihilation of all rights. It means that individuals are entitled to a value regardless of their own actions, or despite their actions. If they don't produce that value or trade for it, then others must provide that value to them. Consider the so-called right to a living wage as an example. If an employee has a right to $15 an hour, then an employer must pay that wage regardless of his own judgment, regardless of the employee's skills. The employer must pay that wage whether or not the employee is worth it. The employee receives a higher wage, not because he has earned it, but because the employer is forced to pay it.

"Or consider the alleged right to housing. If an individual cannot or does not provide for his own housing needs, then others must provide it, lest they be guilty of violating his rights. That means that others must produce housing for him, regardless of their own desires, needs, or judgment.

"Finally, Judge Escobar says that it is impossible to raise a family making minimum wage. This is probably true. But we must ask why someone making less than a thousand dollars a month is trying to raise a family. He clearly does not have the financial resources to do so. His plight is a consequence of his own choices. Judge Escobar's solution is to force business owners to act against their own choices." Once again, Justin took his seat as his timer went off.

WE MUST FREE THE HOUSING PRODUCERS

March 2021

Roger Mason held up a stack of cards. "Now we enter the question round. As I said before, each of our debaters submitted twenty questions. I will select a card at random and read the questions. Each side will have four minutes to answer, and then an additional two minutes for rebuttal. Obviously, we will not get through all the questions this evening." Mason shuffled the cards and then spread them out on the desk before him. With a dramatic flair, he pulled a card from the pile and read, "Houston, like most cities in America, has a severe shortage of housing for low-income families. What do you think is the cause and the cure for this housing crisis? Mr. Walker, you get to answer first."

That's a good question, Justin thought as he approached the podium. I'm glad Pratik suggested it. "The housing crisis is a very complex issue with many factors contributing to it. In most cities, single-family zoning is a primary cause. Houston does not have zoning, so we cannot say that is the cause of our housing shortage. However, the lack of comprehensive zoning does not mean that there are no land-use regulations affecting development and housing in Houston. There is a litany of such regulations. To name a few, setbacks, parking space requirements, and a time-consuming permitting and approval process. Admittedly, Houston's regulations are more friendly towards housing construction than many cities, but these regulations add to the cost of housing.

"The city's building code also adds to the cost. Energy efficiency requirements, for example, force builders to include features that some homebuyers may not want because they cannot afford them. But the city requires them in new construction. The result is higher priced housing.

"Another significant factor is minimum lot size regulations. It varies around the city, but 5,000 square feet is common. This has the same impact as single-family zoning—it makes housing less dense. It would be possible to build two or more housing units on that lot, but regulations prohibit that. By arbitrarily removing land from use for housing, the cost of that land increases. And that too adds to the cost of housing. To illustrate, let us say that a plot of land costs $150,000 to purchase. That price is low inside The Loop, but it will suffice for this example. If construction costs are $120 per square foot, a modest 1,000 square foot house would cost $270,000 to build with land costs. This is unaffordable for a low-income family. However, if that lot could hold three homes, the land cost for each drops to $50,000 and the price of the house would be $170,000. This example illustrates the impact that land-use regulations have on housing costs.

Regulations, in short, make it extremely difficult to build affordable housing profitably for low-income families. That is the cause of the housing crisis. The cure is to remove the regulations that make low-cost housing impossible to build. The cure is to remove the shackles from builders and developers.

"In a free market, producers offer a wide range of products for every price level. This is true of smartphones, automobiles, televisions, and nearly every other product. Manufacturers can do this by including fewer features or lower quality materials.

The same would be true of housing producers if they were free.

"I hasten to add that using lower-quality materials does not mean shoddy construction. Lower quality materials might mean using Formica countertops instead of granite, forgoing double-paned windows, or installing carpet instead of hardwood floors. Developers could build safe, decent housing without all the bells and whistles that building codes often require. They could do so at a price point that is affordable to more people.

"There is an enormous need for low-income housing. Nobody denies that. But low-income families have a need for an abundance of other products and services. They can afford those products because producers can profitably manufacture and sell them. The producers can do so because they are relatively free. If we want to solve the housing crisis, then we must free the housing producers.

Roger Mason nodded toward Marta Escobar. "Judge Escobar, would you like to answer the question?"

Escobar rose from her seat and paused for a moment before approaching the podium. "Mr. Walker is correct when he says the housing crisis is a very complex issue. However, he offers us the simplistic solution of repealing regulations. He is advocating for a return to the days of the Wild West and doggy dog competition. He wants developers to do anything they choose, anywhere they choose to do it. That's not a solution. That's chaos.

"There are many things that we can do to address the housing crisis, but two of them are most consequential. First, we must keep rents as low as possible by controlling the increases that landlords may impose. Rents have nearly doubled in the past ten years, and these unconscionable increases are imposing horrible suffering on low-income families.

"The second thing we can do is encourage builders and developers to offer more housing at below market rates. This is called inclusionary zoning. Before a builder can receive the requisite permits for a project, he must agree that a certain percentage of housing will be offered at below market rates. These two measures won't entirely fix the problem, but they will be a step toward doing so. Of course, we don't know exactly how effective these policies will be. Because this is such a complex problem, we must experiment to find the right combination of policies.

"Let me make this simple for you with an analogy. Let's say that the Astros are trailing by one run in the bottom of the ninth inning. A runner is on second base and there is one out. They have several options to tie the game. They could bunt the runner to third base, but then a sacrifice fly will do no good. However, a wild pitch would allow the runner to score. Or, they could let the batter try to get a base hit, in which case the runner on second could score.

"Of course, Dusty Baker doesn't know which of these, if either, will work. He'll only know after the fact. He will decide based on what his gut tells him will work. That is how we must approach the housing crisis, not with the simplistic solutions offered by Mr. Walker." Escobar returned to her seat.

Before Mason could give him a prompt, Justin was standing at his podium to deliver his rebuttal. "What Judge Escobar means by encouraging housing producers to offer below market rate housing is the use of physical force. Builders will not receive permission to start a project unless they do what the government demands. They won't be allowed to build unless they agree to offer some housing at a loss. The Judge's solution to every problem, whether real or imagined, is forcing people to act as she thinks proper. She did it with the lockdown. She did it with her mask mandates. And then she did it with her renters' protection dictates. And she is advocating for it tonight.

"She claims we can't accurately predict the results of a policy in advance. Instead, we must experiment. We must try something, and if it doesn't work, we'll try something else. Somehow, we'll hopefully stumble across the right policy.

"The truth is, we can predict the future results of a policy. But only if we identify and apply the relevant principles. For example, it was easy to predict the results of the judge's stay-at-home order. When businesses are forced to shut down, they lay off workers. When the workers have no income, they can't pay their rent or mortgage. We don't need an MBA to understand this. One only needs to look at the facts, all the facts. One needs to look at the full context.

"The consequences of the judge's coercive policies are easy to predict. Rent control leads to a decrease in both the quality and the quantity of rental housing. Inclusionary zoning increases the rents charged on market rate apartments. Again, one doesn't need an MBA to understand this. One only needs to look at the facts. Apparently, that is something that the Judge is unable or unwilling to do."

Roger Mason looked toward Escobar as Justin returned to his seat. She remained frozen, staring intently at Justin. "Judge?" Mason finally said. "The floor is yours." She stood and took two tentative steps to the podium.

"Now, Mr. Walker is putting words into my mouth. He is claiming that I advocate using force against the citizens. I never have and never will. Yes, I issued a stay-at-home order. That wasn't force. That was sound public health policy. Same with the mask mandate.

"Regarding inclusionary zoning, there is no force involved. Developers don't have to include below market rate housing in their project. That is their choice. If they aren't willing to meet the very reasonable requirement for below market housing, they can't blame the government.

"Mr. Walker is attempting to appeal to your emotions. All of us must do things we don't like. Sometimes we must do things that serve the greater good. Many people don't like things like stay-at-home orders or mask mandates or inclusionary zoning. But we each need to put aside our personal interests and serve the public interest.

"Again, Mr. Walker is calling for a return to the days of the Wild West, where anyone can do anything. He wants to allow people to walk around infecting other citizens. He wants landlords to be able to throw families into the street for little or no reason. He is putting profits before people." The volume of Escobar's voice had increased with each sentence. By the end, she was shouting, and her hands were shaking. She took a deep breath, smiled, and then returned to her seat.

THE SOLUTION IS MORE FREEDOM

March 2021

"**W**ell," Roger Mason said, "that was certainly interesting." He picked a card and read the question. "Cities across the nation have enacted renters' protections. What can we learn from their experiences? You go first, Judge Escobar."

Escobar stood at the podium and took a deep breath. This was harder than she had envisioned. She had submitted the question but hadn't bothered to give any thought to how she would answer it. "In looking at other cities, we can say with certainty that renters' protections work. They keep people housed. They keep rents affordable. Renters' protections do what they are supposed to do. Most importantly, they are a matter of justice. Let's look at a few of them.

"Just cause eviction laws keep families from being evicted for arbitrary reasons. Landlords often evict tenants simply because they want to bring in a new tenant so they can jack up the rent. That's not a just cause. Many times, landlords invent lease violations to justify evictions. Most renters don't know their rights, so they don't know how to fight back. They are treated unjustly. And that is why we need the right to counsel protections for renters.

"Ninety percent of landlords go to eviction court with a lawyer. Only 10 percent of tenants do. It isn't surprising, then, that landlords almost always win in eviction court. The deck is stacked in their favor. The right to counsel allows tenants to have legal representation. In jurisdictions with the right to counsel, evictions are 80 percent lower than before the measures were enacted. This is proof that many evictions are unjust. Combined, these two measures help keep families housed.

"Let's look at one more renter protection—ban the box. This policy prevents landlords from considering an applicant's criminal history prior to offering a unit. Many landlords reject any applicant with a criminal record, even if it was for possession of marijuana twenty years ago. That is grossly unjust. Once an individual has served his debt to society, he should not continue to be punished. But that is what landlords to. Stable housing is a major factor in reducing recidivism. Ban the box gives those with a record a second chance, an opportunity to move forward as a productive member of society.

"The housing crisis has a disproportionate negative impact on people of color. Blacks and Hispanics have much higher rates of criminal convictions than whites. They comprise nearly 70 percent of the tenants who are evicted. Our housing system is broken, and it perpetuates centuries of systemic racial injustice. Renters' protections address these injustices in a way that is fair and moral.

"As a final point, we have laws against abusing animals. You can't keep your dog chained up outside in July with no shade or water. If you fail to feed your horse and allow it to become emaciated, you will be charged with a crime. You can't set your neighbor's rabbit hutch on fire. I am an animal lover, and I think no decent person would object to laws that protect animals from abuse. We need laws to keep landlords from abusing renters." Escobar sat down with more than a minute on her timer.

Again, Justin was at the podium without a prompt from Roger Mason. "The judge uses the term justice often, but she never bothers to tell us what that word means. I will correct that oversight on her part. Justice means granting to others what they deserve. We understand this in the criminal justice system. We send murderers, rapists, and robbers to prison because that is what they deserve because of their actions. They have used physical force to violate the rights of other individuals.

"Judge Escobar wants to prohibit landlords from considering an individual's past behavior. This, she claims, is a matter of justice. Consider this in the full context. The government has declared that those who engage in certain actions should be sent to prison. Now, Judge Escobar wants to turn landlords into criminals for even considering those past actions—actions which the government punished with a prison sentence. She wants to make it illegal to consider an applicant's character. That isn't justice. It's an injustice to landlords. The same is true of the so-called right to counsel.

"Housing activists like to claim that 90 percent of landlords go to eviction court with an attorney. I have seen this statistic dozens of times, but I have yet to see a single citation regarding the source of this number. I have talked to over thirty different landlords, and between them, they have taken more than fifty tenants to eviction court over the past five years. Only three times did any of them use an attorney. That is less than 6 percent of the time. Granted, this is anecdotal, but it calls that statistic into serious question.

"Again, let's consider the full context of the alleged right to counsel. This program will provide a tenant facing eviction with legal representation. A landlord then faces the prospect of facing an experienced attorney in court or hiring one himself. I know what I'd do. I'd hire a lawyer. Absent the right to counsel, most landlords can and do represent themselves. When the right to counsel is in place, most landlords will incur the cost of an attorney. Adding insult to injury, the landlord is also forced to help pay the legal fees of his tenant through taxes. Again, this is an injustice to landlords.

"How is it that Judge Escobar can advocate for such injustices? The full answer would take far more time than I have now, but I can provide a glimpse at the explanation.

"I have twice mentioned the need to consider the full context. This means identifying and evaluating all the relevant facts. This is a demanding task, but it is absolutely necessary if we are to make the best possible decisions. If we ignore facts or refuse to seek information, we are intentionally blinding ourselves. And this, ladies and gentlemen, is precisely what the judge is doing.

"She looks at each issue in isolation, as if it has no connection to any other issue. Consider, for example, her stay-at-home order. If she identified and considered the full context, she didn't bother to inform us. She didn't warn us that there would be serious economic consequences from her order. Did she acknowledge that shutting down businesses would lead to massive unemployment and the inability to pay for food and housing? I never heard her utter such words. She didn't reveal any alternatives that she had considered and why they were rejected. She didn't do these things because she didn't consider the full context. And she is doing that right in front of our eyes tonight.

"Each of the policies that she has supported is considered in isolation. Paroled criminals have served their time, so we should ban the box. Families struggle to pay the rent, so we should force landlords to charge less. She considers each issue only from the narrow perspective of renters and fails to consider the full context." The timer went off, but Justin added one final statement. "That is a recipe for poor decisions."

"You have two minutes for rebuttal, judge," Roger Mason said. When Escobar did not move or respond, Mason announced, "In five seconds, I am going to start your timer." After fifteen seconds, Escobar stood and took three slow steps to the podium.

"Mr. Walker would like us to believe that it is an injustice to require landlords to treat tenants with respect and dignity. He would like us to believe that those who have served their time should continue to be punished for some youthful indiscretion. He would like us to believe that it is unjust to provide tenants with the same resources corporate landlords have. I do not know what depraved code of ethics Mr. Walker adheres to, but I don't believe it is unjust to help those in need. In fact, it is unjust not to help those in need.

"When I was a child, my grandmother and I would volunteer at a homeless shelter every Friday night. The first time we visited, I was frightened. The men and women there were dirty and unkempt. Many stumbled around or talked incoherently because of drugs, alcohol, mental illness, or some combination. The faces of these people were sunken, and many had open sores. The air was filled with hopelessness. It was, to say the least, a depressing sight.

"Over time, I became friends with a few of the regulars. They would tell me their stories. Sometimes they would tell me about happier days, but mostly they talked about the hopelessness of their situation.

"I don't know why my grandmother took me to the shelter. Maybe it was to make me appreciate the little that we had. Perhaps it was to show me how a person can be rejected by society. Maybe it was to help me understand that even in all their misery and suffering, these were still human beings who deserved our respect.

"Obviously, Mr. Walker has not seen what our system can do to a person. I don't know his background and it really doesn't matter. He seems quick to judge others, but we can never truly understand another person's plight until we have walked in his shoes.

"In closing, I'd just like to say…," Escobar stopped for a moment. "No, never mind," she said while waving her arms. She returned to her seat.

Justin remained seated as he pondered his next move. Escobar had given him nothing to rebut, so he had an open microphone for two minutes. This would be a good time to say something positive.

"Judge Escobar has presented us with a particular vision of the world. She has told us that our purpose in life is to serve others, to sacrifice our personal interests for the poor and needy. I reject this world view."

"In my opening remarks, I mentioned the Declaration of Independence. We are taught that the document declared America's independence from Great Britain. This is true, but it isn't the essential greatness of that document. Fundamentality, it declared the individual's independence from the State.

"Freed from the arbitrary dictates of the State, Americans could pursue their dreams. They didn't need the King's permission to act. Instead, they could act by right. They were free to create products and offer them to willing buyers. They could act as they thought best in the pursuit of their own happiness, no matter who or how many disagreed. The result was the wealthiest nation in the history of mankind.

"Now, you may wonder what this has to do with the issues we are discussing here tonight. The freedom that made America great is under assault. Tonight, we have heard repeated calls for the State to ban actions that some dislike. The advocates of these policies call their ideas progressive, but they are in fact regressive. They want to take us back to a world in which the individual is subservient to the State.

"Consider rent control. A landlord cannot raise rents more than the government permits. His own judgment is irrelevant. Or consider ban the box. A landlord cannot get the information that he thinks necessary to make a wise decision regarding a tenant. His own judgment is irrelevant. Or consider just cause eviction. A landlord can only evict a tenant for reasons that the state permits, thereby rendering the landlord's own judgment irrelevant.

"The solution to our housing problems is not more State control. The solution is more freedom."

SOMEONE WASHES OUR UNDERWEAR

March 2021

For the next seventy minutes, Justin Walker and Marta Escobar verbally sparred. Justin thought some questions submitted by Escobar were absurd. For example, one question asked, "If renters' protections aren't moral, then why did the city council pass them?" When Escobar answered the question, she said that such protections are moral because the city council passed them. She then told a personal anecdote about a trip to Big Bend National Park when she was a teenager. Justin had a field day with that one, explaining why morality and truth aren't decided by a democratic vote.

At fifteen minutes before nine, Roger Mason asked the debaters if they wanted to extend the event for another thirty minutes. Justin quickly agreed, but to virtually nobody's surprise, Escobar declined. "Very well. Then it is time for your closing statements. Mr. Walker, you have five minutes."

Justin was deep in thought. He had prepared his closing statement, but Escobar's performance had allowed him to make those points multiple times already. Repeating a few of those points would emphasize them, but he wanted to say more. He would speak extemporaneously.

"Tonight, you have heard two very different views on what

kind of city Houston should be. One view—the judge's—is that the government should control our lives. If you think that this is hyperbole on my part, remember that she is the one who ordered you to stay home and closed most businesses. She is the one who ordered you to wear a mask in public, whether or not you were infected. She is the one who ordered apartment owners to house the homeless. Tonight, she has defended the city's attempt to exercise even more control over rental property owners. I could go on, but you get the picture.

"For the past year, the judge has been controlling our lives. For months we couldn't go to a movie theater, a restaurant, or the gym. She even told us how many guests we could have at our own home. Also, remember that she is the one who tried to stifle free speech, declaring that only certain individuals could speak about COVID." Justin looked toward Roger Mason. The talk show host nodded.

"Think about what you have had to do without over the past year. These orders and controls will eventually go away, but think about what life would be like if they were permanent. That is the world that the judge wants you to accept and endorse.

"Granted, the renters' protections won't impose conditions as severe as the lock down. But that is only a matter of degree. In principle, the lockdown and renters' protections are the same. Both make the individual subservient to the State.

"I reject that view and so did America's Founding Fathers. They fought for the rights of individuals—all individuals. That is my cause as well because I can think of no cause more noble. I trust that on April 6, you will vote for freedom."

Roger Mason turned to Mart Escobar. "Judge, you may make you closing statement."

Escobar smiled at Mason and remained seated. "I would just like to say…," she began.

"Judge Escobar, please step up to the microphone so everyone can hear you," Mason implored.

Escobar reluctantly stood. "I would just like to say that we should remember that someone washes our underwear. We have a duty to help them. Amen." She turned and walked off the stage.

Mason sat with his mouth agape. "What the hell?" he said before remembering where he was. He shook his head as if trying to get a bad dream out of his mind. "Okay, that concludes tonight's debate. I would like to thank our participants. They provided us with some thought-provoking, and with the judge, bewildering comments. And I thank everyone here tonight, as well as those watching on television or the Internet. Don't forget to vote on April 6. Good night and God bless."

* * *

Tilde greeted Escobar backstage. "What was that all about?" the assistant asked.

"What do you mean?"

"You were a babbling idiot. You say some crazy things at times, but tonight...."

"Shut up, you bitch," Escobar shouted. "I won't tolerate such insubordination. You're fired. Get out of here."

As Tilde stormed away, Jamaal Wilkes approached Escobar. "She may not have worded it well, but Tilde has a point," he said softly.

Escobar looked at him as tears welled in her eyes. She buried her head in his chest and sobbed.

* * *

"My God, boy," Buford Jennings announced, "you ripped her a new one. Even if we lose the referendum, that alone was worth all the money I've paid you. I haven't had that much fun since we tied Jacob Benning to a canoe with a dead alligator and let him float down the Brazos."

"You were magnificent," Pratik said as he slapped his friend on the back. "You got in every point we discussed, and a lot more."

Warren Hicks gave Justin a firm handshake while grinning. "That, young man, was a brilliant performance. I wish I could do that at your age."

Justin smiled. "Overall, I am pleased. I stumbled a few times. That was a lot more difficult than I thought it would be. I had to stay intensely focused for two hours. I am exhausted."

Buford wrapped an arm around each of his intellectual bodyguards. "Come on boys, I'm going to buy you the biggest steak this side of the Pecos."

SOMETIMES THE GOOD GUYS WIN

April 2021

T he days leading up to the referendum on April 6 were a cacophony of claims and counterclaims from supporters on both sides of the issue. Justin and Pratik didn't get drawn into the rancor. They had more speaking requests than they could possibly have time for. Pratik suggested they do virtual talks. They preferred face to face, even when everyone was wearing masks. But doing virtual talks would allow them to satisfy many more requests. Then Justin suggested that, instead of talking to just one group at a time, they talk to several. Instead of both meeting with the same groups, they could each conduct their own meetings. They would get a lot more bang for their time. Pratik agreed, and each spent every evening conducting two ninety-minute meetings.

Based on the questions that were being asked, most of those attending seemed to be undecided. Justin and Pratik were thrilled with that. These were the voters who would decide the election.

* * *

Though he had been on his best behavior as the moderator of the debate, on the following Monday, Roger Mason took the gloves off. "That, ladies and gentlemen, was a total kick ass performance by Justin Walker. He made Comrade Escobar look like the total idiot that she is. I admit that isn't hard to do, given the crazy things she says. My God, did you hear her closing statement? In case you didn't, here it is." The airwaves were filled with Escobar saying, "I would just like to say that we should remember that someone washes our underwear. We have a duty to help them. Amen." Mason laughed hysterically while the clip played. He played it three more times before moving on to deliver another insult. For the rest of the week, his shows focused on berating Escobar, and he said little about the referendum.

* * *

A week before the referendum, the Baker Institute released a new poll. Those opposing the referendum had dropped to 52 percent, with 41 percent in favor. Seven percent remained undecided. This would be the last poll before the one that counted on April 6. While the numbers were moving in the right direction, Justice Inc was running out of time.

* * *

When the polls opened on election day, the clear sky, low humidity, and moderate temperature promised that it would be a good day. At least weather wise. Someone—a lot of someones—would be very disappointed by the end of the day.

When Justin and Pratik stepped out of the house for their morning run, they were greeted by a dozen reporters. The two intellectual bodyguards had grown accustomed to the media milling about on the sidewalk. The reporters had developed a certain level of respect for the two young men. They were clearly passionate about their cause, and they were certainly articulate in expressing their ideas. Some reporters appeared to be a little jealous, but they always treated Justin and Pratik well.

"How are you feeling today?" one reporter asked.

Pratik smiled. "I am a little tired, but it's nothing that a five-mile run won't take care of."

The reporters laughed. They enjoyed Pratik's humor. "I mean, about the election?"

"There's an election today?" Pratik feigned. "It's going to be close. But it's out of our hands now. We will not fret over something we can't control."

"The last poll showed that only 41 percent support your referendum. That's a big margin to overcome in a week. Are you ready to concede defeat?" another reporter asked.

Justin shook his head. "We won't concede until the votes are counted. Polls can be way off base. We addressed that back in January. The results depend on what questions are asked and who is being asked. We put little stock in polls."

After a few more questions, Pratik said, "Hey guys, we'd really like to stick around and chat, but we need to get our workout started. Why don't you come to our victory party tonight at the Galleria Hilton? We'll be a lot more talkative."

The reporters laughed. "That's a rather bold statement, considering how far behind you are."

Pratik shrugged. "Stranger things have happened. See you tonight." And with that, Justin and Pratik took off on their run.

* * *

Justin and Pratik walked into the Galleria Hilton Ballroom thirty minutes before the polls were closing. There were several dozen people already there, and their attitude was somber. Buford Jennings, however, was anything but somber. He walked up to his two friends with a waiter on his heels. Jennings turned, grabbed two flutes of champagne, and handed them to Justin and Pratik. Taking the third glass from the tray, Buford raised it high. "Win or lose, we gave them a hell of a fight. I couldn't be prouder of you two if you were my own sons. Thank you." With that, they clinked glasses, and the intellectual bodyguards had their first ever sip of champagne.

By seven, several dozen more people had entered the ballroom. One of them was Warren Hicks. He fervently shook the hands of Justin and Pratik. "I don't know how this is going to turn out," he said, "but you two are going to have a lot of successes. Lord knows, the way the world is going, you'll have plenty of opportunities."

"Thank you, Warren," Justin said. "Your help was invaluable. We might have done the heavy lifting, but you were our strength coach. We couldn't have done it without you."

"I can't tell you how many times your comments straightened us out," Pratik added. "You were our mentor."

Warren beamed at his two proteges. "It was my pleasure, gentlemen. It was my pleasure."

At seven, the room grew quiet, and all eyes turned to the large screen as a news anchor began to discuss the election. "We have just received the early voting numbers, and the vote is 51.1 percent for and 48.9 percent against. Keep in mind that these are very early results, though the early voting numbers set a record for a special election. We have reports from around the city that the turnout has been heavy. This is clearly an issue that is touching the hearts of many Houstonians. We have a reporter in the ballroom of the Galleria Hilton, where the supporters of the referendum are meeting. Let's go to her to see what the atmosphere is there."

Justin and Pratik suddenly had a microphone stuck in their faces and a camera pointed at them. "I'm here with Justin Walker and Pratik Shah, the two young men who led the effort for this referendum. The early results look promising for you," the reporter said. "Do you think they will hold up?"

Justin and Pratik shared a look that silently said, "Really?" Justin nodded slightly. "Well," Pratik said, "as you might know, elections aren't over until all the votes are counted. Given that, with four or five percent of the votes counted, don't you think it's a little premature to be making predictions?"

The reporter looked stunned. She was the one who should ask the questions. "Um," she stammered, "just trying to get your take on things."

"Well, my take is that it's too early for any kind of

prediction." When the reporter was no longer live, Pratik said, "Look, if you want to talk to us, show us a little courtesy. Don't just show up and stick a microphone in our face." Pratik's size made him very intimidating, but his voice revealed his benevolent nature. "We're happy to talk to you, but don't ambush us."

The reporter nodded meekly and sauntered off.

Three hours later the vote was 50.1 percent in favor of the referendum to repeal the renters' protections and 49.9 percent opposed with 56 percent of the vote counted. As best they could tell, the reported votes were almost equally split between Republican precincts and Democrat precincts. It looked like this was going to go down to the wire.

At midnight, 94 percent of the vote had been counted. The vote was virtually even, with only 104 votes more in opposition. Nearly 200,000 votes had been cast, and this promised to be an election for the history books.

At two in the morning, the final vote count was announced. The ballroom had thinned considerably, and only a few dozen people, including Warren Hicks, Buford Jennings, and a few others from the 1990s zoning fight, remained. They were tired, and a few were a little tipsy. But all gained renewed energy when it was announced that the referendum had passed by a margin of 50.3 to 49.7. Justice Inc. had scored its first victory.

Warren Hicks was standing beside Justin and Pratik when the results were announced. His face showed he was fatigued, but he beamed. "Sometimes the good guys win."

I SUGGEST A VACATION

April 2021

The day after the referendum, Jamaal Wilkes sat in Lia Patel's office. Roderick Jackson sat in the corner looking sullen. "I've accepted a plea bargain. I will plead guilty to involuntary manslaughter and be on probation for two years. My attorney thinks that it's a good deal, and I just want to move past this. The idea of going to prison isn't appealing to me."

Lia nodded. "I understand." She thought for a moment. "Now what do we do?"

"We keep fighting for justice," Jamaal said. "This was just one battle in the bigger war. We almost won and would have if it weren't for those two young men. They proved to be very formidable."

"Somebody should do something about them," Roderick said without looking up. "And I know just the guys to do it."

"If you are thinking of using violence, I can't object more strongly," Jamaal responded. "This is a war of ideas. We have the better ideas, but it takes time for people to digest them. I am more concerned about some of our allies."

"You mean Judge Escobar, don't you?" Lia asked.

"Yes," Jamaal replied. "She was a disaster in the debate. I am sure that was the primary reason we lost. She snatched

"

defeat from the jaws of victory. I think that my dog could have done better than she did. I told her it was a bad idea, and unfortunately, she proved me right."

"Why didn't you debate that kid?" Roderick asked.

"I wasn't asked. The judge was. That was certainly astute on their part. She might be a vocal proponent of renters' protections, but she can be an embarrassment at times. That is part of why I accepted the plea deal. I stayed out of sight the last few months because of my legal problem. Now that it is resolved, I plan to resume my campaign. The next time, if there is a next time, I will be the one debating."

* * *

Over the next week, the *News Journal* ran many articles covering the results of the election. The writers did not try to hide their personal opinions. The articles oscillated between claiming that the supporters of the referendum resorted to lies, misrepresentations, or scare tactics to win. Some of the more ambitious writers combined all three into one story.

At first, Justin and Pratik were upset over these claims. But as they talked about it, they realized it provided them fodder to shoot more holes in the arguments presented in favor of renters' protections. They wrote at least one blog post in response to each article and sent copies to the offending writers. They also sent copies to their email list, which had grown to over 10,000.

One reporter claimed it was a lie to claim that rent control resulted in a decrease in rental housing. Yet, the article did not cite a single example of a city where the rental housing stock had increased under rent control. When Justin and Pratik responded, they cited a dozen different studies that found both the quantity and quality of rental housing declined under rent control.

Another writer admitted that in some cities, renters' protections have gone too far, but claimed that it was a scare tactic to argue that Houston would suffer the same fate. What has happened in Detroit, New York, or Boston has nothing to do with Houston. We can't compare Houston to other cities. Justin and Pratik responded that the writer apparently believes that economic and moral principles stop at the Mason-Dixon line.

But the most outrageous claim was that the referendum supporters had outspent the opposition by a factor of ten to one. The writer didn't provide any specific numbers, nor did she reveal the source of this alleged information. Justin and Pratik had fun with this one and provided some actual numbers to the extent they could track them down. They were the primary supporters of the referendum and had spent just under $50,000. Most of that was on the booths at two conventions, along with the literature and other things needed to make their case. In contrast, the city had used the George R. Brown Convention Center twice at a cost of more than $150,000. From what Josh and Pratik could discern from city records, an additional $500,000 was spent on community outreach, workshops, and other attempts to "educate" voters about renters' protections. Those two expenses alone were thirteen times more than Justice Inc had spent.

Each time a reporter made an unsubstantiated claim, Justin and Pratik refuted it with specific information and the source of their information. As they had during the campaign, they refused to take insults and derision sitting down. They responded with facts and reasoned arguments. And then, the articles ceased.

* * *

Marta Escobar called in sick the day after the referendum. In truth, she had a vicious hangover from drinking the better part of a bottle of Jack Daniels. She had hoped to forget the embarrassment of leading the renters' protection movement. When she had partially recovered from her overindulgence, the memory remained. And so, she repeated the destructive process for five more days. On the following Monday, she announced she was resigning her position, citing health concerns.

* * *

Following their success in stopping the renters' protections, Justin and Pratik were overwhelmed by phone calls and emails from landlords across the nation. Property owners hoped that Justice Inc could help them fight the renters' protections being enacted in their cities.

Justin and Pratik quickly realized that they could not represent everyone who wanted to hire them. They simply could not be everywhere they would need to be. In response, they began holding webinars and their audience exploded. Within a month, fifty people were attending their daily webinars, and hundreds more were paying to watch recordings of those meetings. It was both financially and intellectually rewarding. Justin and Pratik were helping hundreds of landlords, and they were being paid very well for their efforts. However, the demands were wearing on them. They had been working seventy hours a week for months.

One Saturday, they were visiting Warren Hicks. None of the men drank much, but it had become a custom for the three to meet each Saturday evening and split a six-pack of Shiner Bock while they talked about philosophy and current events.

"How are my favorite intellectual bodyguards this week?" Warren asked.

"Tired," the two responded in unison. "It's grueling doing a webinar each day," Pratik added.

Warren nodded. "You two are young and full of energy, but you need to take care of yourselves. You are doing important work. However, if you burn out, you won't do anyone any good."

"What do you think we should do?" Justin asked.

"I suggest a vacation. Go away for a week or two and relax. That alone will do you a world of good. And I'd suggest not even thinking about your work or what you want to do next. You guys run five miles a day, but you take Sundays off. You need to rest your minds just as much as you need to rest your bodies."

"I know where we can go," Pratik said. "Ohio. Justin, you can see Jenna and Meghan."

"And you can see Sally," Justin quickly retorted. "Come on Pratik, I may have been born at night, but I wasn't born last night."

Warren held up his hands. "Hold on, guys. I know you are from Ohio, Justin. But who are these women you named?"

"Jenna is my sister, and Sally is my cousin," Justin replied.

"Meghan is Justin's girlfriend," Pratik quickly added.

"I can't say that she's my girlfriend," Justin replied, "but she's pretty darn close to that. The same is true of Sally and Pratik. Pratik has visited my hometown many times, and he and Sally always spend a lot of time together. So, his attempt at acting like a trip to Ohio would be good for me is just that—an act. Pratik wants to go to Ohio for selfish reasons."

"Then that's all the more reason to go," Warren said approvingly.

Ten days later, Justin and Pratik embarked for Ohio. When they were twenty miles from their destination, Justin received a text from Meghan. The text read: "I may have a client for you. My uncle has a zoning problem. Call me."

BOOKS IN THIS SERIES

The Intellectual Bodyguards

Shortly after graduating college with degrees in philosophy, Justin Walker and Pratik Shah open Justice Inc, a business that provides intellectual bodyguard services. Rather than protect their clients from physical threats, Justin and Pratik protect their clients from intellectual threats.

Justin and Pratik are soon joined by the Three Amigas: Justin's sister, Jenna, his cousin Sally Baker, and Meghan Charlton. Jenna has a master's degree in history. Sally holds a PhD in economics, while Meghan has a master's degree in journalism. All three have minors in philosophy. Combined, the five intellectuals have broad and powerful expertise.

The dangers presented by physical threats are usually obvious and immediate. The dangers posed by intellectual threats are usually hidden and long-term. Potential clients often cannot see the dangers they face, even when they are directly attacked. Undeterred, Justice Inc defends what is right, even when they do not have a client.

Challenging widely held ideas, the Intellectual Bodyguards take on issues that dominate the headlines. They provide thought-provoking arguments in the defense of justice.

The Mendelson Effect

When Antifa creates chaos on their college campus, Justin

Walker and Pratik Shah lead the charge to show that brains will overcome brawn.

Justice Inc

The government imposed lockdown during the COVID pandemic creates economic turmoil in Houston. Intellectual bodyguards Justin Walker and Pratik Shah come to the defense of landlords and small business owners and challenge the morality of the lockdown.

A Moral Sanction

Jack Charlton's dream of manufacturing his revolutionary battery is shattered when government officials seek to derail his plans. Intellectual bodyguards Justin Walker and Pratik Shah defend Jack, declaring that Jack's actions are morally good.

A Matter Of Choice

As concerns about the quality of government schools grow, Texas parents demand more control of their children's education. Justice Inc joins the debate, arguing that education is a matter of choice—the parent's choice.

The Three Amigas

When Justice Inc is accused of cultural appropriation, the intellectual bodyguards find themselves drawn into a raging controversy. They respond by doing what they do best—they challenge the premises of their accusers.

BOOKS BY THIS AUTHOR

All Men Are Created Equal

Thirteen-year-old Samuel Dawson abhors slavery. When he is put in temporary control of his father's plantation, Samuel begins an audacious experiment to treat the slaves like human beings.

Dawson Town

Following the end of slavery, Samuel Dawson and his former slaves build a thriving community. But many of his fellow Texans are reticent to recognize the natural rights of Blacks, and they threaten to destroy Dawson Town.